Reflections on Malcolm Forsyth

MARY I. INGRAHAM
& ROBERT C. RIVAL,
EDITORS

REFLECTIONS ON MALCOLM FORSYTH

UNIVERSITY *of* **ALBERTA** PRESS

Published by

University of Alberta Press
Ring House 2
Edmonton, Alberta, Canada T6G 2E1
www.uap.ualberta.ca

LIBRARY AND ARCHIVES CANADA
CATALOGUING IN PUBLICATION

Title: Reflections on Malcolm Forsyth / Mary I. Ingraham & Robert C. Rival, editors.
Names: Ingraham, Mary I., editor. | Rival, Robert, 1975– editor
Description: Includes bibliographical references and index.
Identifiers: Canadiana (print) 20190148705 | Canadiana (ebook) 20190148713 | ISBN 9781772124866 (soft cover) | ISBN 9781772125030 (PDF)
Subjects: LCSH: Forsyth, Malcolm. | LCSH: Composers—Canada—Biography.
Classification: LCC ML410 F735 R33 2019 | DDC 780.92—dc23

First edition, first printing, 2019.
First printed and bound in Canada by Houghton Boston Printers, Saskatoon, Saskatchewan.
Copyediting and proofreading by Joanne Muzak and Alana Gralen.

University of Alberta Press is committed to protecting our natural environment. As part of our efforts, this book is printed on Enviro Paper: it contains 100% post-consumer recycled fibres and is acid- and chlorine-free.

University of Alberta Press gratefully acknowledges the support received for its publishing program from the Government of Canada, the Canada Council for the Arts, and the Government of Alberta through the Alberta Media Fund.

This book has been published with the help of a grant from the Canadian Federation for the Humanities and Social Sciences, through the Awards to Scholarly Publications Program, using funds provided by the Social Sciences and Humanities Research Council of Canada.

Canadä

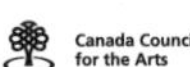

Contents

Figures IX

Acknowledgements XIII

Prelude XV
AMANDA FORSYTH

Introduction XVII
MARY I. INGRAHAM & ROBERT C. RIVAL

1 Reflections on a Life and Career 1
ROBIN ELLIOTT

2 Sonorous Pleasure 17
Portrait of a Master Orchestrator as Pedagogue
ALLAN GORDON BELL

3 Remembering and Continuing 23
Rhapsody for 14 Strings
RYAN MCCLELLAND

4 Finding Inspiration in Canadian Folk Songs 49

An Analysis of Three Métis Songs from Saskatchewan

ROXANE PREVOST

5 Breathing in G 79

Harmonic Tension and Repose in the Cello Concerto Electra Rising

ROBERT C. RIVAL

6 Allusion and Reflection in *Je répondrais...* for Solo Piano 109

EDWARD JURKOWSKI

7 "Here, All Is a Beginning" 129

Reflections of Forsyth in A Ballad of Canada

MARY I. INGRAHAM

8 Interlude 169

Reminiscences

CARL HARE

TOMMY BANKS

NORA BUMANIS & JULIA SHAW

ALLAN GILLILAND

JOHN MCPHERSON

FORDYCE C. (DUKE) PIER

TANYA PROCHAZKA

RAYFIELD RIDEOUT

CHRISTOPHER TAYLOR

9 A Life Experience 183

The Early Orchestral Works

KATHY PRIMOS

10 Splendour in the Brass 197

A Legacy of Brass Music

DALE SORENSEN

11 The Choral Music 215
LEONARD RATZLAFF

Postlude 231
VALERIE FORSYTH

List of Works 233

Contributors 241

Permissions 247

Index 249

Figures

26 Figure 3.1. *Rhapsody for 14 Strings*, mm. 1–27.

29 Figure 3.2. *Rhapsody*, juncture between first and second sections, mm. 34–56.

30 Figure 3.3. *Rhapsody*, primary and secondary variants on "jazz-like" figure.

31 Figure 3.4. *Rhapsody*, culmination of *Allegretto giusto*, mm. 103–14.

33 Figure 3.5. *Rhapsody*, winding down of *Allegretto giusto*, mm. 129–38.

35 Figure 3.6. *Rhapsody*, start of third section, mm. 150–64.

38 Figure 3.7. *Rhapsody*, F major material, mm. 180–202.

41 Figure 3.8. *Rhapsody*, first melody of the fourth section, mm. 216–20.

41 Figure 3.9. *Rhapsody*, new theme of the fourth section, mm. 257–60.

42 Figure 3.10. *Rhapsody*, isomelody and isorhythm, mm. 331–8.

44 Figure 3.11. *Rhapsody*, recapitulation in the fourth section, mm. 421–53.

46 Figure 3.12. *Rhapsody*, thematic and tonal resolution, mm. 490–510.

51 Figure 4.1. Cass-Beggs's transcription of "Chanson du petit cordonnier."

52 Figure 4.2. Cass-Beggs's transcription of "Adieu de la mariée à ses parents."

54 Figure 4.3. Cass-Beggs's transcription of "Chanson de la Grenouillère."

55 Figure 4.4. "Chanson du petit cordonnier." Showing Forsyth's use of harmonic and tempo changes in response to the text.

57 Figure 4.5. "Chanson du petit cordonnier," mm. 1–11. Showing Forsyth's use of harmonic and tempo changes in response to the text.

59 Figure 4.6. "Chanson du petit cordonnier," mm. 35–47. Showing Forsyth's change in texture to A♭M7 harmonization.

60 Figure 4.7. "Adieu de la mariée." Showing Forsyth's changing metres in relation to the text.

61 Figure 4.8. "Adieu de la mariée," mm. 1–17. Showing Forsyth's change in metre.

63 Figure 4.9. "Adieu de la mariée," mm. 18–31. Showing the couple's dissonant chord material.

65 Figure 4.10. "Adieu de la mariée," mm. 46–60. Showing the change in metre in the fourth verse.

68 Figure 4.11. "Chanson de la Grenouillère." Showing Forsyth's use of the song and its variants.

69 Figure 4.12. "Chanson de la Grenouillère," mm. 1–17. Showing Forsyth's use of harmony in the first verse.

71 Figure 4.13. "Chanson de la Grenouillère," mm. 26–36. Showing Forsyth's walking bass.

72 Figure 4.14. "Chanson de la Grenouillère," mm. 59–78. Showing Forsyth's use of semitone movement between sections.

74 Figure 4.15. "Chanson de la Grenouillère," mm. 87–105. Showing Forsyth's use of metre.

80 Figure 5.1. Rival, Overture, m. 1 and m. 22.

81 Figure 5.2. Forsyth, *Atayoskewin*, "The Spirits," mm. 1–3. Flutes, oboes, percussion, piano, harp.

82 Figure 5.3a. Prominent occurrences of the motto-tetrachord in *Atayoskewin*.
83 Figure 5.3b. *Atayoskewin*, "The Dream," mm. 1–4. Strings.
84 Figure 5.3c. *Atayoskewin*, "The Dance," F^{+3-6}.
87 Figure 5.4. *Electra Rising*, mvt. 1, mm. 1–20.
89 Figure 5.5a. *Electra Rising*, mvt. 1. Reduction of orchestral chords and collections.
90 Figure 5.5b. *Electra Rising*, mvt. 1. Orchestral triads plotted on a cubic lattice.
91 Figure 5.5c. *Electra Rising*, mvt. 1. Voice-leading size between pairs of triads.
93 Figure 5.6. *Electra Rising*, mvt. 1, mm. 49–58.
97 Figure 5.7. *Electra Rising*, mvt. 3, mm. 1–9.
99 Figure 5.8. *Electra Rising*, mvt. 4, mm. 1–28.
101 Figure 5.9a. Collection voice leading in *Electra Rising*, mvt. 4, mm. 1–28.
101 Figure 5.9b. All scales (except one) in *Electra Rising*, mvt. 4, mm. 1–71, plotted on a portion of a cubic lattice.
102 Figure 5.10. *Electra Rising*, mvt. 4, mm. 142–68.

111 Figure 6.1. Purcell, *Fantazia upon One Note*, mm. 1–8.
112 Figure 6.2. Forsyth, *Je répondrais...*, mvt. 1, mm. 1–49.
115 Figure 6.3. "à Purcell," mm. 69–83.
116 Figure 6.4. "à Purcell," mm. 84–96.
118 Figure 6.5. Illustrating the 12-note tuning of a kalimba.
119 Figure 6.6. "à Schumann," mm. 1–12.
122 Figure 6.7. "à Schumann," mm. 31–51.
124 Figure 6.8a. "à Chopin," mm. 1–11.
125 Figure 6.8b. Tonal centres and motivic movement in "à Chopin."

133 Figure 7.1a. *Atayoskewin*, m. 1. Flute, piccolo, and oboes. Northern Lights motive.
133 Figure 7.1b. *A Ballad of Canada*, mvt. 1, mm. 2–3. Flutes and oboes. Northern Lights leitmotif.

134 Figure 7.1c. *A Ballad,* mvt. 5, m. 132. Flute, piccolo, and oboes. Northern Lights leitmotif.
137 Figure 7.2. "In the Yukon," poem by Ralph Gustafson. Text used by Forsyth in *A Ballad* in roman.
140 Figure 7.3a. *A Ballad,* mvt. 1, mm. 25–7. AB voices with brass choir. Section A.
141 Figure 7.3b. *A Ballad,* mvt. 1, mm. 47–50. SA voices. Section B.
143 Figure 7.4a. *A Ballad,* mvt. 2, mm. 1–4. Violins and violas. Section A motive.
144 Figure 7.4b. *A Ballad,* mvt. 2, mm. 17–19. SA. Section B motive.
145 Figure 7.4c. *A Ballad,* mvt. 2, mm. 31–2. Brass and percussion.
148 Figure 7.5. "The Toll of the Bells," poem by E.J. Pratt. Text used by Forsyth in *A Ballad* in roman.
150 Figure 7.6a. *A Ballad,* mvt. 3, mm. 14–18. Trumpets and trombones.
151 Figure 7.6b. *A Ballad,* mvt. 3, mm. 30–7. SATB.
153 Figure 7.7. *A Ballad,* mvt. 4, mm. 44–7.
156 Figure 7.8. "Newfoundland," poem by E.J. Pratt. Text used by Forsyth in *A Ballad* in roman.
161 Figure 7.9a. *A Ballad,* mvt. 5, mm. 16–20. SATB.
162 Figure 7.9b. *A Ballad,* mvt. 5, mm. 39–40. SATB with full orchestra.
163 Figure 7.9c. *A Ballad,* mvt. 5, mm. 67–9. SA.
163 Figure 7.9d. *A Ballad,* mvt. 5, mm. 115–7. SATB.

188 Figure 9.1. *Sketches from Natal,* mvt. 2, mm. 1–15.
189 Figure 9.2. Symphony No. 1, mvt. 4, m. 6.
194 Figure 9.3. Symphony No. 1, mvt. 1, mm. 1–21. Violas.

Acknowledgements

MARY I. INGRAHAM & ROBERT C. RIVAL

THIS PROJECT BEGAN in July 2011 when Robert Rival, then the composer-in-residence at the Edmonton Symphony Orchestra, initiated conversations with colleagues to honour the life and work of Malcolm Forsyth, one of Edmonton's and Canada's foremost classical composers. Forsyth had recently passed away, and Rival was interested in organizing an event to bring together music scholars and performers to reflect on the breadth of Forsyth's influence. In the course of these discussions, he made Mary Ingraham's acquaintance at the University of Alberta. To gauge interest, she suggested organizing an academic panel at a conference, which the two of them did for the Canadian University Music Society annual conference in 2012. The panel included contributions from Robin Elliott, Mary Ingraham, Edward Jurkowski, Roxane Prevost, and Robert Rival. This work ultimately led to further conversations with University of Alberta Press and additional authors to develop the collection of essays and reminiscences included here. We are very grateful to our editor at University of Alberta Press, Peter Midgley, for his unwavering support for this project since its inception, and for his ongoing guidance and enthusiasm for Forsyth's work in general.

Several others have been devoted to bringing this collection to fruition. First and foremost are the authors and contributors. Whether they provided extensive analytical or personal essays, brief recollections of Forsyth's teaching, performing career or personal friendships, or works of poetry, the impact of Forsyth's life and music on audiences, scholars, and close friends is truly inspiring. Our sincerest thanks also to Forsyth's daughter, Amanda, and his wife, Valerie, for their written contributions and encouragement for the project as a whole. Finding a satisfactory balance and coherent flow in work involving such a large number of contributors springing from so many different backgrounds proved a stimulating task but also a challenging and time-consuming one. We thank everyone involved for their undying patience.

We also wish to thank the institutions that supported this project: the University of Alberta Music Department, the Canadian Music Centre (Prairie Region), the University of Calgary Music Department, and the affiliated institutions of all our contributors. Special thanks to Jean-Marie Barker at Counterpoint Music Library Services for assistance in providing access to scores and recordings to several authors, for creating the List of Works included in this volume, and for granting permission to reproduce the musical excerpts from Forsyth's published scores. Additional research for this collection was undertaken by Rival at the Malcolm Forsyth Fonds at the Richard Johnston Canadian Music Archives, University of Calgary. To date, this is an underutilized resource that, with focused investigation, will undoubtedly expand appreciation and understanding of Forsyth's legacy.

And lastly, thanks to David Owen for his generous work preparing the index. His varied experiences as a professional editor, indexer, and performing musician have proven invaluable in sifting through the concepts, keywords, and connections across this multi-authored collection.

Prelude

AMANDA FORSYTH

MALCOLM FORSYTH HAS BEEN DESCRIBED by both his friends and colleagues as an icon: intellectually and musically brilliant. To me, he was my mentor, my composer, my music teacher, and confidante. He was my biggest fan and my harshest critic, but, most of all, he was my father. Dad possessed a musical intellect of the highest order. In fact, whenever I needed an answer to anything theoretical or musical, I would bypass the *Grove Dictionary* and just ask Dad.

While I have enjoyed playing all of his compositions, from solo cello to chamber and orchestral, one of the most memorable times that I shared with Dad was when he was composing the cello concerto *Electra Rising*, a work for which he later received a JUNO Award as Best Classical Composition.

Tragically, my father was diagnosed with terminal cancer in 2010. Throughout his illness, his spirit never yielded, nor was it diminished by his failing health. Despite all the unpleasant effects of his treatments, he somehow managed to make the journey from Edmonton to Ottawa to be present at the premiere of his final work for orchestra and choir, *A Ballad of Canada*, performed by the National Arts Centre Orchestra, where I was then principal cellist, and my husband,

Pinchas Zukerman, music director. Upon conclusion of the performance, my father, who was seated in the royal box, removed his oxygen and graciously rose to accept standing ovations from audience and performers alike. I will always keep that memory close to my heart, as it was the last time I would ever see him hear his own music.

My father was a complex and enigmatic person, and in my mind will be remembered as a champion of excellence. His legacy is his music, and what better way for him to live on? He said that the greatest compliment he ever got from a musician came from me: while playing the last movement of his cello concerto, I told him I felt as if I was flying, that my feet had actually left the ground. It is true, and I will continue to fly every time I perform it. Finally, I share a quote from him, which I think of often: "If I can change an audience's feeling for a brief moment with my music, then my job is done." Well, Dad, job well done.

In loving memory of Malcolm Forsyth.

Introduction

MARY I. INGRAHAM & ROBERT C. RIVAL

ON JULY 5, 2011, Canada lost one of its finest composers. A three-time JUNO Award winner and Member of the Order of Canada, Dr. Malcolm Forsyth was a prolific composer whose music—orchestral, vocal, and chamber—is admired by musicians and the public alike: by the former for its fine craftsmanship, and by the latter for its immediate appeal.

Forsyth's life path was typically Canadian. Born in 1936 in Pietermaritzburg, South Africa, as an adult he fled the turmoil of the apartheid regime to immigrate to Canada, eventually settling in Edmonton, Alberta, where he accepted positions as a theory and composition professor at the University of Alberta and as a trombonist with the Edmonton Symphony Orchestra. Paradoxically, from this new vantage point he rediscovered the music of his homeland, its vibrant rhythms ultimately becoming a defining feature of his music. But he also turned for inspiration to the sounds of his adopted home, inspired by Indigenous and other music in the broad multicultural soundscape around him. These influences he combined with his training in Western European art music, both classical and modernist in style, to develop a compelling voice that was uniquely Canadian, and uniquely Forsyth.

Reflections on Malcolm Forsyth is a collection of essays that reflect Forsyth's life and work, evidencing the multiple intersections of his personal and professional lives as a friend, colleague, teacher, and composer, and the influences of his creative work on those who knew him personally as well as those who did not. It includes both biographical and musical reflections on this sometimes enigmatic composer, critical exploration of individual works, surveys of repertoire for ensembles (orchestral, brass, choral) that he wrote across his career, and a list of his works. Genres of writing in the collection are also diverse, and include writing in biographical and theoretical styles, close analyses of complete works as well as analytical vignettes of specific moments or ideas within works and personal reminiscences. In essence, this variety of stylistic writing models Forsyth's deeply held personal belief in accessibility of expression as well as the spread of his influence across general and academic audiences. In this regard, *Reflections on Malcolm Forsyth* also acknowledges unique approaches to scholarship on music in Canada: in its inclusion of voices across the artist's life and work, and through its exploration across the composer's work of creative musical responses to multiple cultural influences. Invited authors in this collection include former students, performers and performing colleagues, composers, musicologists, music theorists, educators, close family and friends. Included here are essays by composers Allan Gordon Bell (Calgary) and Robert C. Rival (Ottawa); music theorists Ryan McClelland (Toronto), Roxane Prevost (Ottawa), and Edward Jurkowski (Winnipeg); musicologists Robin Elliott (Toronto), Mary I. Ingraham (Lethbridge), and Kathy Primos (Johannesburg); and musicians, trombonist Dale Sorensen (Charlottetown) and choral conductor Leonard Ratzlaff (Edmonton). Each of these authors has been drawn to Malcolm's music for different reasons—from its beauty and design to its texts and inimitable modes of expression—and all have come away refreshed and inspired.

The collection opens with introductory essays on Forsyth's life and work, followed by musical analyses and analytical vignettes of specific pieces, and concludes with overviews of repertoire for orchestra, brass, and choir. Brief personal reminiscences by friends and colleagues, including a poem written for his memorial by friend and colleague Carl Hare, provide an interlude. Daughter Amanda, a renowned professional cellist, offers a Prelude to the collection and Forsyth's widow, Valerie, its Postlude.

Robin Elliott's essay opens the collection with a biographical account that considers Forsyth's personal and professional experiences, highlighting the significant intercultural encounters reflected in his music from his native South Africa as well as his adopted home in Canada. Elliott experiences Forsyth's career as the intersection of these dual realities: as a South African and a Canadian, a performer and a composer, and as an academic and a mentor to students. While he discusses aspects of Forsyth's life prior to emigrating from South Africa, Elliott's focus is on Forsyth's career in Canada, largely from 1980 onward.

This essay is followed by an extended reminiscence from composer and former student Allan Gordon Bell in the form of a personal account of Forsyth as a teacher and mentor. Bell writes specifically about Forsyth's approach to orchestration, one that privileges a deep commitment to listening for the beauty of sound, and offers musical examples and personal anecdotes that recreate his experiences with Forsyth as a creative teacher and composer.

Five essays follow that explore individual works through close analytical study; these range from early compositions in Canada in 1975 to his final, completed work that premiered shortly before his death. Stylistically, these essays include both analytical vignettes and more extensive theoretical studies on Forsyth's compositions.

Ryan McClelland's thorough analysis of Forsyth's *Rhapsody for 14 Strings* (1982) traces the thematic and tonal development of a small number of motives across this single-movement work. McClelland explores the relationship of their various transformations to the work's overall formal design, arguing that Forsyth's approach builds imaginatively upon tradition.

Roxane Provost offers a discussion of folk song influence from transcriptions of texts and melodies Forsyth used for his *Three Métis Songs from Saskatchewan* (1975). Prevost studies how Forsyth's settings depart from the transcriptions in Barbara Cass-Beggs's collection of Métis songs from Saskatchewan and what that reveals about the composer's aesthetic priorities.

Robert C. Rival's reading of one of Forsyth's most intensely personal works, the cello concerto *Electra Rising* (1995), written for Malcolm's daughter, Amanda, analyzes patterns of voice leading among chords and scales, arguing that sequences of relative tension and repose suggest an abstract psychological narrative that can be interpreted on multiple levels.

Edward Jurkowski examines one of Forsyth's most celebrated works for solo piano, *Je répondrais...* (1997), by considering the role of traditional South African music influences as well as the programmatic attention Forsyth gives to three Western art music composers: Henry Purcell, Robert Schumann, and Frédéric Chopin. Jurkowski's insights into pitch and rhythm reveal integration rather than distinction across its three movements.

Mary I. Ingraham's study of Forsyth's last major work, *A Ballad of Canada* (2011), explores how the composer generates meaning as much by its many fascinating musical layers—including musical self-quotation, a continued reliance on intervallic structures, rich orchestral writing—as through his judicious selection of excerpts from the five Canadian poems he sets for chorus and orchestra. Taking as its point of departure the text of Ralph Gustafson's poem used for its first movement ("Here, all is a beginning"), Ingraham considers what lies between the text and its musical setting as the remainders of a lived, musical life and as a reminder of the composer's unique place in the music of Canada.

Three final chapters provide overviews of Forsyth's orchestral, brass, and choral music across his career. The first is a reprint of a 1994 survey of the early orchestral music by South African musicologist and educator Kathy Primos that was drawn from the author's impressive master's thesis, "The Compositional Styles of Malcolm Forsyth's Orchestral Works: 1968–1982." Primos provides a concise but illuminating summary of important tendencies in Forsyth's orchestral music, notably its African influences, rhythmic attributes, harmonic technique, and timbral refinement, linking these to his lifelong desire to create music attractive to performers and listeners alike.

Trombonist Dale Sorensen writes informatively about Forsyth's many, diverse, and highly regarded compositions for brass instruments in an essay that will appeal to non-performers as well as brass players. Acknowledging Forsyth's personal commitment to the trombone and extraordinary talent as a trombonist, Sorensen blends musical highlights of each work considered with often entertaining commentary and anecdotes derived from his own interviews with performers.

Leonard Ratzlaff offers a conductor's view of Forsyth's substantial output of choral and vocal music arguing that they deserve to be far better known. Ratzlaff's career-long relationship with the choral music of Canada as a performer and celebrated choral conductor, and his personal friendship with Forsyth at the University of Alberta, result in keen perceptions on some of the musical highlights in these works, including a more extended exploration of the merits of the cycle *Hesperides* for chorus and two harps on texts by Robert Herrick.

Our goal in this collection is to document multiple perspectives on Forsyth's life and work from across his often-inseparable personal and professional worlds, and in so doing to offer readers a kaleidoscope of images that reflect the diverse spheres of his creative influence. The richness of Forsyth's creative output and his impact on performers and audiences are evident, manifest even in the short reminiscences included in the Interlude section. Here, performers, composers, colleagues, and close friends share personal stories about Malcolm as they knew him.

As a collection, *Reflections on Malcolm Forsyth* attempts to chronicle some of the many stories of Malcolm Forsyth's life and work, exposing the humanity in his creativity and confirming his lifelong desire to communicate with listeners and performers through challenging yet accessible creative work. His legacy survives beyond these pages through the revelations they might inspire for further listening, performance, or analysis of his music.

1
Reflections on a Life and Career

ROBIN ELLIOTT

WITH HIS COMMANDING PERSONALITY, flair for writing accessible, brilliantly orchestrated music, and prominence as an educator at the University of Alberta, Malcolm Forsyth was a force to be reckoned with on the Canadian music scene from the time of his arrival in 1968 until his death in 2011. His musical education and the start of his career as an orchestral trombonist took place in South Africa, but most of his compositions were created in Edmonton, his home for the last 42 years of his life. His music frequently makes reference to the soundscapes of his native South Africa, but on occasion also includes Indigenous Canadian themes and musical idioms. Indeed, his life can be read as a series of negotiations—between his South African origins and adopted Canadian identity, and among his three simultaneous careers: as professional trombonist, gifted composer, and highly respected university professor.

My contact with Malcolm Forsyth during his lifetime was, regrettably, minimal: I never met him in person, and my communication with him was confined to personal correspondence regarding program notes that I wrote about his music. I recall him as being forthright, modest, and pleased with the attention that was being paid to his music. I have managed to fill out my picture of the man by listening to an extensive selection of his music, speaking with some of those who knew him, listening to audio materials about him, and reading everything I could find about him, both in print and online, including the many obituaries that appeared immediately after his death, several of them by his close friends and colleagues.[1]

Malcolm Denis Forsyth (pronounced For-SYTH, with the accent on the second syllable) was born in Pietermaritzburg, South Africa, on December 8, 1936; it was the 71st birthday of Jean Sibelius, whose music Forsyth admired.[2] Forsyth was born two months after Steve Reich and two months before Philip Glass, composers with whom he has, apart from the proximity of their birthdates, little in common. There is not a single piece in Forsyth's output that could be considered to be minimalist in orientation.[3] Curiously enough, though, both Reich and Forsyth began to be influenced by African music in 1970; for Reich the inspiration came from a trip to Ghana that summer to study drumming, but for Forsyth the use of African musical ideas was a glance back at the homeland he had left by then—a glance that mixed a certain degree of nostalgia with sometimes stringent cultural commentary. I shall return to Forsyth's engagement with the music of Africa at the end of this essay.

Prominent South Africans of Forsyth's generation include Desmond Tutu (b. 1931), the politicians F.W. de Klerk (1936) and Winnie Mandela (1936–2018), the writers Athol Fugard (1932), Breyten Breytenbach (1939), and J.M. Coetzee (1940), and the musicians Miriam Makeba (1932–2008, a singer and civil rights activist known as "Mama Africa"), Chris McGregor (1936–1990, a jazz pianist), Hugh Masekela (1939–2018, a jazz trumpeter), Mike Masote (1941–2017, the first black South African to be awarded a BMUS degree and the founder of several youth orchestras), and Joseph Shabalala (1941, the founder of Ladysmith Black Mambazo). His contemporaries among fellow Canadian composers include R. Murray Schafer (1933), Srul Irving Glick (1934–2002), Michael Conway Baker (1937), Ann Southam (1937–2010), and Jacques Hétu (1938–2010).

Forsyth experienced what he termed an "anal-retentive, Presbyterian upbringing."[4] He was born into a second-generation South African family that was of Scottish origin, but had no artistic inclinations. The composer's father worked for South African Railways and was deputy mayor of Pietermaritzburg from 1948 to 1950, and his brother, Donald, became an accountant. Exposure to music as a child was confined to desultory piano lessons that inspired him to drop music and take up soccer instead. His brother states, "When they re-established a military band at Maritzburg College where he was a pupil, he was given a euphonium to play and his musical interests really took off from there."[5] Forsyth graduated from Maritzburg College in 1953 and began to work in a civil service job. It was not until a couple of years after graduation that an interest in music became a passion for music. As is often the case with those who come to music later in life, a single transformative experience set him on the path to his future career: it was hearing a live performance of Rimsky-Korsakov's *Scheherazade* by the Durban Civic Orchestra under the Dutch conductor Frits Schuurman.[6] As Forsyth related, "I had never heard anything so absolutely mind-blowingly beautiful in my life. It was absolutely stunning, and I was completely knocked out by it. I've never recovered; that was it, and I remember saying 'That's what I'm going to do.' I was nineteen."[7]

Forsyth acquired a trombone and taught himself to play the instrument from a book; soon he was playing in a wind ensemble. By 1959 he had quit his job as a municipal clerk and moved to the opposite side of South Africa to study music at the University of Cape Town. He completed his BMUS degree there in 1963, graduating in the same class as Alan Lessem, who emigrated to Canada shortly after Forsyth did and taught from 1970 until his death in 1991 in the music department at York University in Toronto. Forsyth went on to do his MMUS degree at Cape Town in 1966, and emigrated to Canada early in 1968. He was back in Cape Town from June 1971 to September 1972 on a Canada Council grant to complete his DMUS degree.

Forsyth's composition teachers at Cape Town included Stanley Glasser, Stefans Grové, and Erik Chisholm. The instruction, at least at the undergraduate level, was thoroughly British in nature; the South African–born Glasser was educated at the Guildhall School and

King's College Cambridge, Chisholm was born in Glasgow and was a pupil of Donald Tovey at Edinburgh University, and Grové studied with Chisholm.[8] Students were required to compose pastiche exercises in historical idioms that had little relation to musical reality and still less to contemporary musical idioms. Forsyth, though, found the pastiche exercises useful, for they awakened his interest in quotation and allusion, which were to become important aspects of his own mature compositional style. He studied trombone and conducting at Cape Town as well. His initial career choice in music was to be an orchestral trombone player, and he played for seven years in the Cape Town Symphony. During the 1960s in South Africa, he married his first wife, Lesley Eales, a ballet dancer, and the couple had a daughter, Amanda (b. Cape Town, October 12, 1966); he also began to have his compositions performed professionally, initially by the Cape Town Symphony, of which he was a member.[9]

These developments in Forsyth's life unfolded against the backdrop of the increasingly repressive apartheid regime in South Africa, which resulted in the country becoming a pariah state among the nations of the world. The Afrikaner Nationalist Party came to power in 1948, when Forsyth was 11 years old, and quickly moved to consolidate the existing apartheid practices. Marriage and sexual relations between whites and non-whites were forbidden, and all other aspects of life were strictly segregated by race: residential areas, medical care, beaches, and all facets of public service, including education.[10] In 1959, when Forsyth began his studies at the University of Cape Town, the Extension of University Education Act excluded all non-whites from white universities. In 1960 the Sharpeville massacre galvanized opposition to the apartheid regime, both within South Africa and internationally. As Forsyth was completing his BMUS degree, Nelson Mandela was tried, found guilty of treason, and sentenced to life in prison. In June 1967 the Defence Amendment Act introduced compulsory military service for all white South African men; shortly thereafter, in January 1968, Forsyth and his family left South Africa. They travelled on the SA *Oranje*, a Union-Castle Line ship, from Cape Town to Southampton, and then flew to Toronto, arriving there in the midst of winter.[11]

From his base in Toronto, where he eked out a living by working at a record store (the famous Sam the Record Man store on Yonge Street) and doing occasional supply teaching, Forsyth sent out his CV to universities across Canada. He was soon offered a position as an assistant professor of theory and composition at the University of Alberta. Together with his wife and young daughter, he drove to Edmonton in 1968 to take up the university position that he would hold for the next 34 years. He also played in the Edmonton Symphony Orchestra for 11 of those years (bass trombone, 1968–1971 and principal trombone, 1973–1980) and continued to play the trombone in various other ensembles on an occasional basis until 1996. At the University of Alberta, he taught theory and musicianship, composition, and trombone; he also conducted the university's symphony orchestra and was University composer-in-residence at the time of his retirement at age 65 in 2002. He continued to compose until his death in 2011. His last major work was *A Ballad of Canada*, written for the National Arts Centre Orchestra; it is a setting for chorus and orchestra of five poems by Canadian authors (including a new poem by his friend and former University of Alberta colleague Carl Hare).[12] By the time of the premiere, Forsyth had been hospitalized with pancreatic cancer and knew he did not have long to live.[13] He was released from hospital on oxygen tanks, a flight to Ottawa was arranged, and he was in the National Arts Centre to receive a standing ovation after the first performance of the work on June 9, 2011. He then returned to Edmonton and died less than a month later.

By all accounts that I have read and heard, Forsyth was a formidable individual. The obituary issued by his family notes, "As a friend, he was often a challenge, never letting go a casual statement that was ill-thought out. He loved to debate and loved to win. He loved a crowd, and he loved the stage, and when he walked into a room, the room became full. He loved to tell stories and make people laugh."[14] The choral conductor Leonard Ratzlaff, a friend and colleague, remarks that Forsyth was a "crusty individual" and a "brilliant and somewhat intimidating presence," but also recalls "his love of life, his raucous laughter, his fondness for great food and drink (especially wine and scotch), and the numerous parties at his house that were legendary for his generosity."[15] Ratzlaff notes that Forsyth had "deeply held views on what he perceived to be declining standards of musical training of students for professions in music, and [an] unerring commitment to raising those standards."[16] Trumpet player and conductor Fordyce Pier, who was chair of the University of Alberta's Department of Music at the time of Forsyth's retirement, added that, "He mellowed somewhat over the years, but still I would say that the outstanding feature was kind of an uncompromising standard of excellence. He believed a lot in basics [and] a lot of hard work, and was not afraid to give [a student] the bad news that, this time, they didn't measure up."[17] The pianist Janet Scott Hoyt, who was a student in Forsyth's first classes at the University of Alberta and later became a colleague, also uses the word *uncompromising* to describe Forsyth: "He was uncompromising in his expectations as he tried to fill the gaps in our musical education."[18] Massage therapist Valerie Simons met Forsyth after a concert that he had conducted in 2000, and soon afterwards become his partner; after living with him for many years, she became his third wife in January 2011.[19] She remarks that "his list of interests was endless: poetry, history, religion, politics, woodworking, watercolours, languages, and travel. He was a voracious reader—in his areas of knowledge, he was encyclopedic."[20]

At the time of Forsyth's death, I was familiar with only a small portion of his creative output. I had written liner notes for recordings of three of his works—*Atayoskewin, Fanfare and Three Masquerades,* and *Jubilee Overture.*[21] I knew that *Three Métis Songs from Saskatchewan,* which has been recorded commercially several times, is probably his best-known work and counts as a standard repertoire piece in the genre of Canadian vocal music.[22] *Sun Songs,* a setting of poems by Doris Lessing for mezzo-soprano and orchestra that was composed for Judith Forst, was also familiar to me; I had heard the broadcast premiere on CBC Radio and it made a strong and lasting impression.[23] In preparing to write this essay, I acquired 37 of Forsyth's works that have been commercially recorded (117 CD tracks—about nine hours' worth of music) and listened to them at least three or four times each.

A handful of his works that I particularly enjoyed I listened to a dozen times or more. In addition to the commercially recorded music, 20 further works by Forsyth are available on CentreStreams, the Canadian Music Centre's streaming audio service—another four hours or so of music.[24] It was a very rewarding experience to get to know Forsyth's catalogue of works in greater depth. If I had to sum up his music with a single adjective, it would be *exuberant*. Bursting with energy, brilliantly scored and orchestrated, full of lively rhythms and memorable lyrical melodies, his music is written to be rewarding to play for the performers and immediately accessible to the audience members. Wide ranging in style and idiom, his music can be thoughtful and introspective at times, but at its most characteristic the music evokes a mood of celebration and outgoing enthusiasm.

Just under half of Forsyth's total catalogue is available on commercial and archival recordings. Not counting the 30 or so arrangements that he made of music by other composers, he wrote about 135 original compositions, 57 of which have been recorded; to put it another way, he wrote about 28 hours of music in total, just over 13 hours of which has been recorded. Some of his major works remain unavailable on recording, including his longest work, *Evangeline*, a cantata with text by Henry Wadsworth Longfellow for soprano, trumpet, and chamber orchestra, and *A Ballad of Canada*, his only major work for choir and orchestra and his last major completed work.[25] But a representative selection has been recorded for posterity and can easily be accessed. Everything that he wrote for public performance has been heard in the concert hall, most of it several times over. At the height of his career in the 1980s, his music was receiving over 100 live public performances each year.

Forsyth's love of and great respect for the venerable traditions of European art music are evident in his preference for standard orchestral and chamber music groupings (though there is no opera and not a single work for string quartet in his catalogue), and also in the deft use of allusion and quotation in his music—often for humorous purposes but always a humour born of fondness and respect rather than mockery. His stylistic idiom is extraordinarily varied; influences on his music range from baroque music to Olivier Messiaen, and from jazz to African music. His command of traditional orchestration techniques is impressive; particularly notable is his flair for using the brass choir of the orchestra and also solo brass instruments to great effect. His intimate understanding of the cello is striking, as shown in the cello concerto *Electra Rising* and the many other works he wrote for his gifted daughter, Amanda, a Juilliard graduate who was the principal cellist of the National Arts Centre Orchestra in Ottawa from 1999 to 2015.[26]

Notwithstanding the inevitable ups and downs of inspiration that accompany the pressures of the commissioning process, his music consistently attains high professional standards, is engaging to listen to, and bears up well after many repeated hearings. His emotional range is enormous; the music is by turns profound, sorrowful, witty, dreamlike, virtuosic, cheeky, and introspective. It is never boring, and always respects the players' abilities and the audience's expectations. At its best, it is on a par with the finest music of its day and age.

Some particularly memorable moments for me are the conclusion of the *Jubilee Overture*, when the opening brass fanfares and flourishes return in a stirring culminating gesture; the third movement of *Atayoskewin*, a rollicking and witty dance for full orchestra with some wonderful writing for the brass instruments; the last movement of *Electra Rising*, a hymn-like and radiant movement that ends with upward rising melodies and great sweeping double stops in the solo cello that imbue the music with a profound sense of struggle and triumph; and the third and final movement of *Sun Songs*, which ends with a wonderful soaring vocal line that is reminiscent of Richard Strauss at his most transcendentally beautiful.

Speaking of his music in an interview that aired on CBC Radio on the occasion of the premiere of his *Serenade for Strings* on May 12, 1986, Forsyth stated, "There are two kinds of pieces really; there are two kinds of compositions. There's the one where one is trying to expand one's own musical environment—I call them my research pieces—and then there are pieces which have to hit the target, have to hit the bull's eye on the first shot, and for these pieces I draw on my experience now. I have written a great deal of music, and I have a language of my own, and I can expand on ideas from previous pieces."[27] Richard Taruskin notes that Aaron Copland similarly "maintained two compositional approaches, one diatonic and the other twelve-tone. He called them his 'popular' and 'difficult' styles; on occasion he referred to them as his 'public' and 'private' manners."[28] In his so-called research pieces, Forsyth uses a variety of compositional idioms, including not only twelve-tone techniques, but also Messiaen's modes of limited transposition, atonality, and other contemporary idioms, whereas the accessible pieces feature an eclectic idiom that could broadly be labelled tonal, ranging from traditional tonality through to bitonal and polytonal idioms, sometimes including stretches of ambivalent tonality.[29]

Taking this statement at face value, one could divide his output into the research pieces on the one hand, such as the *Quintette for Winds*, the trumpet and piano concertos, and *Steps...* for viola and piano; and the accessible works on the other hand, including *Three Métis Songs from Saskatchewan*, *Jubilee Overture*, and *Atayoskewin*. Ultimately, though, this simple binary division is not really workable. Many of his works combine both the research and accessible styles—for instance, *Electra Rising*, *Fanfare and Three Masquerades*, and *Sun Songs*. Even in his most adventurous research pieces, the idiom remains intelligible to the average non-specialist listener, for this was his ultimate goal in writing music. In an oft-quoted artistic credo from October 1996, Forsyth placed great store on the audience's response to his music:

> *I always have had a sense of responsibility to the audience, coming from a deep sense of belief. I am myself a dedicated audience member, dedicated to the idea of concert music that does sweep people away. I'm never more happy than when I can be transported by a performer or performance. Everything I've done is with that experience in mind: changing the space that the audience sits in for those brief few moments.*[30]

Forsyth's frequent recourse to tonal procedures was not fashionable for a Canadian university-based composer during the 1970s and 1980s, and may have cost him the respect of some of his academic colleagues. The use of expanded tonality was not uncommon among composers of Forsyth's generation, but in the university environment it was unfashionable at best, perhaps even suspect for a good deal of Forsyth's career. Nonetheless, together with Violet Archer, who arrived at the University of Alberta six years before he did, he was among the first generation of composers in Alberta to achieve a significant national and international reputation. Archer and Forsyth also trained the next generation of Alberta composers, including Allan Gordon Bell, Allan Gilliland, and Robert Rosen.

Forsyth's association with the Edmonton Symphony Orchestra (ESO) was an important part of his career in Canada; during his years as a trombonist in the orchestra, the playing standards steadily improved, and in 1971 it became a full-time professional ensemble, rehearsing during the daytime rather than in the evenings. Forsyth truly had an insider's knowledge of how the orchestra works and of the kinds of music that orchestra players find rewarding to perform. After he left the ESO, his association with the ensemble continued; the orchestra premiered seven of his compositions and two ESO recordings of his music won JUNO Awards for Best Classical Composition.

Beginning with *Sketches from Natal* of 1970 (written for the CBC and his first work to be commissioned in Canada), Forsyth often incorporated ideas inspired by African music into his compositions, something that, curiously enough, is not a feature of the handful of works that he completed while still resident in South Africa.[31] One must be cautious about the reductive nature of the phrase "African music," however; the music of an entire continent, in all its richness and diversity, cannot be reduced to a few stock rhythmic and textural ideas that will somehow convey the authenticity of lived experience in that part of the world. Nevertheless, there is a substantial body of scholarship in ethnomusicology, from Erich von Hornbostel to Kofi Agawu, that takes it as given that something called "African music" does indeed exist.[32] Ethnomusicological scruples aside, it is debatable whether this "African music" can retain its geographical specificity when it has been sundered from its original cultural, social, political, and historical context and transplanted into a concert music tradition that is closely associated with the European colonizers of the continent.

This is not to say that Forsyth was insensitive in his use of African materials. He was actively opposed to the policy and practices of apartheid, left the country for this reason, and wrote the orchestral work *Siyajabula!* to celebrate the end of the apartheid era and the election of Nelson Mandela as the president of South Africa in 1994. For the most part, he draws upon musical idioms of the Zulu people with whose music he was in daily contact as a child growing up in Pietermaritzburg. The titles of several of his pieces and movements of other pieces are in the Zulu language, which he learned to speak as a second language. Unlike Steve Reich or, for that matter, ethnomusicologists who experience African music as part of what could be broadly construed as "tourist culture," Forsyth came to this idiom as part of his birthright.

Nevertheless, the problematic nature of white composers adopting an African identity by drawing upon the music of black Africa has received a good deal of commentary from South African writers. Hans Roosenschoon, in an article on cross-culturalism and the South African composer, asks some pointed questions: Should those composers who wish to absorb African elements become ethnomusicologists, making field trips or diligently studying tape recordings? Are only the musical materials of interest, or should the composer consider also the broader cultural context? Should the incorporated indigenous material be recognizable, and if so only to Western or African ears? Roosenschoon concludes that "it is impossible for a composer of Western art-music, when taking material from African sources, to be anything else except an 'exoticist,'" for the simple reason that it is not possible to do equal justice to both worlds, either aesthetically or musically.[33] In Forsyth's case, however, I would suggest that, *pace* Roosenschoon, his use of African-inspired musical materials was not exoticism, but rather an honest attempt to reflect an important aspect of his own African identity and to express his solidarity with black Africa. More research remains to be done on this aspect of Forsyth's creative life, but I believe that he was one of those composers who, in Roosenschoon's words, "voiced their conceptual rejection of apartheid not only verbally, but also, and perhaps more deeply, via the elemental voice of their art."[34]

There are many ways to measure a composer's success: some of these factors include the number and prestige of commissions, critical reception, the number of performances and repeat performances, the prestige of the performers who premiere and perform the music, the number of broadcasts and recordings, commercial publication and distribution of representative works, and awards and other types of external recognition, both musical and honorific. Forsyth scored in the middle to high range of Canadian composers of his generation in each of these rubrics. From the mid-1970s onwards, all of his music was commissioned, with increasingly prominent performers involved; his music was frequently heard in concerts and broadcasts; he won three JUNO Awards for Best Classical Composition (in 1987 for *Atayoskewin*, in 1995 for *Sketches from Nulul*, and in 1998 for *Electra Rising*), was named Composer of the Year by the Canadian Music Council in 1989, and was named a Member of the Order of Canada in 2003. His music was performed across Canada and in the United States, in his native South Africa, and on occasion in Europe as well. Plentiful though the recognition and successes were during his life, now that he is dead the full measure of his abilities and achievements will be taken. This book is the beginning of that ongoing process of assessment, and as these essays demonstrate, his legacy richly deserves to be celebrated because he was one of the truly outstanding Canadian composers of his day.

NOTES

1. My sources include the following: an interview between Malcolm Forsyth and Richard Moses that aired in 1988 on Edmonton radio station CKUA, archived on the Canadian Music Centre's streaming audio service at https://musiccentre.ca/centrestreams; an excellent 55-minute audio documentary about Forsyth produced by Eitan Cornfield on the first CD of the two-CD set *Canadian Composers Portraits: Malcolm Forsyth* (Centrediscs CMCCD 8802, 2002) (hereafter "Forsyth Documentary"), and a transcription of the documentary by Darius Truhlar online http://www.musiccentre.ca/sites/www.musiccentre.ca/files/resources/pdfmedia/forsyth-portrait-en.pdf; an hour-long 2008 interview between Malcolm Forsyth and John Gray, interspersed with musical excerpts from five works by Forsyth, available on a

Canadian Music Centre podcast, http://www.musiccentre.ca/node/65921; an outstanding 45-minute television documentary, *Conquering Beauty: The Life and Music of Malcolm Forsyth*, written, directed, and produced by Theresa Wynnyk for Company of Women on the Screen in association with the CBC, which aired on July 27, 2015, in the CBC series *Absolutely Alberta* (the documentary includes interviews with 20 friends and family members and excerpts from 20 works by Forsyth); a series of three podcasts titled "Remembering Malcolm Forsyth" (October 27, 2011), 48 minutes total duration, featuring Robert Rival in interview with Allan Gordon Bell and Allan Gilliland, both of whom studied composition with Forsyth, available on Robert Rival's website at http://www.robertrival.com/writing.html#podcast; a biographical sketch and list of compositions available at http://malcolmforsythcomposer.ca; and a finding aid to the Malcolm Forsyth fonds at the University of Calgary, https://searcharchives.ucalgary.ca/malcolm-forsyth-fonds.

2. Sibelius's Fifth Symphony (which was premiered on the composer's 50th birthday) inspired the second movement of Forsyth's orchestral suite *Atayoskewin*. In an interview with John Gray (at 52:28) for the podcast *The Composer's Chair*, Forsyth remarks in passing, "Although I share the same birthday as Sibelius, I'm not the same as him, either, because I don't drink quite as much vodka as he did, poor man...In other respects I would be delighted to think of myself as similar to him." See John Gray, "Episode 3: Malcolm Forsyth," *The Composer's Chair* (podcast), Canadian Music Centre, 2008, http://www.musiccentre.ca/node/65921. The Czech composer Bohuslav Martin (1890–1959) was also born on December 8.
3. In an interview on the CBC Radio program *Two New Hours* on November 28, 2004, about his work *umGcomo* (1999) for two pianos and percussion, Forsyth states, "There are melodic fragments; it's the closest I've ever come to minimalism, I suppose, which is a style I absolutely abhor." Forsyth emphasizes that the repetitive melodic idiom of *umGcomo* was inspired by African music, rather than the influence of minimalist composers. The interview can be heard on the Canadian Music Centre's streaming audio service at https://musiccentre.ca/centrestreams.
4. As quoted by his daughter Amanda Forsyth in Cornfield, "Forsyth Documentary."
5. Donald Forsyth, as quoted in "Obituary: A Composer of High Acclaim at Home and in Canada," *The Witness* (Pietermaritzburg), July 12, 2011. Other notable alumni of Maritzburg College include Alan Paton (1903–1988, the author of *Cry, The Beloved Country*) and the composer Kevin Volans (b. 1949).
6. Schuurman (1898–1972) was conductor of the Durban Civic Orchestra from 1955 to 1966. In 1955 the Durban Civic Orchestra had 31 players; presumably the ranks were filled out with contract players for the performance of *Scheherazade* on tour in Pietermaritzburg. For information about Schuurman's career in South Africa, see Sjoerd Alkema, "Conductors of the Cape Town Municipal Orchestra, 1914–1965: A Historical Perspective" (PHD diss., University of Cape Town, 2012), 149–53.
7. Cornfield, "Forsyth Documentary."

8. See the respective entries on these three men in the first two volumes of Jacques P. Malan, ed., *South African Music Encyclopedia* (Cape Town: Oxford University Press, 1979, 1982).
9. Lesley and Malcolm Forsyth divorced in 1981; Lesley moved to Adelaide, Australia, and lived there for 15 years before returning to Canada in 2000 to manage her daughter Amanda's career as a cellist; see Roberta Walker, "The Sensuous Cellist," *Ottawa City* (April/May 2002). Malcolm Forsyth was married to his second wife, Connie Braun, for five years before that marriage also ended in divorce in 2001.
10. Of the six concerts that Stravinsky conducted in South Africa in 1962, for example, five were for whites-only audiences; a sixth concert for blacks was added as window dressing, apparently at Stravinsky's suggestion; see John Hinch, "Stravinsky in Africa," *Muziki: Journal of Music Research in Africa* 1, no. 1 (2004): 71–86. Forsyth played in the trombone section of the Cape Town Symphony under Stravinsky during this tour.
11. Gray, "Malcolm Forsyth," *The Composer's Chair*; Cornfield, "Forsyth Documentary."
12. Hare also wrote a poem for Forsyth's memorial service in Edmonton in 2011. This poem, "Malcolm Forsyth," is reproduced in this volume. See also Mary Ingraham's study of *A Ballad of Canada* in this volume.
13. See Colin Eatock, "Composer Malcolm Forsyth: Out of Crisis, A Musical Creation," *Globe and Mail*, June 8, 2011, http://www.theglobeandmail.com/arts/music/composer-malcolm-forsyth-out-of-crisis-a-musical-creation/article598565/. Pancreatic cancer has the lowest survival rate of the 21 different common types of cancer.
14. See Obituary of Malcolm Forsyth, Connelly-McKinley online obituaries, n.d., accessed January 15, 2016, http://www.connelly-mckinley.com/obituary_intro.php?id=589.
15. Leonard Ratzlaff, "My Friend Malcolm," *Reflections on Choral Music* (blog), July 10, 2011, http://choralhelix.blogspot.ie/2011_07_01_archive.html. See also Ratzlaff's survey of Forsyth's choral music in this volume.
16. Ratzlaff, "My Friend Malcolm."
17. Cornfield, "Forsyth Documentary."
18. Janet Scott Hoyt, "Some Thoughts about Malcolm Forsyth," University of Alberta Department of Music, July 2011, accessed January 31, 2014, www.music.ualberta.ca/en/news/2011/July/OnaPersonalNoteDepartmentofMusicTeachingFacultyShareMemoriesofMalcolmForsyth.aspx.
19. See also Valerie Forsyth's Postlude in this volume.
20. See Obituary of Malcolm Forsyth, Connelly-McKinley online obituaries, n.d.
21. *Atayoskewin: Suite for Orchestra* was recorded by the Edmonton Symphony Orchestra under Uri Mayer and was released on CBC SM-5059 in 1986; *Fanfare and Three Masquerades* was recorded by the Canadian Chamber Ensemble and issued on

Centrediscs CMC 3488 in 1988; and *Jubilee Overture* was recorded by the Edmonton Symphony Orchestra under Uri Mayer and issued on CBC SM-5069 in 1986.

22. See Roxane Prevost's study of this work in this volume.
23. *Sun Songs* was written in 1985 on a commission from CBC Vancouver. The premiere was given December 6, 1987, by Judith Forst with the CBC Vancouver Orchestra conducted by Mario Bernardi in a concert to celebrate the 10th anniversary of the Canadian Music Centre's British Columbia regional office. The program is available online at http://musiccentre.ca/node/60434. The CBC broadcast of the concert took place on December 22, 1987.
24. See Canadian Music Centre, CentreStreams, www.musiccentre.ca/centrestreams/. Some of Forsyth's works can also be heard on the CBC's streaming audio service, CBC Music.
25. Part One of *Evangeline* (about half of the work) can be heard on the Canadian Music Centre's streaming audio service, CentreStreams (www.musiccentre.ca/centrestreams/), but the complete work has not been recorded. The last work Forsyth wrote is *Bis for Brahms*; it is an encore for violin and cello, written to be played after the Brahms Double Concerto, Op. 102. *Bis for Brahms* was composed for the cellist Amanda Forsyth (the composer's daughter) to perform with her husband, the violinist and conductor Pinchas Zukerman. See Peter Amsel, "Malcolm Forsyth: In Memoriam," *The Inner Voice of the CrazyComposer* (blog), July 6, 2011, http://crazycomposer.blogspot.ca/2011/07/malcolm-forsyth-in-memoriam.html.
26. See also Robert Rival's study of *Electra Rising* in this volume. When her husband, Pinchas Zukerman, stepped down as the music director of the National Arts Centre Orchestra in 2015, Amanda Forsyth also left her position as the orchestra's principal cellist. The couple relocated to New York City and continue to appear around the world, both separately and together, as soloists and chamber musicians.
27. The interview can be heard on the Canadian Music Centre's streaming audio service, www.musiccentre.ca/centrestreams/, which can be accessed via Forsyth's showcase page, http://www.musiccentre.ca/node/37179/.
28. Richard Taruskin, *The Oxford History of Western Music*, vol. 5, *Music in the Late Twentieth Century* (Oxford: Oxford University Press, 2010), 111–12.
29. In an interview with John Gray in 2008, Forsyth stated "I have never, at any stage, abandoned tonality. That's why I am sort of on the outskirts of modern music practice, and always have been and always shall be." See "Malcolm Forsyth," *The Composer's Chair.*
30. This quotation is reproduced, in whole or in part, on many websites and in the composer's biography in the online version of the *Encyclopedia of Music in Canada* (http://www.thecanadianencyclopedia.com/en/article/malcolm-forsyth-emc/, accessed January 15, 2016), which gives the source as the composer's website and the date as 2003. The quotation seems to be from a radio interview dating

from October 1996, but the exact original source has not been located. See also, "Composer Malcolm Forsyth Dies at 74," CBC *News*, July 5, 2011, https://www.cbc.ca/news/entertainment/composer-malcolm-forsyth-dies-at-74-1.1109680.

31. A partial list of his African-influenced works includes *Sketches from Natal* (1970), *Music for Mouths, Marimba, Mbira and Roto-Toms* (1973), Concerto for Pianoforte and Orchestra (1973–79), *African Ode (Symphony No. 3)* (1981), *ukuZalwa* (1983), *Three Zulu Songs* (1988), *Valley of a Thousand Hills* (1989), *The Kora Dances* (1990), *Natal Landscapes* (1993), *Electra Rising* (1995—the second movement is subtitled "Mayibuye Afrika!"), *Siyajabula! We Rejoice* (1996), *umGcomo* (1999), and *Je répondrais...* (1997—the second movement of which is "à Schumann: Thumb-Piano" and the third movement is "à Chopin: White-Key Study in African Mode").

32. There were no ethnomusicologists in South Africa before the German academic Veit Erlmann was appointed to the University of Natal in Durban in 1981; see Carol A. Muller, *Focus: Music of South Africa*, 2nd ed. (New York: Routledge, 2008), 13. Akin Euba stated that ethnomusicology is "irrelevant to African culture," though he himself is both a leading composer of African art music and an ethnomusicologist; see his "Issues in Africanist Musicology," in *Proceedings of the Forum for Revitalizing African Music Studies in Higher Education*, ed. Frank D. Gunderson (Ann Arbor: US Secretariat of the International Center for African Music and Dance, The International Institute, University of Michigan, 2001), 139. Martin Scherzinger voices similar reservations about ethnomusicology's treatment of African music, writing of its "implicit academic imperialism," in "Towards a Supplementary Approach to the Study of African Music within Modernity," paper delivered at the Music Studies and Cultural Difference conference, London, 1997, accessed January 15, 2016, http://www.open.ac.uk/Arts/music/mscd/scherz.html.

33. Hans Roosenschoon, "Keeping Our Ears to the Ground: Cross-Culturalism and the Composer in South Africa, 'Old' and 'New,'" in *Composing the Music of Africa*, ed. Malcolm Floyd (Aldershot: Ashgate, 1999), 267.

34. Roosenschoon, "Keeping Our Ears," 265.

2

Sonorous Pleasure

Portrait of a Master Orchestrator as Pedagogue

ALLAN GORDON BELL

When old age shall this generation waste,
Thou shalt remain, in midst of other woe
Than ours, a friend to man, to whom thou say'st,
"Beauty is truth, truth beauty,"—that is all
Ye know on earth, and all ye need to know.

—JOHN KEATS, "Ode on a Grecian Urn" (lines 46–50)

IN THE FALL OF 1974, at my first composition lesson with Malcolm Forsyth, he declared, "I can teach you nothing about composition. Understood? Good. Now, let's get started." What transpired over the course of several years of study, and then as a feature of just about every subsequent conversation that we had, was an intensive examination of music: mine, his, the works of the masters that he pulled from the shelf or played from memory at the piano, or new works we had just heard at concerts. I began to understand that the lessons he wished to impart, first as a teacher and then as an engaging colleague, were contained in the questions that he asked: What is the essential idea? Does it *sound*? Is it expressive? Is it clear? Does it contain wit, in the sense of being evidence of a keen intelligence, in other words, of being worth saying? Is it well made overall? The one question that he never asked—yet I remain convinced that this is what lay at the very heart of his own compositional aspirations—was: Is it beautiful?

Of course Keats's assertion in "Ode on a Grecian Urn" that "beauty is truth" is completely untenable, fraught as it is with complex aesthetic and epistemological issues if taken at face value and out of context. But, combined with "in the midst of other woe / Than ours, a friend to man," the assertion speaks to the reasons that most of us sincerely turn to art, poetry, and music: for pleasure, for consolation, for intimations of transcendence, for expression of ineffable values beyond and through material struggle, or for the affirmation that comes from an encounter with the beautiful. In the postserialist, poststructuralist, postmodernist realm that was the context for composers in the mid-1970s in North America (especially those who worked also in academia), no one with a Keatsian sensibility was taken seriously, which is no doubt why I never heard Forsyth discuss the notion of beauty in his own work until our very last conversation at his home in February of 2011. I do not think that this was a matter of intellectual cowardice or of some kind of careerism on his part—his ferocious skepticism and eloquent defence of his cultural, political, and philosophical positions belie that notion—but rather I think that he chose to "speak" about the issue of beauty *through his music*. And, I think that his expressive, indeed often exquisite, approach to instrumental timbre is a major component of his musical "voice."

Forsyth taught orchestration in an idiosyncratic manner, no doubt derived from both his own traditional education and from his years of experience as an orchestral player and conductor. Students had to learn instrumentation—range, register, transposition, notation—as well as rudimentary principles of scoring, all of which are contained in every orchestration textbook. However, he also emphasized the need for careful and capacious listening, especially to the standard repertoire; for Forsyth, all of this was merely the beginning. It was in his advanced classes that his particular approach to the problems of making something *sound* well became evident. At this point, he stressed the importance of recognizing that composers were not scoring for instruments but for the players of those instruments, so that an understanding of idiomatic usage was paramount. Students needed to understand how the sound was embodied—breath, embouchure, bow arm, fingering—and how the sound would be shaped by the performer according to each musician's understanding of the intent of a passage. For Forsyth, every musical idea was also a choreographic idea: ease of playing implied background material, while the use of challenging yet idiomatic fingerings and articulations brought more intensity to the sound, suggesting foreground material. Choreographing the appropriate kind of playing results in clarity of musical intent and, in Forsyth's opinion, orchestrators reverse these at their peril. Consequently, and as Forsyth's teaching encouraged, a piece that is well made has a chance of being well played. Such statements may appear to be truisms, yet they are notoriously difficult to realize in large-scale composition because of the inherent complexity that arises in combining timbres.

Composers typically learn to score music (to choose the appropriate combinations of instrumental sounds to convey the musical intent of a passage) by doing orchestration exercises and listening to the results as well as by carefully analyzing the work of other composers, in particular those of the acknowledged masters, much as was promoted by Forsyth in his teaching. Difficulties emerge in the latter case because, unlike pitch and rhythm, there is no analytic solfège for timbre that is commonly accepted. Instead, textbooks generally revert to adjectives (dark, clear, brilliant, etc.) when speaking of an instrument's register or of a specific scoring (harmonic or inharmonic with respect to the overtone series). Forsyth bypassed this issue by asking his students to imagine as many possibilities for the sound of a passage as they could and then to make the appropriate choice for their own work. A prodigious memory for the sounds of instrumental combinations, of course, is only attainable through careful listening as a lifelong pursuit; Forsyth himself had this capacity, and continuously encouraged his students to develop theirs.

But listening was not enough. Forsyth taught his advanced students to try to reimagine the pathway that lead a composer to make a specific decision on timbre, suggesting a three-stage process: generating an harmonic reduction of the passage (normally playable on one piano and, sometimes, two) and eliminating all doublings; reimagining the orchestration of this reduction through a study of the musical styles of major composers from the past, reincorporating their doublings and applying their likely choices for timbres and specific musical perspectives (whether foreground, middle-ground, or background); and after giving due consideration to the historical approaches of these composers, identifying the idiosyncratic choices that result in the individual sound of the composer under examination. For example, in considering an excerpt from Bartók's *Concerto for Orchestra,* after reducing the passage students might reimagine the score according to the approaches and resources of Haydn, Berlioz, and Debussy, resulting in at least three examples (or more if one chose to think through the myriad choices that each of these composers might have used), all of which pointed towards the peculiar way in which Bartók used conventional means and the innovative choices in his orchestration. Painstaking as it was, the process taught by Forsyth led to deeper listening and a larger store of memorized sound.

Preparing this essay sent me back to the score of *Atayoskewin,* one of Forsyth's most frequently performed orchestral compositions, and my first, and almost paralyzing, shock was seeing his notation. He composed it while still using pen and ink, and there is something intensely personal about his manner of inscribing the notes, simultaneously fastidious and flamboyant. I was his copyist for two years and I spent many hours with this handwriting, and for me it is virtually inseparable from his voice. He insisted that I attend first rehearsals to learn how much time is wasted when parts contain mistakes, and his voice was always in my mind's ear as I copied subsequent pieces. A singular pain that arises from the death of someone important is that those who are left behind can never hear that voice again.

The last time I saw him was a cold February afternoon and evening just a few months before he died, and among the many things of which we spoke was that, creatively speaking, he only had one regret: that he had spent too much time trying to please others, time that he should have spent composing what he really wanted to. When I asked him what that would have been, he replied that it would be more of what he was composing now. Later that day we listened to a telephone message from Duain Wolfe, the conductor who had just directed the Ottawa chorus at the National Arts Centre in its initial rehearsal of what turned out to be Forsyth's last major composition, *A Ballad of Canada*, effusively praising the work, and closing with the statement that many of the performers considered it to be "the most beautiful piece—*ever*!" Forsyth's delight was such that we listened to that recording a dozen times.

When I arrived that February afternoon to visit Malcolm and his wife, Valerie, I was welcomed to their home by a majestic black standard poodle, who was obviously very protective of his masters. The dog sat quietly during our conversations, holding us all under careful observation. The dog's name is Keats.

3

Remembering and Continuing

Rhapsody for 14 Strings

RYAN MCCLELLAND

ALTHOUGH PERHAPS BETTER KNOWN for his orchestral music and vast output of chamber music for brass instruments, Malcolm Forsyth also created highly effective works for string ensembles. Among these is his *Rhapsody for 14 Strings*, composed in 1982 and commissioned by the Canadian Music Centre for Stephen and Sue Jane Bryant, a violinist and violist based in Edmonton at the time.[1] The ensemble consists of four first violins, four second violins, three violas, two cellos, and double bass; owing to the considerable doubling among the instruments, the ensemble is generally treated more as a small string orchestra than as a large chamber group. A single-movement work lasting approximately 14 minutes, the Rhapsody is a masterful study in thematic development, transporting the listener through an intricate web of relationships and transformations. The principal thematic materials are plainly presented at the outset: a high-register octatonic scale segment descending from E, horn fifths pitched in E major in the middle register, and a low sustained E minor triad. The familiarity of these gestures facilitates their recognition as they are varied, and it encourages hearing them in dialogue with the conventions of earlier musical practices. This essay follows thematic development in the Rhapsody, exploring how its materials come into conflict, exchange characteristics, and are transformed. Central to my interpretation of these processes is the directionality provided by neo-tonal pitch organization as well as the continuity achieved through the blurring of formal boundaries. These contexts reveal the expert linking of musical structure and meaning in a composition that is as solidly crafted as it is immediately expressive. With an improvisatory quality befitting its title, the Rhapsody seems immersed in remembering and continuing, both its own history and that of the musical tradition to which it belongs.

In the program note accompanying the score, Forsyth outlines the form of the Rhapsody. His descriptions of the four principal sections provide a good initial orientation, and I cite them in their entirety below (with measure numbers, timings, and metronome markings from the score added):

> *Lento, pensato* (mm. 1–38; 0'00" – 2'15"): 4/4 (quarter = 72), in which the material of the entire work is presented, *viz.*, a descending pattern of whole and half steps, a repeated E-minor chord, and a motif in the violas based on so-called "horn" fifths.
>
> *Allegretto giusto* (mm. 39–149; 2'15" – 5'35"): 6/4 (dotted half = 66), wherein various *ostinatos* present themselves and jazz-like figures cascade in violins and cellos.
>
> *Lento, come prima* (mm. 150–200; 5'35" – 8'20"): 4/4 (quarter = 66), an elaboration of the first section, incorporating an extended interlude for solo violin.
>
> *Allegretto, leggero* (mm. 201–510; 8'20" – 13'05"): 6/8 (dotted quarter = 132), further variation and development in a fairly complex chain of events. Rhythmic *ostinatos* are again much to the fore; there is a new theme in the violins, and cross rhythms abound. The piece ends by simply and restfully fading into silence.[2]

At each of these formal boundaries there is considerable continuity, arising through sustained pitches and overlapping thematic material, features that are explored in more detail below. In addition, the maintenance of a common basic pulse (MM = 66) supports continuity, and this feeling of a consistent pulse even remains after the first section with its slightly faster pulse (MM = 72). The first section concludes with two statements of a two-measure gesture, and the second of these ends with a sustained chord beneath a fermata. Besides the loosening of the metric environment provided by the sustained chord and the fermata, the larger musical context invites a slight ritardando by sensitive performers.

Lento, pensato: Sowing Seeds

As noted above, the materials of the opening section infuse the entire work. They also establish E as the work's pitch centre. Less immediately apparent but no less significant are their interactions that suggest paths for future development and contrast. Furthermore, some relationships among the seemingly disparate materials emerge already within the initial section. Figure 3.1 presents a reduced score of the Rhapsody's first 27 measures.[3] The labels S, HF, and TR identify statements of the descending octatonic scale segment, the violas' horn fifths and the low sustained E minor triad, respectively.

In terms of tonal design, the establishment of E as pitch centre could hardly be clearer: the octatonic scale segment departs from E, and the low strings enter on E and subsequently sustain an E minor triad. The horn fifths in the violas suggest E major, but only indirectly. Horn fifths in E major typically proceed G♯/E–F♯/B–E/G♯,[4] but there is no such statement here. Instead, the focus is on F♯/B, initially embellished by an accented A♯/F♯ whose function as an appoggiatura to G♯/E only becomes explicit later, in m. 27. This unmasking of the underlying horn fifth gesture is beautifully underscored by a shift from pizzicato to arco, a change remarkable not only for the timbral contrast but also because the bowed sound better suits the pastoral associations of horn fifths. From a purely acoustic perspective, the violas bring tonal emphasis to B, yet the allusion to conventional horn fifths suggests that they

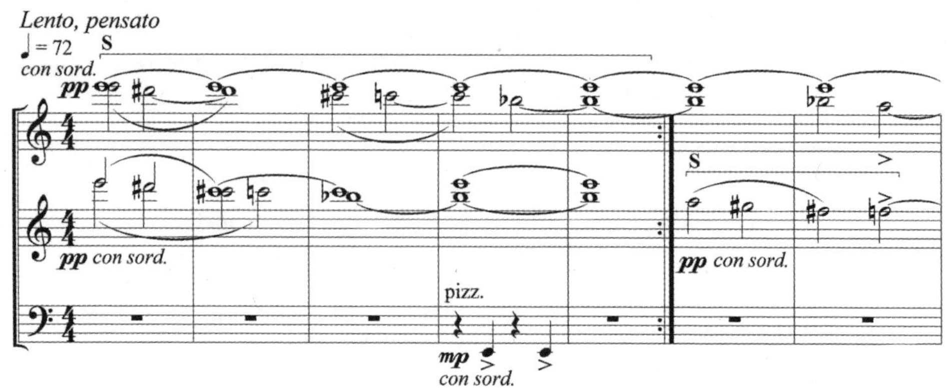

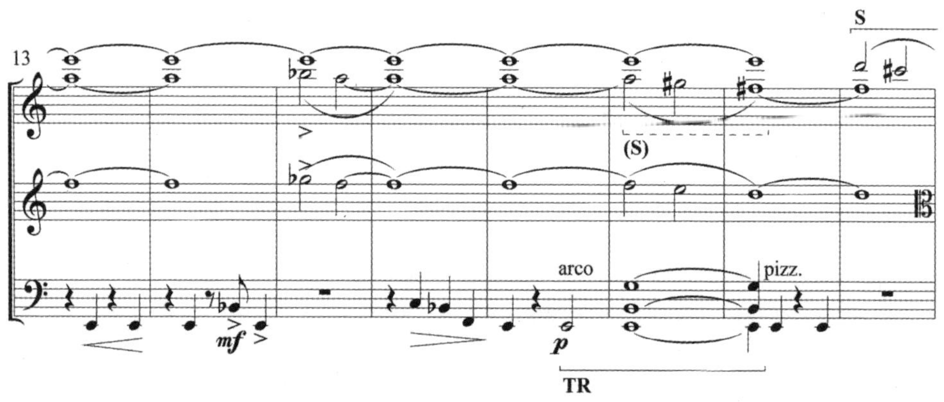

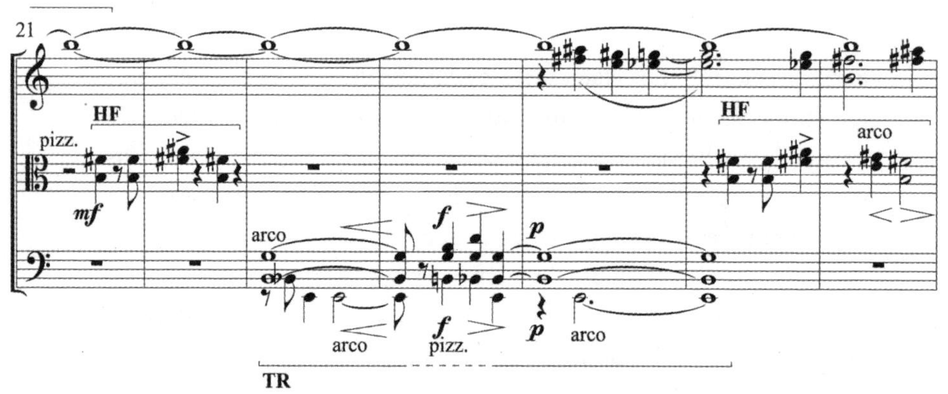

FIGURE 3.1. Rhapsody for 14 Strings, *mm. 1–27.*

represent the tonal orbit of E major. Notably, when the violas enter, the upper strings have shifted their sustained pitch from E to B, further strengthening the tonal impact of the F♯/B fifth in the violas. The resultant tension between E and B as pitch centres is one thread that calls for further elaboration.

The plain octatonicism of the opening measures raises the possibility that the work will have a predominantly octatonic language. The unfolding of the section, however, makes it clear that the framework is essentially a diatonic one, albeit with considerable chromaticism. The initial descending scale traverses half of the C–C♯ octatonic scale; the scale is not completed. Instead, when the segment's terminal B♭ descends, it initiates an octatonic scale segment from A (m. 11), and when the segment's upper boundary descends, it spawns an octatonic scale segment from D (m. 20). The descending half and whole steps from E, A, and D represent all three octatonic collections. Moreover, neither the E minor triad of the lower strings nor the G♯/E dyad in the violas is a subset of the primary C–C♯ octatonic collection. Although it seems unlikely that octatonicism will come to function as the work's essential pitch language, the degree of octatonic infiltration represents another fruitful avenue for exploration.

In the sustained texture and relatively soft dynamics, accented events are especially salient. As noted above, the A♯/F♯ embellishment of the violas' horn fifths is consistently accented, highlighting its ornamental function. Earlier, in m. 12, there is an accented event in the upper strings that is also a major third: A/F. At that moment, the three-voice texture sounds E/A/F, which outlines a sonority familiar from common-practice harmony, namely the F major triad with major seventh (FMM7). The upper strings sustain these three pitches for six measures, except for brief accented appoggiaturas B♭/G♭ in m. 15. There are several important implications of these events, both local and global. First, the obvious appoggiatura function of B♭/G♭ to A/F foreshadows the initially less obvious elaborating role of the enharmonically equivalent A♯/F♯ when the violas enter. Second, the FMM7 sound provokes a response by the lower strings that articulates the dominant seventh of F: C–B♭–F–E in mm. 16–17. Third, although this suggestion of F as tonal centre by the lower strings is immediately rebuffed by the ensuing sustained E minor triad, the seed for exploration of F as pitch centre in the Rhapsody's third section has been sown.

Allegretto giusto: Transforming and Then Remembering

The *Lento, pensato* ends with a focus on the violas' horn fifths and the E minor triad, and both elements continue smoothly into the *Allegretto giusto*, as shown in Figure 3.2. The E minor triad is only rearticulated once, but the horn fifths persist for some twenty measures (and after that the F♯/B fifth sounds as a tremolo). Almost immediately, the horn fifths figure undergoes expansion, as its melodic peak becomes B/G. These pitches function like appoggiaturas to the already embellishing A♯/F♯ dyad. Melodically, this expansion introduces the upper line B–A♯–G♯, a short octatonic fragment that subtly recalls the one thematic element that is not explicitly present.

Befitting the faster tempo, the music falls into clear four-measure units defined by an ostinato version of the horn fifths figure. Each statement of the ostinato has a distinct textural configuration: as noted above, in the initial statement the E minor triad is sounded for a final time. The second four-measure unit presents the ostinato by itself. Subsequent statements incorporate new textural elements. The first of these is a *leggero* repeated note idea accompanied by pizzicato chords in the violins in m. 47. This material is notable in its strong projection of E minor, as well as its launch from E–D♯, the two pitches associated with the violins' octatonic scale segment at the start of the piece. The pizzicato chords, too, are a five-note subset of E harmonic minor, arranged in a way that suggests a dominant ninth chord (with a persistent E embedded in an inner voice). Next, the bass enters with a four-note ostinato, whose simple structure features the two fifths at the heart of the tonal conflict between E and B: the fifths E–B and B–F♯. This ostinato underlies almost half of the *Allegretto giusto*, guiding a crescendo from m. 51 to m. 96; the pattern undergoes slight alterations only briefly in mm. 71–3, 82–5, and 94–5. Finally, a solo violin interjects with a wayward eighth-note exclamation in m. 55. This is the entrance of the "jazz-like figures" to which Forsyth refers in his program note.

FIGURE 3.2. Rhapsody, *juncture between first and second sections, mm. 34–56.*

FIGURE 3.3. Rhapsody, *primary and secondary variants on "jazz-like" figure.*

The last of the elements to be introduced, these "jazz-like figures" become the most salient textural component. The pitch content of the original figure is preserved in most subsequent statements, although the number of iterations of the pitch A at its onset varies, as does its metric placement. Tonally, the figure outlines a dominant ninth chord in E minor, the G♯ and E♯ easily taken as embellishments connecting A to F♯. When the pitch content varies, the figure most often unfolds as shown in the primary variant given in Figure 3.3. The memory of its original version still permits the G♯ and E♯ to be understood as embellishing tones, and the remainder of the figure moves through the same dominant ninth harmony. The figures are "jazz-like" not only because of the slight, quasi-improvisatory changes that occur but also because these modifications all refer to the same underlying harmony, just as a jazz musician performs solos above a fixed harmonic framework. Moreover, these figures are consistently presented by solo instruments, in contrast to the pervasive doublings elsewhere. The figures gradually occur with greater frequency, starting from an eight-measure separation between m. 55 and m. 63 to a climactic seven-voice stretto in mm. 98–100 (not shown in Figure 3.3). From m. 95 onward, the figure has a markedly different pitch content, shown in the secondary variant in Figure 3.3. The emphasis on B and the harmonic fifth B–F♯ remains, as does an intervallic similarity in the first three pitches (A–G♯–E♯ in the initial version becomes B–A♯–F♯ in the secondary variant). The slight intervallic change and the transposition of the figure up a whole step to B creates a subtle connection with the violas' horn fifths: throughout much of the section, the upper strand of the viola ostinato consists of these pitches. In addition, the eighth notes of the secondary variant of the jazz figure recall the earlier *leggero* idea, which began E–D♯–B.

FIGURE 3.4. Rhapsody, *culmination of* Allegretto giusto, *mm. 103–14.*

The continuous dynamic, textural, and rhythmic intensification of the *Allegretto giusto* culminates in a *fortissimo* transformation of the horn fifths, which emerge as a Bartókian melody in the violins at m. 103. As shown in Figure 3.4, the melody begins with a two-measure unit consisting of a single oscillation (F♯/B–A♯/F♯–F♯/B), is elaborated with additional major thirds in m. 105ff much like the violas' earlier ostinato, returns to its original version in m. 109ff, and then appears in a considerably ornamented version in m. 111ff. At the same time, the *leggero* idea returns in the second violins in m. 104, but fragmented so that its opening and closing segments sound as responses to the principal melody.

With this climactic transformation achieved, the section begins a continuous dynamic, textural, and rhythmic reduction that leads smoothly into the *Lento, come prima* third section beginning in m. 150 (shown in Figure 3.6). Tonally, the Bartókian melody descends by fifth from F♯/B to B/E in m. 117 and finally E/A in m. 129 (shown in Figure 3.5)—again, all harmonic fifths that bear a strong connection to E minor. The move to the E/A fifth coincides with a return of this material to its source location, the violas; this is the point at which Figure 3.5 begins. Although the E/A fifth remains quite close to E minor, the descending fifth motion has nonetheless moved away from E minor. The Bartókian melody re-attains the "home" F♯/B fifth through a smooth pivot. Throughout the statements of the melody oriented around E/A, the major third G♯/E frequently appears in the additive melodic embellishments (for example, in mm. 129, 131, 133, and 134). Yet, in relation to the F♯/B fifth, G♯/E functions as the major third involved in the purest form of the horn fifths. This dual function of G♯/E is employed in m. 135 to bring back the "home" F♯/B fifth, and the remainder of the section features oscillations between the E/A and F♯/B fifths. The pacing of these oscillations ultimately becomes slower and then separated by silence (in m. 146). When this strand of the texture eventually stops, it does so on the F♯/B fifth, that is, on the downbeat of m. 150 that occurs as shown at the start of Figure 3.6.

The return of the horn fifth material to the violas at m. 129 frees up the violins for other thematic material. At first, the material is new and

FIGURE 3.5. Rhapsody, *winding down of* Allegretto giusto, *mm. 129–38.*

accompanimental: four-note pizzicato chords that include the pitch classes of the F♯/B, B/E, and E/A fifths featured melodically in the immediately preceding and ongoing principal strands of the texture. But then the violins begin to remember the thematic materials of the first section (mm. 1–38), moving progressively further back in time, as if to make the process as continuous and gradual as possible. The secondary variant of the "jazz" figure re-emerges first; this figure had led up to the Bartókian transformation of the horn fifths, and it had occurred in a few places as an interjection thereafter (for example, in mm. 116 and 125 and in inversion in mm. 118, 120, 123, and 125). The violins then seize upon the figure's initial pitch, B, and recall its usage as a sustained upper pedal throughout much of the Rhapsody's first section (mm. 21–8). There follows a series of alternations between the "jazz" secondary variant and the pedal B, the latter growing progressively longer (see mm. 131–3, then mm. 134–9, and finally mm. 142–9, where it sounds as a harmonic). The slowing within the violas' fifths noted above thereby has an analogue in the violins. The B in the violins, although acoustically consonant with the F♯/B fifth of the violas, does not represent a return to the "home" upper pedal tone, E. Two measures before the end of the second section (mm. 148–9), however, two violins enter with the high E sustained as a triple *piano* (*ppp*) harmonic floating a perfect fourth above the tremolo B. The E and B both sound throughout the final two measures of the second section, but the B drops out when the third section begins. The "home" upper pedal, slipped in at the very end of the second section, hovers throughout the onset of the third section and is sustained throughout mm. 150–4. Within the span of about one minute, the music has progressively found its way back to materials identified with the Rhapsody's beginning.

Lento, come prima: Finding an Oasis in Thematic Memory

The smooth thematic transition and resultant blurring of formal division does not come to an abrupt end when the Rhapsody's third section begins. Instead, there is a complex interweaving of remnants from the second section and recollections of elements of the opening section not yet remembered as the second section was winding down. Figure 3.6 provides the beginning of the third section, and annotations identify various thematic elements. In the upper register, the violins recall the FMM7 sonority, which had received emphasis as an accented event early in the work, in m. 12ff (see Figure 3.1). As before, this sonority is embellished by appoggiaturas, although curiously they are now enharmonically respelled as A♯/F♯ instead of B♭/G♭. One might, perhaps fancifully, speculate that the music is still in the process of remembering; this major third has most recently been spelled with sharps in its role within the horn fifths material. As the

FIGURE 3.6. Rhapsody, *start of third section, mm. 150–64.*

section unfolds, these appoggiaturas regain their spelling with flats (mm. 162–3, for example), but this is also related to changes in tonal context, as explored below.

The middle strand of the texture, carried by two violas in unison, is the slowest to shake off the memory of the second section. Here the "jazz" figure remains, initially even at the same speed as before (in the prescribed tempo proportion, a sextuplet sixteenth note is equivalent to the preceding eighth note). The material decelerates and fragments, thematic processes observed above in the discussion of the closing stages of the second section. Both in terms of thematic material and compositional technique the start of the third section is completely intertwined with the end of the second section.

As can be seen in Figure 3.5 above, the cellos and bass play an ostinato as the second section winds down. Gradually, silences are introduced into their pattern, and with the onset of the third section the note E♭ is withdrawn, too, leaving only the tritone B♭–E in m. 150. These were the first pitches sounded by the cellos and bass at the work's outset in m. 14, and, as earlier, they trigger the note C, the gesture in mm. 153–4 being a distorted recollection of mm. 14–17. Owing to its placement in the lower register and its pitch content, this gesture exerts a pull towards F major, responding to the FMM7 sonority above just as it did at m. 14 (see Figure 3.1). The cellos and bass are content not to repeat this gesture further, moving instead back to the E minor triad; they reiterate the tritone swell gesture only near the end of the Rhapsody's third section in mm. 191–3 (see Figure 3.7).

Amidst the lingering fragments from the second section and the reminiscences of elements of the first section, a melody emerges in the upper register of a solo violin in m. 155. Although built from a combination of whole and half steps and therefore having a connection to the descending octatonic lines of the Rhapsody's opening, this melody's ascending direction, clear connection to E minor and employment of a solo violin rather than a pair in unison give it the impression of newness. Its elevated expressive content is highlighted through the performance indication "with utmost mellowness"; worth bearing in mind is the utmost economy with which Forsyth deploys such indications in the Rhapsody, and in general. Yet this new melody soon returns to the pedal E: when it moves again in m. 158 it outlines the same descending octatonic scale fragment as the work's opening phrase.

With the reassertion of E minor achieved through the soaring violin solo and the sustained low-register E minor triads, the music revisits the most distant tonal relation inherent in the Rhapsody's opening materials: F major. In the first section, F major was only represented by the FMM7 harmony and some iterations of the swelling gesture in the cellos and bass; both of these reappear early in the third section, as noted above. The third section goes much further in its deployment of F major, and it does so incrementally. At m. 159, the high E pedal drops out, and a pair of violins sounds the major third D/B♭. B♭, of course, presents a possible turn towards F major, but in the thematic network of the Rhapsody one of the strongest implications for continuation from D/B♭ is C/F, due to the pervasiveness of the horn fifth material. This indeed occurs, though surreptitiously at first. Mid-register violins enter with *pianissimo* sul ponticello tremolos, above the violas' reminiscences of the "jazz" figure and beneath the leading solo violin (see mm. 162–3). Moreover, the D/B♭ to C/F motion is submerged beneath a B♭/G♭ to A/F move, which is a diminution of the earlier appoggiaturas to the FMM7 sonority. This ponticello version occurs twice more in mm. 167–8 and m. 175 but always *pianissimo* and sandwiched between descending octatonic scale segments in the upper register and reiterations of the E minor triads in the low register. Finally, in mm. 180–2, the F major material assumes a leading role, a passage provided in Figure 3.7.

The blossoming of F major is the central moment in the Rhapsody's third section. It is set off from the preceding and following music in numerous ways. Besides the reduction in rhythmic activity and the textural thinning, there is the luminous purity of the complete B♭ major and F major triads in succession—tinged with a slight commingling of the two by sounding a C as an added ninth in the B♭ triad. The consolidation of F major is reflected in the material breaking through its earlier consignment to ponticello tremolos. The selection of F major

FIGURE 3.7. Rhapsody, *F major material, mm. 180–202.*

beautifully expands upon tonal details from earlier in the Rhapsody, but it also triggers the associations F major has in common-practice repertoire, especially the pastoral. The sense of calm is reinforced by the plagal harmonic implications of the gesture derived from the horn fifth. Through tonal context and rhythmic emphasis, the D/B♭ functions as part of a plagal motion towards a stable C/F. Earlier in the Rhapsody, as is conventional, the fifth within a horn fifth gesture is the least stable harmonically, as it represents dominant harmonic function; the initial third and the ensuing sixth express tonic harmonic function. As noted earlier, the horn fifth gesture at the outset of the piece is always incomplete, comprising only the first two intervals (a third then a fifth); the tonal context is the conventional one, though, where the fifth is harmonically active. There is a tension between the inherent acoustic stability of the fifth and its meaning in the overall tonal context. In the F major gesture, the acoustic stability of the fifth entirely fits with its tonal environment, but of course that environment—the pitch centre F—is in conflict with the establishment of E as the overall pitch centre for the Rhapsody. The Rhapsody's F major oasis calls to mind the many common-practice works of a moderate to large scale where an expressively unsettled minor mode beginning leads to a soft, strongly marked, major mode moment about half-way through. The presence of such a moment raises the potential of an expressive breakthrough towards a major mode ending, a potential that ultimately is realized in the Rhapsody.

The concluding portion of the Rhapsody's third section withdraws F major and moves back towards the orbit of E minor. In a nod to the expressively charged melody near the outset of the third section, the solo violin returns, at first confirming F major in mm. 182–3 but then continuing its descent octatonically rather than diatonically with the substitution of F♯ in place of an expected F natural in m. 184. The remainder of the third section explores various major third relationships, all outfitted with triads. After a point of imitation starting from G in m. 187, three violins coalesce on an E♭ major triad, which is then juxtaposed with a return of the low-register E minor triad, and then this pair of triads is superimposed in a sinister ponticello tremolo (see mm. 193–4). The conclusion of the third section features the superimposition of E minor and C major triads, producing an overall CMM7 sonority. There is thus a clear move away from the F major oasis in the direction of E minor, but the tonal return is incomplete owing to the lingering presence of C.

Allegretto, leggero: Finding Thematic and Tonal Resolution

The Rhapsody's final section might better be viewed as having two distinct subsections. The first, mm. 201–430, emerges smoothly from the end of the preceding *Lento, come prima* and gradually develops into music of great rhythmic excitement. This subsection introduces new material, and it owes relatively little to the Rhapsody's initial components. The second subsection, mm. 431–510, provides a return of many of the initial elements that begins as a recapitulation—albeit somewhat transformed—of the Rhapsody's opening. Although the discussion below will comment briefly on the rhythmically driven music in the middle, the emphasis will be on the aspects of remembrance: the thematic continuities at the outset of the fourth section and the recapitulatory segment at the end.

As is apparent in the final two measures of Figure 3.7 above, both the CMM7 of the violins and the E minor triad of the cellos and bass are sustained into the start of the Rhapsody's fourth section. The CMM7, in fact, persists at the top of the texture for the first 17 measures of the new section. The new material, slipped into the middle of the texture, consists of rapid broken triads (initially B major and G augmented with C major added later). Unlike the rest of the work, which is entirely dominated by melodic themes, the writing here is momentarily oriented around texture. Despite much activity, the overall effect is stasis. When a melody does emerge (see Figure 3.8), it is closely related to one of the last utterances of the *Lento, come prima,* namely the bass E–B♭–C–E figure from mm. 191–3 (shown in Figure 3.7), which has its origin in the initial utterances of cellos and bass at the Rhapsody's outset. In the new transformation, the syncopations and additive melodic design provide decisive rhythmic impulse that cuts through the busy, yet static, accompanying texture.

FIGURE 3.8. Rhapsody, *first melody of the fourth section, mm. 216–20.*

FIGURE 3.9. Rhapsody, *new theme of the fourth section, mm. 257–60.*

In his description of the fourth section, Forsyth refers to a "new theme in the violins." This theme, shown in its initial statement in Figure 3.9, is introduced by a solo viola before occurring multiple times in the violins. It incorporates a couple of elements encountered earlier: an initial descending semitone and an octatonic scale segment. Yet, like the soaring violin melody in the third section, despite the reference to an octatonic scale, the theme comes across as essentially new. A considerable expanse of music is dedicated to transposed restatements and rhythmic variations of this melody in alternation with the syncopated tritone-based theme. Particularly important as the section progresses are the rhythmic devices Forsyth employs. A representative passage, shown in Figure 3.10, shows melodic and rhythmic patterns that repeat independently above a backdrop of three ostinatos, each of which has a unique periodicity (shown by the brackets in Figure 3.10). The melody features G major and A♭ major triads organized so that G and D are rhythmically and metrically emphasized; the overall harmonic effect, however, is complex since the cellos and bass gravitate around a whole-tone subset (B–D♭–F). The tonal language of the early stages of the fourth section is the least pitch-centric in the Rhapsody, but here and elsewhere it is G and D that have a certain degree of centricity. Both are pitches that play minimal roles in the Rhapsody's initial materials, and they therefore offer tonal contrast.

FIGURE 3.10. Rhapsody, *isomelody and isorhythm, mm. 331–8.*

Rhythmic devices remain in the forefront even as the moment of recapitulation approaches; Figure 3.11 begins with the last ten measures leading up to the recapitulation. The upper register melody is a further transformation of the one provided in Figure 3.10, transposed to fit the E–E, rather than the D–D, octave. Here the rhythmic and melodic patterns coincide; it is the five eighth-note periodicity that grinds against the 6/8 metre. The accompanying ostinatos, notated in 2/4 metre, initially outline a 2+3 rhythm (in eighth notes, but bear in mind these eighth notes are duplets in the 6/8 metre sounding in the upper register). While the cellos and bass maintain this rhythmic organization until the recapitulation, the pizzicato triads in the violins and violas contract to a 2+2 rhythm (at m. 424). Compared to music heard earlier in the fourth section, the tonal focus is much clearer—and that centre is now E, the Rhapsody's principal pitch centre. With the exception of the octatonic scale in the cellos and bass in mm. 429–30, the pitch content of the 10 measures preceding the recapitulation falls entirely within E harmonic minor. The dominant triad, B major, has much presence, and the C major triad is easily heard as a neighbouring embellishment. Although B major and C major triads appeared frequently, earlier in the fourth section, there they did not clearly serve a particular tonal centre (and certainly not E).

The onset of the recapitulation, while unmistakable, is again a site of formal blurring. The techniques that give rise to this blurring are similar to those present at earlier major formal junctures, a feature that supports the idea of understanding Forsyth's fourth section as comprised of two distinct subsections. The high E tremolo was already incorporated into the lead-up to the recapitulation at mm. 425–6, and the sixteenth-note oscillations in the lowest register of the violas continue those of the low strings. After the descending octatonic scale briefly has the scene to itself, C major and B major triads re-emerge. The repeated chords in the violins in mm. 444–51 contain a C major triad; the scoring is obscured in the reduced score provided, but in actuality the first violins play the C major triad, while the second violins sound the A♯/F♯. The B major triad is implied by the F♯–B fifth in the bass and also by the returning horn fifth material in the violas. In the last two measures of Figure 3.11, the first violins outline another variant on the new melody from the fourth section. This version incorporates a full B major triad with the suggestion of a C major triad. The B major and C major triads emphasized in the preparation of the recapitulation thus reappear soon after the recapitulation is underway.

As in the Rhapsody's first section, the recapitulation moves from an initial emphasis on E to greater focus on the fifth F♯/B. The recapitulation, however, soon returns to an E centre. Furthermore, the E major triad plays a central role from m. 464 until the end. Specifically, the cellos and bass repeat G♯3/B2/E2 continuously throughout mm. 464–8, 471–5, 478–9, 482–3, 486–500, and 503–10 (not all shown in Figure 3.12). When the E major triad is not sounding in the low register, the F♯–B fifth is present; Forsyth invokes the conventional dominant–tonic relationship repeatedly and prominently. The competition between E and B, present at many points in the Rhapsody, is here resolved deci-

FIGURE 3.11. Rhapsody, *recapitulation in the fourth section, mm. 421–53.*

FIGURE 3.11. *Continued.*

sively in favour of E. Given the work's strong ties to common-practice tradition, the emergence of E is expected, but the turn towards the major mode is not structurally necessary. The major mode gives the ending a radiant warmth that fits nicely with a consoling idea of remembrance that seems to be at the core of this work.

The Rhapsody's ending provides not only tonal resolution but also thematic completion. This is not surprising given the importance of thematic relations in this composition. Just as a coda in a work by Beethoven or Brahms often brings stability to thematic material that originally appeared in a destabilized version, so too does Forsyth's closing section. Here it is the horn fifths material that is accorded greater stability. Throughout the Rhapsody the F♯/B fifth consistently serves as the endpoint of the horn fifths figure; conventionally, it would be followed by the sixth E/G♯. As shown in Figure 3.12, the Rhapsody's close stalls on the F♯/B fifth, expanding it across mm. 490–502 as it is transferred up an octave. In a dramatic twist, the supporting strings

FIGURE 3.12. Rhapsody, *thematic and tonal resolution, mm. 490–510.*

cease their E major triadic accompaniment for the last two measures of this span, and at this point the F♯/B fifth is allowed to move onwards to an interval expressing tonic harmony. The F♯/B fifth does not move to the E/G♯ sixth but instead the G♯/E third; nonetheless, the sense of resolution is still present. The colouration is simply different by leaving the bright raised third scale degree at the top of the texture rather than arriving at E.

The one element that still rubs against the E major tonal context is the pitch A♯. In the horn fifths material A♯/F♯ very often precedes the F♯/B fifth and acts like an appoggiatura that displaces an implied G♯/E. In the resolution at m. 503, the A♯ from the preceding measure indirectly attains G♯, but this motion goes against the tendency of A♯ to resolve upwards in an E major context. In other words, the modal quality seems more lydian than major. The violas engage this remaining instability, resolving A♯/F♯ up to B/G♯ (see mm. 504–5). Forsyth draws attention to this special moment through the *fortissimo* dynamic and the marking en dehors; although the texture is busy, all of the other instruments are marked *pianissimo* or triple *piano* (*pp* or *ppp*). This final melodic gesture not only resolves the A♯ in an E major context, but it also returns this thematic material to its original register and placement in the violas. Due to the pure E major triad already present at m. 503, there is a feeling that the violas' final utterance comes after the tonal course of the composition is over. It is an event that looks only to the past and no longer extends implications for the future. A fadeout brings the Rhapsody smoothly into silence.

|| Forsyth's Rhapsody shows the hand of a mature and confident composer writing with sincerity and without hesitancy. The thematic development, though extensive, can be followed readily by an engaged listener. The melodic materials avoid cliché but fall within the gestures conventionally associated with sensuous and idiomatic string writing. The harmonic language draws on familiar tonal elements, such as the tonic–dominant relationship, major and minor triads, and the acoustic strength of perfect fifths, yet it avoids banality. In short, this is music that manages to communicate directly to the first-time listener and also to reward repeated hearings, and analytic contemplation. Perhaps what is most striking is the continuity and teleology of the writing, both in terms of thematic development and formal organization. Although there is considerable use of ostinatos, the approach to musical time and formal process is essentially conventional. Even when multiple ostinatos are layered, they tend to align at the measure level and do not serve to complicate the sense of metric flow; the complex relationships between ostinatos found in Stravinsky's music are not present, nor are the discontinuities caused by introducing irregularities into ostinatos or by suddenly breaking away from them. At the same time, Forsyth's persistent ostinatos do not generate the glacial continuities of minimalist works, owing to the compelling thematic development present above them. While some individual melodic and rhythmic figures bring Bartók's oeuvre to mind, the Rhapsody is not open to easy relegation to the soundworld of an earlier composer, compositional approach, or aesthetic. The Rhapsody demands consideration according to its

own premises, and I contend that these are primarily thematic and tonal. Following the many transformations of the Rhapsody's thematic materials and their tonal bases reveals a work that is internally continuous in both domains, always engaged in remembering its own past even as it extends connections with the musical traditions from which it emanates.

NOTES

1. Malcolm Forsyth, *Rhapsody for 14 Strings* (Toronto: Canadian Music Centre, 1982). There are no commercially available recordings of the work, but recordings of two live performances can be accessed through CentreStreams on the Canadian Music Centre website (www.musiccentre.ca), including the 1983 premiere conducted by the composer.
2. Malcolm Forsyth, *Rhapsody for 14 Strings* (Toronto: Canadian Music Centre, 1982).
3. All score reductions were prepared by the author.
4. Note that pitches separated by a diagonal slash signify upper/lower voices.

4

Finding Inspiration in Canadian Folk Songs

An Analysis of Three Métis Folk Songs from Saskatchewan

ROXANE PREVOST

IN 1975 MALCOLM FORSYTH selected the text and music of three folk songs collected by Barbara Cass-Beggs in *Seven Métis Songs of Saskatchewan* (1967) as the basis for his work *Three Métis Songs from Saskatchewan* (1978).[1] He dedicated the work to the Canadian contralto Maureen Forrester, who premiered the voice and piano version in Calgary in September 1975 with Yehudi Wyner and the orchestral version with the CBC Vancouver Chamber Orchestra under the baton of Michael Kymlicka in February 1976.[2]

Cass-Beggs's collection includes an informative preface in which she associates the transcribed songs with Joseph Gaspard Jeannotte, one of the most popular folk singers at the time of her transcriptions. She also provides a brief historical introduction of the Prairie Métis and their struggles and reprints her transcriptions of the music and text (in French) for seven Métis songs from Saskatchewan with English summaries, illustrations, and short notes on the roots of each song.

From this collection, Forsyth selected three songs of contrasting musical materials and moods: "Chanson du petit cordonnier" (Song of the Little Shoemaker), "Adieu de la mariée à ses parents" (Bride's Farewell to Her Parents), and "Chanson de la Grenouillère" (Song of the Frog Plain). The first song deals with forbidden love, the second with a young woman's reluctance at being forced into an arranged marriage, and the third with a victory of a band of Métis over British soldiers. Forsyth arranges the songs in a fast-slow-fast design, with the last movement reflecting a dance-like style. He originally set the work for voice and piano, but later orchestrated different versions, including one for voice and chamber orchestra noted above and another for voice, organ, and trumpet.[3] In the following, I focus on the voice and piano version. By comparing Cass-Beggs's transcription of the three songs with Forsyth's setting, I examine how the composer uses musical elements, such as melodic connections between the voice and piano, harmony, modulations, texture of the accompaniment, metrical placement of the words, and addition of other materials, to highlight the text while preserving most of the original melodies and text. Ultimately, Forsyth retains the songs' folk qualities by remaining true to the transcriptions even as he recasts them within a composed Western European art song context.

Cass-Beggs's Folk Song Transcriptions

Cass-Beggs transcribed the songs in the collection from the Métis community of Lebret, a small village in the Qu'Appelle Valley in Saskatchewan. The Métis, who were descendants of an Indigenous mother and French (or French Canadian) father, disseminated their songs predominantly through fiddling and travellers' songs performed mostly by men.[4] Many of these songs would have been passed down from the father and rooted in the French-European tradition.[5] Cass-Beggs notes that the songs probably originated from the Red River region and were brought to the Qu'Appelle Valley perhaps as recently as the late nineteenth century; in the mid-1960s, when Cass-Beggs was collecting songs in the region, these songs were still performed by

FIGURE 4.1. *Cass-Beggs's transcription of "Chanson du petit cordonnier."*

Joseph Gaspard Jeannotte for weddings and special occasions, as well as for private gatherings.[6]

The text of "Chanson du petit cordonnier" recounts the story of a young shoemaker who falls in love with a young woman; he asks for her hand in marriage, but her father refuses, believing that the young man only wants to marry his daughter for her wealth.[7] The young woman's brother attempts to convince the father, but without success. The two lovers are heartbroken and in the last verse the young shoemaker leaves on his horse, composing his song. Cass-Beggs sets her transcription in a 3/4 metre with the indication "rhythmically" (Figure 4.1). The song is in G dorian with an F♯ added to change the mode to G minor. The melody centres around the tonic and dominant (D–F♯–A) triads. This through-composed melody is grouped into four-measure phrases subdivided into two with the exception of the last three measures, which combine as one phrase, and is repeated for the five other verses of text.

FIGURE 4.2. *Cass-Beggs's transcription of "Adieu de la mariée à ses parents."*

"Adieu de la mariée à ses parents" recounts the story of a young woman being forced to marry.[8] She must bid farewell to her parents and siblings, as well as to her youth, her personal possessions, and her dreams for the future, leaving for the rest of her life to live in misery. Cass-Beggs's transcription is set in a 3/4 metre with the indication "wistfully" (Figure 4.2). The song is in F♯ minor with the leading tone E♯ and centres on the pitches of the tonic triad. The form of the song unfolds as a–a'–b–b' (3+3+4+4), subdivided as groups of 2+1 and 2+2, for a total of 14 measures, which are repeated five times to accompany the six verses of text.

"Chanson de la Grenouillère" recounts a battle between the Métis Bois-Brûlés[9] and British soldiers that took place at la Grenouillère (present-day Winnipeg) on June 19, 1816; the Métis were victorious.[10] The song was written by Pierre Falcon, "le chanteur des plaines" (the singer of the plains), and exists in several versions and titles, including "La bataille des Sept-Chênes" (The Battle of Seven Oaks) and "La chanson de Falcon" (Falcon's song).

The song recounts the pride of a small band of Métis, the Bois-Brûlés, who, after having captured three prisoners, surprised and surrounded British troops at la Grenouillère. The Métis wanted to negotiate terms with the British governor, but he refused and ordered his troops to fire. The British perished in the battle that followed.[11]

Cass-Beggs's transcription is set in a 6/8 metre with the indication "triumphantly" (Figure 4.3). The song unfolds in G major and centres around the pitches of the tonic triad and dominant seventh chord. This through-composed melody is grouped into phrases of 4+4+2 measures in length demarcated by rests. Unlike the other songs in the collections, Cass-Beggs includes three variants of the melody for this song, each of which preserves the same main melodic contour. The first variant, however, adds more passing tones to fill in leaps and includes a C♯ to emphasize the implied dominant chords that follow, while the second variant retains the C♯ and some of the passing tones, but is a simpler version than the first variant. The third variant adds a metre change in the second line, most likely to emphasize the dotted quarter note duration of the performance she transcribed; these eight measures could also have been notated as four measures of 6/8. With six verses, it is likely that performers would begin with the principal version for the first verse, but turn to the variants for subsequent verses.

FIGURE 4.3. *Cass-Beggs's transcription of "Chanson de la Grenouillère."*

"Chanson du petit cordonnier"

Forsyth uses Cass-Beggs's transcribed melody for "Chanson du petit cordonnier" with few changes in terms of intervals and durational values.[12] As previously mentioned, the original version, transcribed in G dorian with raised leading tones, giving it a G minor flavour, spans 11 measures. The most significant alteration made in Forsyth's setting is harmonic, and involves a change in key structure beginning in E minor (first and second stanzas) and shifting to G minor (third stanza), F minor (fourth and fifth stanzas), and back to E minor (sixth stanza). These and other structural alterations are summarized in Figure 4.4. Note also the dramatic tempo change to "A little slower; freely" that occurs in the fourth and fifth verses.

FIGURE 4.4. *"Chanson du petit cordonnier." Showing Forsyth's use of harmonic and tempo changes in response to the text.*

Verse	*Measure*	*Key*	*Tempo*	*Text Summary*
1–2	1–11	E minor	Brisk (quarter note = 116)	The shoemaker admires the young woman; father rejects the marriage proposal.
3	13–23	G minor		The brother tries to convince father to allow the two lovers to marry.
4–5	24–46	F minor	A little slower; freely	The shoemaker bids farewell to his beloved.
6	48–58	E minor	Tempo I	The shoemaker composes his song.

Forsyth sets the first two verses of text to the same music by including a repeat sign for the first 11 measures. These measures include mostly plagal progressions (tonic–predominant–tonic), making the harmonic movement static (Figure 4.5). These repeated plagal progressions mirror the simplicity of the shoemaker in the eyes of the father. Subtle harmonic colouring also contributes to Forsyth's interpretation of the song. The accompaniment in the first 11 measures consists of primarily octaves and fifths in the left hand of the piano and a triplet motive, an E minor triad and an A minor triad in the right hand. The triplet motive connects to the melody by reproducing its first four pitches in diminution. The interval of the perfect fourth plays an important role here since it marks the opening of the melody, but also the movement in the bass, which sets up the plagal progression. This interval also comes into play in the other movements, as will be discussed later.

The most significant change in the piano accompaniment over the course of the first two verses occurs at m. 8, where the pitches of the ostinato-like triplet motive (B–E–F♯) are altered to B–D♯–E, supported by a B major chord, the dominant chord of E implied by this melody. Forsyth also decorates the ensuing A minor chord with triplet sixteenth notes. This change in motivic and harmonic content aligns with the point in the text in which the young shoemaker asks permission to marry Lisette in the first verse and receives the father's rejection of his request in the second. Since the piano ostinato repeats for most of the first 11 measures, at times it conflicts with the melody, which implies a different harmony. For example, the D♯ of the vocal line in the second measure conflicts with the A minor chord that accompanies it. This aligns with the emotions of the two lovers whose love is forbidden by the woman's father.

Forsyth also adds a short transition between the second and third stanzas (mm. 11–13, not shown) to facilitate his modulation from E minor to G minor, the key of the original transcription and of the third verse. He essentially transposes mm. 1–11 by an ascending minor third to accompany the text with the brother defending the shoemaker by considering him an honourable man. Once more, the simple repeated plagal harmonic progressions mirror the pedigree of the shoemaker in the eyes of the father. A sudden change occurs in the piano part of m. 24 at the opening of the fourth verse involving a succession of ninth chords and rapid melodic lines, which consist primarily of arpeggios, underscoring the shoemaker bidding farewell to Lisette. An even more

FIGURE 4.5. *"Chanson du petit cordonnier," mm. 1–11. Showing Forsyth's use of harmonic and tempo changes in response to the text.*

striking change in texture appears in the accompaniment of the fifth verse at mm. 35–47 (Figure 4.6) when Lisette cries and bids farewell to her beloved. Forsyth highlights this poignant moment with a change in tempo, allowing the melody to unfold more freely and by adding a chord that preserves four of the pitches from the final chord of m. 34: G–C–A♭ in the left hand of the piano combine to create an A♭M7 chord in third inversion, and a melodic figure that alternates between C and D♭ as sixteenth-note triplets followed by a C half note in the right hand of the piano supports this.[13] The A♭M7 chord in the left hand replaces the plagal progressions of the previous verses and provides sustained tension, not only because the seventh occurs in the lowest voice, but also because the melody is still in F minor. Thus, the chord is built on the mediant with a seventh in the bass. The upper neighbour note D♭ in the right hand of the piano does not occur in the melody in these measures (mm. 35–47), but rather its chromatic alteration (D natural) is sung in the melody at the end of m. 40, adding further harmonic tension to the passage. These dissonances reflect the woman's sorrow as she bids farewell to the shoemaker. The dissonant and thin texture, consisting of primarily sustained block chords, allows the singer to express more effectively the young woman's pain.

Musical material from mm. 1–11 returns for the last verse, in the original key of E minor, as the shoemaker leaves on his horse to the accompaniment of a triplet figure. Forsyth modulates back to E minor by leaping down a diminished fourth (A♭ to E natural) between the roots of the chords in mm. 47–8. The common tone G natural, which occurs in the lowest voice in m. 47, provides a connection to the start of the last verse (m. 48) by appearing in the same register in the left hand of the piano, as it did in m. 1. The E–G interval is also mirrored by the first modulation between the first two verses and the third.

With these nuanced alterations to Cass-Beggs's transcriptions, Forsyth thus transforms the original folk song into an art song capable of more dramatic expression. This is primarily achieved through the piano accompaniment's harmonic progressions and modulations. The key of E minor represents verses that are grounded in reality (verses 1 and 6) or the authority of the father (verse 2), while the modulation to the key of G minor aligns with the brother, who has less authority. The suspended A♭M7 with the motive C–D♭–C projects well the loss of the beloved with its semitone motion pulling to the C. These harmonic motions effectively convey the reality of the loss for the two lovers.

FIGURE 4.6. *"Chanson du petit cordonnier," mm. 35–47. Showing Forsyth's change in texture to A♭M7 harmonization.*

"Adieu de la mariée"

Of Forsyth's three song settings, "Adieu de la mariée"[14] departs the most from Cass-Beggs's work (compare Figures 4.2 and 4.8) despite the fact that he preserves her original harmony (F# minor) and most of her melodic materials. His principal area of departure lies in the change of metre from 3/4 to 6/8, which substantially alters the durational values in the melody, allowing greater flexibility in the delivery of the text and suggesting a feeling of improvisation (Figure 4.7). Forsyth also omits the fifth verse and sets the entire text to a very slow tempo of dotted quarter note = 30.

FIGURE 4.7. *"Adieu de la mariée." Showing Forsyth's changing metres in relation to the text.*

Verse	*Measures*	*Time Signature*	*Summary*
1	4–17	6/8	The couple prepares for the wedding.
2	18–31	6/8	Preparations are made for the wedding day.
3	32–45	6/8	The day after the wedding arrives.
4	47–60	9/8	The young woman acknowledges that she was forced to marry.
5	omitted by Forsyth		The bride regrets the marriage and feels trapped.
6	63–76	9/8	The bride bids farewell to her parents and siblings.

Forsyth's setting begins with chords constructed of superimposed fifths (B–F#–C#) with octave doublings and a descriptive tempo indication of "slow and sad." The octave doubling of the pitch classes B and F# highlight the tonic–subdominant relationship that prevailed in the first movement. The composer creates greater harmonic tension in this movement, in part, by setting a B pedal in the lowest voice, implying the key of B minor harmonically, while the melody unfolds in F# minor. The interval of the perfect fourth (C#–F#) in the right hand of the piano foreshadows the opening interval in the vocal line.

FIGURE 4.8. *"Adieu de la mariée," mm. 1–17. Showing Forsyth's change in metre.*

The first verse, which tells of a young couple about to get married, reproduces Cass-Beggs's transcribed melody in varied rhythm to suit his changes in metre and tempo (Figure 4.8). Forsyth maintains her barlines for the notes of the melody, but his rhythmic alterations give the melody a more tentative feeling. His changes also include altering the relationships between shorter and longer durations, which have the effect of adding metrical instability, effectively representing the bride's anxiety. Further, the melody is accompanied by sombre chords built on a subdominant B pedal that, in combination with the more erratic melody just described, reflect the young woman's mood. The highest voice of the piano doubles the pitches of the vocal line in most cases, but the durations unfold as regular dotted quarter notes. This contrasts with the vocal line, which is more free flowing with many short durations on the strong beats, as if to represent the young woman leaving her life of freedom to conform with someone else's life. In the second verse, which describes the day of the wedding, we learn that the bride does not want to get married; she refers to the "hat of worry" ("*chapeau de souci*") and the "necklace of suffering" ("*collier de souffrance*") that await her.[15] Forsyth's use of durational values in her melodic material differ only slightly from Cass-Beggs's transcription here, made to accommodate the text; the sombre chords with superimposed fifths and the B pedal heard in the first stanza persist.

In mm. 22–3, Forsyth adds quadruplets in the right hand of the piano to highlight the man's "white suit" ("*habit blanche*") and his "suit of happiness" ("*habit de jouissance*") (Figure 4.9). Further changes in harmonic content highlight the groom's happiness in contrast to the bride's sorrow. In these measures, Forsyth superimposes a B chord (no third) and F augmented chord with a major seventh chord (second inversion), thereby creating a clash between F–F♯ (m. 22). These brief harmonic gestures, while subtle, nonetheless underscore the bride's feeling of incompleteness (B chord without the third for stability) and the groom's short-lived happiness (dissonant augmented chord). Their chords conflict, as do their expectations for their upcoming marriage.

In the third verse of this song, which recounts the day after the wedding and the young woman's regret, Forsyth once more reproduces

FIGURE 4.9. *"Adieu de la mariée," mm. 18–31. Showing the couple's dissonant chord material.*

the pitches of the transcription, but with extensively varied durations from both the transcription and the two previous verses. The woman's despair at leaving her family and everything she knows is conveyed by simplifying the durational values of the melody, perhaps a reflection of the woman's resignation to her new life. Forsyth also adds a descriptive tempo indication for this verse as "lightly and quicker." Despite these superficial changes in mood, the piano accompaniment continues to underline the young woman's anxiety, now with agitated arpeggiated chords. He includes a fermata at m. 46, allowing time to stop briefly and to suggest the weight of her impending life that is making it hard for her to breathe (see Figure 4.10).

In his fourth verse, Forsyth changes the time signature to 9/8 with the indication "Flowing with childlike simplicity." This aligns with changes in the text, which turns to someone talking to the young woman, most likely an older woman who has experienced the same sentiments at some point, instead of the young woman's words. Here the composer again alters the rhythmic duration of the melody, but preserves the pitches within their original barlines with the exception of the G♯ in m. 52. With the change in metre and tempo, however, we perceive a deceleration. Further, although he preserves the barlines and the metrically accented first beats remain the same, the rhythms inside each measure must change to fit the triple metre. Originally, a dotted quarter note equalled 30 beats per minute; for the second verse, the dotted quarter note increases to 56. Although the pulse is quicker with the dotted quarter note equalling 72 beats per minute in the fourth verse, the durations that align with the text are in reality longer through the addition of one dotted quarter note to accommodate the 9/8 metre. The new, rhythmically uneven piano accompaniment figure underlines the older woman's sacrifices in her own marriage through the quick ascending perfect fifth in the left hand and a pair of staccato dyads in the right hand. The repeating figure contrasts with the blocked chords of mm. 1–33 and the arpeggiated chords of mm. 32–46, further highlighting the sacrifices that a woman at that time had to make for marriage. The harmonic movement of mm. 47–62 is plagal with the alternation of F♯ minor chords with B minor chords, once more emphasizing the

FIGURE 4.10. *"Adieu de la mariée," mm. 46–60. Showing the change in metre in the fourth verse.*

importance of the interval of the perfect fourth in this work. Moreover, Forsyth includes harmonic conflicts between the harmonic progression and the melody that unfolds above it, such as in m. 48, where the B minor harmony occurs below the pitches A and G in the vocal line. The harmonic progression and conflicts allow the listener to draw parallels between the first two movements, both of which focus on sorrow and loss.

Cass-Beggs's original transcription of this song includes appoggiaturas on the strong beats of the second, third, and fifth measures. These align with the last words of each of the first three lines of the first three verses. In the first verse, appoggiaturas on the A (m. 2), G# (m. 3), and A (m. 5) align with the words "*rivage*," "*ruisseau*," and "*oiseau*." This shifts the syllable accent of the words, which should have a stronger emphasis on the second half of the words. Forsyth takes advantage of these dissonances by adding an additional appoggiatura to the fourth verse on the word "*volonté*" ("will") (m. 52). In doing so, he draws attention to the contradiction between the speaker's claim that it is the young woman's will to marry the young man even though she does not perceive it as such. The many short appoggiaturas on strong beats, accompanied by the static accompaniment, evoke a sense of anxiety and further represent the young woman's emotional state as she is forced to marry.

The fermata that occurs in mm. 60–2 coincides with the omitted fifth verse, allowing for a pause in the narrative before the final stanza. With the exception of the introduction and one measure at the end of the song, these are the only measures in Forsyth's setting that do not include text. Although the sixth verse repeats much of the text of the fifth (the bride's regret), the sixth verse is now rendered more poignant as she bids farewell to her family and her previous life, and resigns herself to her future. For this last stanza, Forsyth restores the original tempo while preserving the 9/8 time signature of the fourth verse.[16] The time signature of the last two verses in triple compound (9/8) instead of duple compound (6/8) gives the composer the means to preserve many of the durations of the transcribed version in 3/4, especially in this sixth verse. The piano chords resemble those that supported the first verse, echoing the woman's resignation to her new life. The song ends with a one-measure postlude that sustains the quintal chord from the opening measures: that the young woman will never achieve her dreams is conveyed through the repetition of the ambiguous chord with no third.

Forsyth musically depicts the young woman's consistent emotional state in this song through his use of such quintal and dissonant harmonies, sustained chords, a B pedal, and the rhythmic instability of the vocal line with the appoggiaturas, all of which accurately capture her anxiety at the realization of facing a life of misery.

"Chanson de la Grenouillère"

Unlike the previous two songs, the final one selected by Forsyth embodies a positive theme, that of victory in battle, and the possibility of working with multiple song variants must have been appealing. As noted above, Cass-Beggs's transcriptions include a primary version and three variants (see Figure 4.3), and Forsyth uses all four of these in his setting. His also uses four of the original six verses, thus pairing each verse with a different variant (Figure 4.11).

A six-measure introduction presents a quintuplet motive over a tonic chord alternating with a dominant ninth chord and chromatic chords. This motive with quintuplet sixteenth notes surrounded by staccato eighth notes is reminiscent of the opening motive of the first movement through its durations, which included triplet sixteenth notes surrounded by staccato eighth notes, both representing galloping horses. Forsyth begins the first verse of text with Cass-Beggs's primary melodic version, in her original key of G major, and accompanies this mostly with arpeggiated chords in 6/8 metre (Figure 4.12). As with the previous movements, the accompaniment foreshadows the material of the vocal line, although more subtly this time: the first three pitches of the quintuplet figure in the right hand of the piano (D–G–D) are transposed down an octave to produce the beginning of the vocal part. Furthermore, the material in mm. 4–5 of the right hand of the piano connects the introduction to the first verse (mm. 16–17) through repetition of the same pitches and durations. Melody and accompaniment are reminiscent of traditional French folk song in the lightness of their texture and harmonic simplicity and here they accompany a text announcing the Métis' arrival. An eight-measure interlude (mm. 17–26, not shown) connects the first and second verses by means of the opening quintuplet motive and a tonic prolongation (I–♭VII–I) in the left hand, also taken from the introduction.

FIGURE 4.11. *"Chanson de la Grenouillère." Showing Forsyth's use of the song and its variants.*

	Verse	*Measures*	*Key features*	*Text Summary*
Original	1	7–17	G major; 6/8	The Bois-Brûlés arrived on June 19, 1918.
Variant 1	2	26–36	G major; 6/8; two pitches changed (m. 32)	They took three prisoners.
Variant 2	3	48–58	G major; 6/8; one eighth note added (m. 48), one durational value changed (m. 49), one pitch added (m. 51)	The English came to attack.
		59–78	New material in two parts: G major (mm. 59–68) and A flat (mm. 68–78); 6/8	La-la-la
Variant 3	4	87–101	G major; omits changing time signatures; repeats the last 10 measures of the transcription; one durational value changed (m. 96), four pitches changed (m. 100)	The governor refused to negotiate and lost the battle.

FIGURE 4.12. *"Chanson de la Grenouillère," mm. 1–17. Showing Forsyth's use of harmony in the first verse.*

Forsyth's second verse uses Cass-Beggs's first variant of the melody, accompanying this with a descending line in the left hand that resembles a walking bass and a motive consisting of a sixteenth note followed by a dyad in thirds in the right hand (Figure 4.13).[17] The piano accompaniment that supports this second verse resembles the one used for the first verse with arpeggiated chords. However, to increase their complexity Forsyth changes the durations in the right hand by replacing the quarter note rest followed by two sixteenth notes with a dotted eighth note rest followed by a sixteenth note and an eighth note, thereby highlighting the prisoners' capture. A second interlude with three eighth notes and six sixteenth notes doubled at the octave (mm. 36–47, not shown) emphasizes different chords (G major, E minor, and A minor), embellished by chromatic tones.

The quintuplet motive from the introduction returns with a similar accompaniment between verses two and three, and Forsyth follows this with a third stanza melody based on Cass-Beggs's second variant, with minor changes to better reflect textual details. In the accompanying text of this verse, the Bois-Brûlés are warning their colleagues of approaching English soldiers, and the piano marks this dramatic moment primarily with ascending arpeggiated chords in septuplet sixteenth notes separated between the two hands. Although Forsyth inserts chromatic notes between some of the harmonies, G major and D major serve as the primary harmonies. Here, the stable chords represent the determination and pride of the warriors, while the chromatic chords represent challenges they face to protect their land.

In mm. 59–78 (Figure 4.14), Forsyth adds new material set to the text "la-la-la," although some material can be traced back to the verses, such as mm. 60–2, which replicate mm. 28–30 and mm. 50–2 (and eventually mm. 89–91) with slightly altered durations; these measures mark the end of the first phrase of the three variants. Forsyth includes them also in the right hand of the piano, this time transposed up a minor second in mm. 70–2 to accommodate the modulation to A♭ major. The "la-la-la" section may be divided into two, the first subsection in G major (mm. 59–67) and the second in A♭ major (mm. 68–78). In the first subsection, Forsyth modulates to A♭ major through E♭, the lowered

FIGURE 4.13. *"Chanson de la Grenouillère," mm. 26–36. Showing Forsyth's walking bass.*

sixth scale degree in G major.[18] The material of the second subsection (mm. 68–78) synthesizes the main motives and accompaniment of the song, including the dotted eighth-note motive, the arpeggiated chord, and the octave doublings, while the primary harmonies consist once more of tonic and dominant. The interlude (mm. 79–86) that follows unfolds primarily as eighth-note octave doublings of single pitch classes, which group as arpeggiated chords, mostly as E minor and A♭ minor.

FIGURE 4.14. *"Chanson de la Grenouillère," mm. 59–78. Showing Forsyth's use of semitone movement between sections.*

The "la-la-la" subsection, which separates the last two verses, reflects a gap in the action, marking the moment *between* the British soldiers' approach and the Bois-Brûlés' victory, as if the fighting occurred during this section; this section is the only place in the setting where Forsyth modulates to another key. Perhaps Forsyth associated the key of A♭ major with the soldiers, who are eventually defeated, and the victorious Bois-Brûlés with the home key of G major.

Cass-Beggs's third variant, used by Forsyth for his fourth verse, contains a changing metre from 6/8 to 3/8 (Figure 4.15). Forsyth overrides this change in metres by grouping two 3/8 measures as 6/8 for mm. 5–14 of the transcribed variant (see Figure 4.3). To achieve this, he shortens the rhythmic value of the last pitch of m. 96 and alters those of the melodic pitches in m. 100. This downplays the role of the governor, who eventually is defeated by his arrogance. The piano accompaniment here consists of octave doublings with accented dotted quarter notes in the left hand and a new quintuplet motive in the right hand. This accompaniment pattern changes at the end to the grace-note figure that first appeared in mm. 12–16, when the Bois-Brûlés are first referred to as warriors. Here, the warriors prevail. The last four measures recapitulate some of the most prominent motives of the song—the quintuplet motive, the dotted motive, octave doublings—with the text "la-la-la," this time in the home key of G major that celebrates the Métis' victory.

By using the primary version and all three variants transcribed by Cass-Beggs as the basis for different verses of the song, Forsyth is thus able to highlight the Bois-Brûlés' victory over the British soldiers described in the text in a manner that is subtle yet more effective than it might have been with a simple strophic song. This also allows his story to unfold as a series of different events with new material for each verse, instead of a narrator simply recounting a story.

Forsyth's borrowing of melodies and texts from Cass-Beggs's transcriptions as the primary source for his work *Three Métis Folk Songs from Saskatchewan* was clearly just a starting point for his work. Even subtle changes to these materials resulted in dramatic changes in the character of the songs owing to his creative use of harmony

FIGURE 4.15. *"Chanson de la Grenouillère," mm. 87–105. Showing Forsyth's use of metre.*

and addition of new material (accompaniment as well as melodic and harmonic changes), all while keeping the majority of the original pitches, durational values, phrases, and text. By including modal harmonies, modulations, chromatic chords (passing and sustaining long passages), and tempo changes, Forsyth further captures and enhances the emotions of the main characters within each song text such that they are no longer simply narrated stories but an unfolding of events as experienced by different characters within each song. The listener is therefore taken on a journey through their lives in a manner that provides a fascinating reworking of the Métis tradition recast as Western European art song for concert audiences.

NOTES

1. Barbara Cass-Beggs, *Seven Métis Songs of Saskatchewan* (Don Mills, ON: BMI Canada Limited, 1967); Malcolm Forsyth, *Three Métis Songs from Saskatchewan (for Voice and Piano)* (Willowdale, ON: Leeds Music, 1978); Malcolm Forsyth, *Three Métis Songs from Saskatchewan (Full Orchestra Version)* (Toronto: Counterpoint Music Library Services Inc., 2004). In this chapter, I focus on the voice and piano version, rather than the orchestral version, to facilitate the discussion of the work.
2. Recordings of these performances are available online through the Canadian Music Centre CentreStreams recordings (www.musiccentre.ca/centrestreams).
3. Available scores for the *Three Métis Songs from Saskatchewan* consist of one version for voice and piano (1978) and archival copies available through Counterpoint Music Library Services Inc. (in B♭ major for medium high voice and piano; in B♭ major for medium high voice and chamber orchestra; in G major for medium voice and chamber orchestra). Available recordings include Maureen Forrester (contralto) and Yehudi Wyner (pianist), Canadian Music Centre CentreStreams, 1975, online recording; Forrester and CBC Radio Orchestra, dir. Michael Kymlicka, Canadian Music Centre CentreStreams, 1976, online recording; Forrester and John Newmark (pianist), Canadian Music Centre CentreStreams, 1980, online recording; Forrester and the McGill Symphony Orchestra, dir. Richard Hoenich, YouTube, http://www.youtube.com/watch?v=FmjXKxKf1dU, 1986, online recording; Phyllis Mailing (mezzo-soprano) and CBC Vancouver Orchestra, dir. Mario Bernardi, Canadian Music Centre CentreStreams, 1986, online recording; Judith Forst (mezzo-soprano), and CBC Vancouver Orchestra, dir. Mario Bernardi, SMCD 5081, 1989.
4. Lynn Whidden, "The Songs of Their Fathers," *Ethnologies* 25, no. 2 (2003): 108. In "The Songs of Their Fathers," Whidden also examines how the working songs of Métis women in Saskatchewan in the nineteenth to mid-twentieth centuries reflected how women adapted to their new role in society. These songs, passed down to future generations, were rooted primarily in old French folk songs, but some were also melodies popular at the time as well as "'ditties' of no particular origin but known by everyone" (108).

5. Since Métis folk songs are part of an oral tradition, the transcriptions of these songs vary tremendously from region to region, as well as from performer to performer. For example, Cass-Beggs's transcription of "Adieu de la mariée à ses parents" (a transcription of Joseph Gaspard Jeannotte's interpretation of the song in Lebret, Saskatchewan, in the mid-twentieth century) shares the same words as Whidden's "Tout le long du rivage" (a transcription of Mme Alphonse Carrière's performance of the song in St. Boniface, Manitoba, in 1971), but the two versions are dramatically different. The changes include the key of F♯ minor versus E minor, the time signature of 3/4 versus common time, the tempo indication "wistfully" versus "slowly," the opening melody on an anacrusis versus the first beat, and different melodic contours.
6. Cass-Beggs, *Seven Métis Songs of Saskatchewan*, 3. Although Cass-Beggs titled her collection *Seven Métis Songs* of *Saskatchewan*, Forsyth extracted three of the songs and named them *Three Métis Songs* from *Saskatchewan* (emphasis mine).
7. "Chanson du petit cordonnier" exists in several versions in Canada, Belgium, and France; it is also known as "Lisette, ô ma Lisette" and "Galant retirez-vous" (Young man, take your leave). Forsyth, *Three Métis Songs from Saskatchewan*, 2.
8. "Adieu de la mariée à ses parents" also exists in several versions in Canada, the United States, Belgium, and France. At least 52 versions appear in Quebec alone. Forsyth, *Three Métis Songs from Saskatchewan*, 2.
9. The term *Bois-Brûlé* was used primarily in the nineteenth century to describe a Métis with an Indigenous mother and French father. The term literally translates to "burnt wood" and was associated with the skin colour of the Métis. John Robert Colombo, "Bois-Brûlé," in *Canadian Encyclopedia*, Historica Canada, 1985—, article published February 7, 2006, last modified July 17, 2015, https://www.thecanadianencyclopedia.ca/en/article/bois-brule.
10. In the *Minnesota Heritage Songbook* (2008), Robert B. Waltz argues that the battle was not between the Métis and British soldiers, but rather between the Hudson's Bay Company and the Northwest Company, both of which used Métis to "raid the others' outposts"; according to this account, the Bois-Brûlés had been hired by the Northwest Company. Robert B. Waltz, "(French) Falcon's Song," in The Minnesota Heritage Handbook, accessed July 5, 2013, http://mnheritagesongbook.net/the-songs/addition-song-without-recordings/falcons-song/.
11. Forsyth, *Three Métis Songs from Saskatchewan*, 2.
12. Forsyth transposes Cass-Beggs's transcription in G dorian to E dorian, presumably to accommodate Maureen Forrester's vocal range. The other changes are not significant and include a missing grace note at m. 7, small deviations in the durations in mm. 15, 26, 34, 38, 42, and 50, and missing or added non-harmonic tones at mm. 30, 38, 42, and 54, and an added accidental at m. 58.
13. The enharmonic equivalent of the D♭ (C♯) was first highlighted in m. 5, where it changed the subdominant chord from a minor chord to a major chord.

14. Forsyth drops the latter part of the song title ("de la mariée") for the title of the second movement.
15. The melodic pitches in this passage are once more identical to the transcribed version, with the exception of the E, which should be an E♯ in m. 19. Since there is an E♯ in the orchestral version, it is likely that this alteration was simply a copying mistake.
16. The composer also changes one word from the original transcription by replacing *"ce n'est point pour un an"* with *"ce n'est* pas *pour un an."*
17. With the exception of two durations in m. 32, the melody remains identical to Cass-Beggs's transcribed version.
18. The use of the flattened submediant scale degree to the dominant (descending semitone) was also prevalent in the first movement when the lovers bid farewell (C–D♭–C motive).

5

Breathing in G

Harmonic Tension and Repose in the Cello Concerto Electra Rising

ROBERT C. RIVAL

IN EARLY 2004 I harangued a reluctant and recently retired professor of composition into taking me on as a private student.[1] He eventually acquiesced—on one condition: that he could speak his mind. Of course, I exclaimed—but then wondered anxiously what I had signed up for. Distance was no object. Although he lived in Edmonton and I in Montreal, I bought him a telephone with a hands-free headset and mailed him some of my scores. My new teacher, whose music I greatly admired, was the late Malcolm Forsyth.

Although I recall these lessons with fondness, some of Forsyth's comments continue to haunt me to this day. I think often about his critique of one piece in particular, my blandly titled Overture, a simple, driving concert-opener heavily influenced by Prokofiev, which I wrote when I was 21. Recently, when a community orchestra requested to perform it, and I discovered that the parts were in disarray, I decided to take the opportunity to make some small revisions in the course of which I came across the copy of the score annotated by Forsyth. On the first few pages he had numbered what he deemed unrelated ideas. Continuing in this manner, by m. 41 he had found an eleventh.

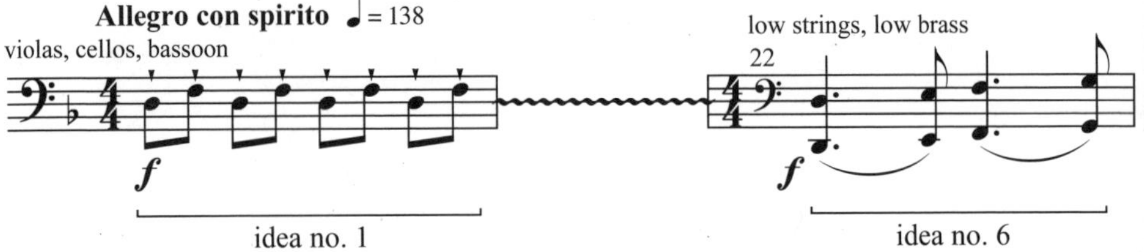

FIGURE 5.1. *Rival, Overture, m. 1 and m. 22.*

During our lesson he had ridiculed as "extravagant" the exposition of so many ideas in such a short span of time. The ideas had character, he conceded, but there were simply too many.

Years later I remain somewhat puzzled by his critique. Consider, for instance, two ideas he labelled as unrelated, nos. 1 (m. 1ff.) and 6 (m. 22ff.): the opening D–F ostinato and the principal theme, respectively (see Figure 5.1). I can only assume that he got a little trigger-happy with his label gun: he must have noticed that no. 6 fills in the minor third in no. 1 with a passing tone. Having studied Forsyth's style more closely, I now speculate that what he was really saying was that it was a pity I had abandoned the first idea so soon as surely there was much more to be done with the minor third.

I reminisce about my lessons with Forsyth because I believe that a teacher cannot help but reveal something about their own preoccupations in the very comments they make about their student's work. However open-minded they may be, it seems inevitable that a teacher will ultimately concentrate on those aspects of the craft that they value most.

A Composer Obsessed

What, then, do Forsyth's comments on my Overture reveal about his compositional values? I believe they point to his economical style of writing. In the music of Forsyth with which I am familiar nothing is thrown away. He sticks, almost obsessively, with an idea once introduced, as if trying to squeeze from it every bit of potential. This may be a melodic or rhythmic figure, or, very often, a composite gesture.

FIGURE 5.2. *Forsyth,* Atayoskewin*, "The Spirits," mm. 1–3. Flutes, oboes, percussion, piano, harp.*

Consider the opening of the first movement, "The Spirits," from Forsyth's most frequently performed orchestral composition, *Atayoskewin: Suite for Orchestra* (1984) (see Figure 5.2). A distinctive gesture, a flurry, is repeated over and over but each time, with only a few exceptions, slightly varied, an approach similar to that taken by Varèse in the opening of *Intégrales.* Once Forsyth discovers a winning idea he sticks with it relentlessly, through subtle variation exposing its every facet. Only when its potential is utterly exhausted does the idea cede to, or develop into, something else.[2]

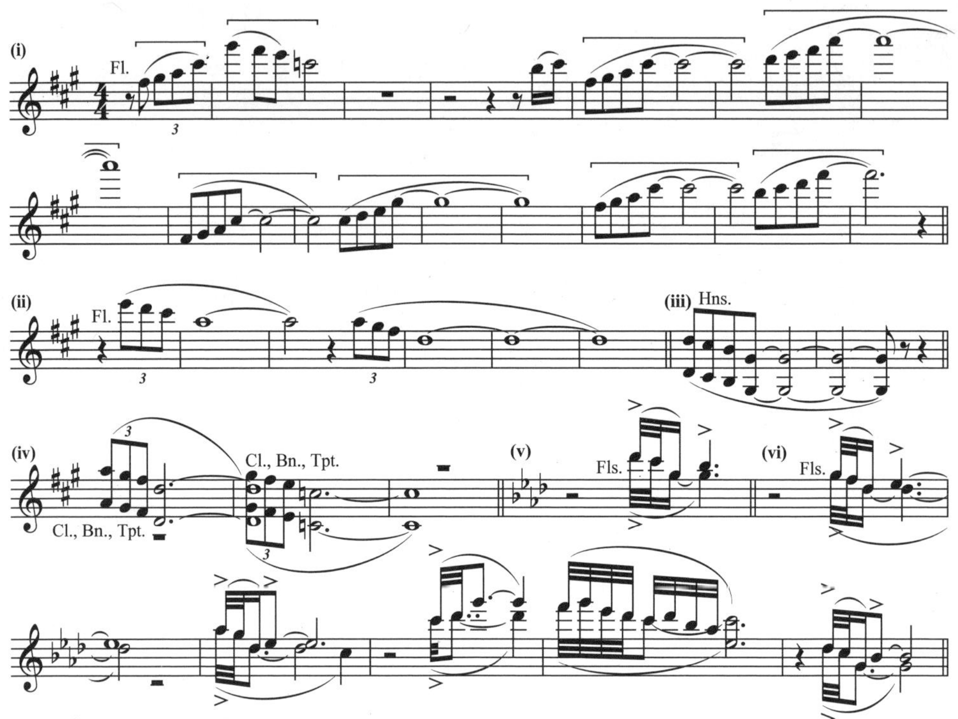

FIGURE 5.3a. *Prominent occurrences of the motto-tetrachord in* Atayoskewin. *In "The Spirits": (i) Letter* A^{+5}*; (ii) Letter* B^{+11}*; (iii) Letter C; (iv) Letter* E^{-2}*. In "The Dream": (v) Letter* A^{+5}*, with the clarinets doubling an octave below, and in relief against the motto in background (see Fig. 5.2); (vi) Letter* C^{+2}*, with doubling in oboes and clarinets.*

The principle of never letting go extends to motivic unity across the entire work. Forsyth, however, does not simply quote a passage from an earlier movement in a later one, the hallmark of cyclic form, or derive the theme of one movement, or section, from that of another. Rather, *Atayoskewin*'s three contrasting movements, "The Spirits," "The Dream," and "The Dance," are, by the composer's own admission, unified by the motto-tetrachord that in its simplest form—*step–step–leap*—lies buried in the harp in the work's opening gesture, discussed above (see Figure 5.2). Other instruments play the motto, too, either truncated or with octave-displaced pitches. Figure 5.3a compiles a few prominent

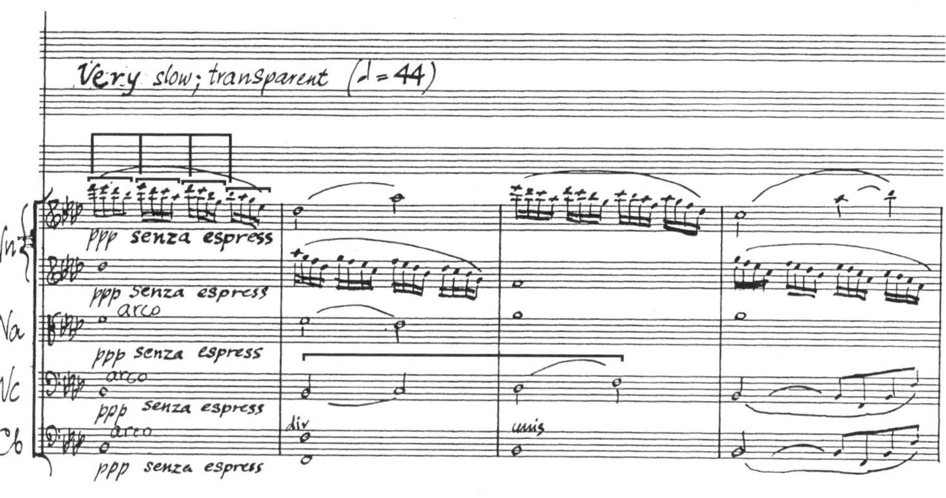

FIGURE 5.3b. Atayoskewin, *"The Dream," mm. 1–4. Strings.*

occurrences of the motto, variously transformed, in the work's first two movements. The degree of thematic unity across movements—atypical in a suite—may escape the ears of the casual listener but becomes obvious once pointed out. Such is the mark of a consummate craftsperson: sophistication hidden beneath a veneer of simplicity, Mozart-like.

An inverted form of the motto-tetrachord saturates the dreamy second movement (Figure 5.3b). The strings unfurl it in an unbroken chain that forms a gentle background tapestry; the movement's closing strains feature the superimposition of the motto, in multiple transformations (not shown). In the last movement the motto serves as the basic building block of the episodes, providing contrast to the jovial, arpeggiated rondo theme: it appears notably in rectus *and* inverted forms simultaneously (see Figure 5.3c).

Forsyth's economical—or one might say obsessive—tendencies extend into other compositional realms. He is infatuated with ostinato textures of all kinds. Some are static, repeating with no variation whatsoever. As we shall see, the harp has one such ostinato in the first movement of the cello concerto. Others repeat a basic idea but with slight variations. Still others are built up by adding layers, as in the

FIGURE 5.3c. Atayoskewin, *"The Dance,"* $F^{+3\text{-}6}$.

opening of the second movement, entitled "Mayibuye Afrika!" and marked "scherzo-like, strictly rhythmic," in which the solo cello finally enters, interrupting the juggernaut at the point at which it becomes intolerable.

Obsessed with Harmony

Forsyth's economical approach is not limited to his manipulation of thematic, rhythmic, and gestural material but extends to the realm of harmony as well.[3] I shall explore this hypothesis through a sustained study of voice leading and harmony in one of the composer's most beloved works, the cello concerto *Electra Rising* (1995), composed for his daughter, Amanda Forsyth, and winner of the 1998 JUNO Award for Best Classical Composition.

A large-scale, 30-minute work in four movements, *Electra* was premiered by Amanda Forsyth and the Calgary Philharmonic Orchestra led by Mario Bernardi in Calgary on November 9, 1995, and again shortly thereafter with the CBC Vancouver Orchestra for its first radio broadcast. Since then Ms. Forsyth has also performed it with the National Arts Centre Orchestra and the Edmonton Symphony Orchestra, the latter with which she recorded it for CBC Records.[4]

"It's full of elation," Ms. Forsyth commented about the finale. "When I play it I feel like I'm flying."[5] Critics have unanimously shared in her enthusiasm. A review of the premiere noted the finale's "grandly expansive optimism" and the first movement's "powerfully nostalgic melodies, set against the constantly shifting patterns and colours of the orchestral accompaniment,"[6] colours variously described as "ethereal"[7] and "tenuous, shimmering."[8] A CD review in *Gramophone* lauded *Electra* as "a lyrical and sensuously scored work in which echoes of Sibelius and Messiaen merge into a personal language."[9]

Murray Dineen, writing for the *Ottawa Citizen*, offered a more poetic assessment. "There are at least two striking features of Forsyth's work," he observed, "the sense of a constant wind, a lightness, an optimism blowing throughout. Secondly, there is always a sense of mystery, of whispered truths, things seen darkly through a glass, a dark continent filled with human cares and triumphs."[10] Eric Dawson, the reviewer of the premiere, noticed these dueling forces as well, drawing attention to the "potent dramatic interplay of tension and repose."[11]

The contrast between light and dark, between tension and repose, I argue, may be traced, at least to a substantial degree, to Forsyth's handling of harmony. The harmonic material in *Electra* is concentrated to the point that the outer movements are almost unrelentingly rooted in G. In the first movement, entitled simply "Cadenza" and marked "With gossamer lightness," the G major triad is preeminent. In the fourth movement, "Paean," and marked "Hymn-like; radiant," various G-centred scales take precedence. In both there is a continual pull away and return to a stable G triad or G scale. Meanwhile, harmonic stability is repeatedly challenged by progressions to remote triads or inflections of scale degrees, and further coloured by chordal extensions and non-chord tones.

First Movement: Of Youth and Maturity

Take the opening of the first movement (see Figure 5.4).[12] The orchestra articulates regular 2+1 phrase groups: two bars of a G major triad (the first played tremolo, the second, non-tremolo) followed by one bar of a secondary triad: in turn, E♭ minor, D♭ major, B♭ major, and C♯ minor. The complete harmonic progression, G–e♭–G–D♭–G–B♭–G–c♯, repeats two more times before breaking down. Only one other triad (B♭ minor) ever sounds in the orchestra, and not until the movement's closing moments, during what we might call its coda (mm. 50ff., Figure 5.6).

Figure 5.5a plots all the orchestral triads across the movement. Each cycle consists of G major triads alternating with four secondary (non-G) triads, numbered 1, 2, 3, and 4. All secondary triads are mediated by G. The G major triad thus dominates the harmonic landscape in the orchestra, and through sheer repetition, establishes G major as the de facto tonic. None of the other triads belongs to the key of G major, the continual alternation between G and remote triads contributing to the movement's otherworldly aura.

Figure 5.5b plots the six orchestral triads on a cubic lattice of the type used by Dmitri Tymoczko, illustrating graphically the relative

FIGURE 5.4. Electra Rising, *mvt. 1, mm. 1–20.*

FIGURE 5.4. *Continued.*

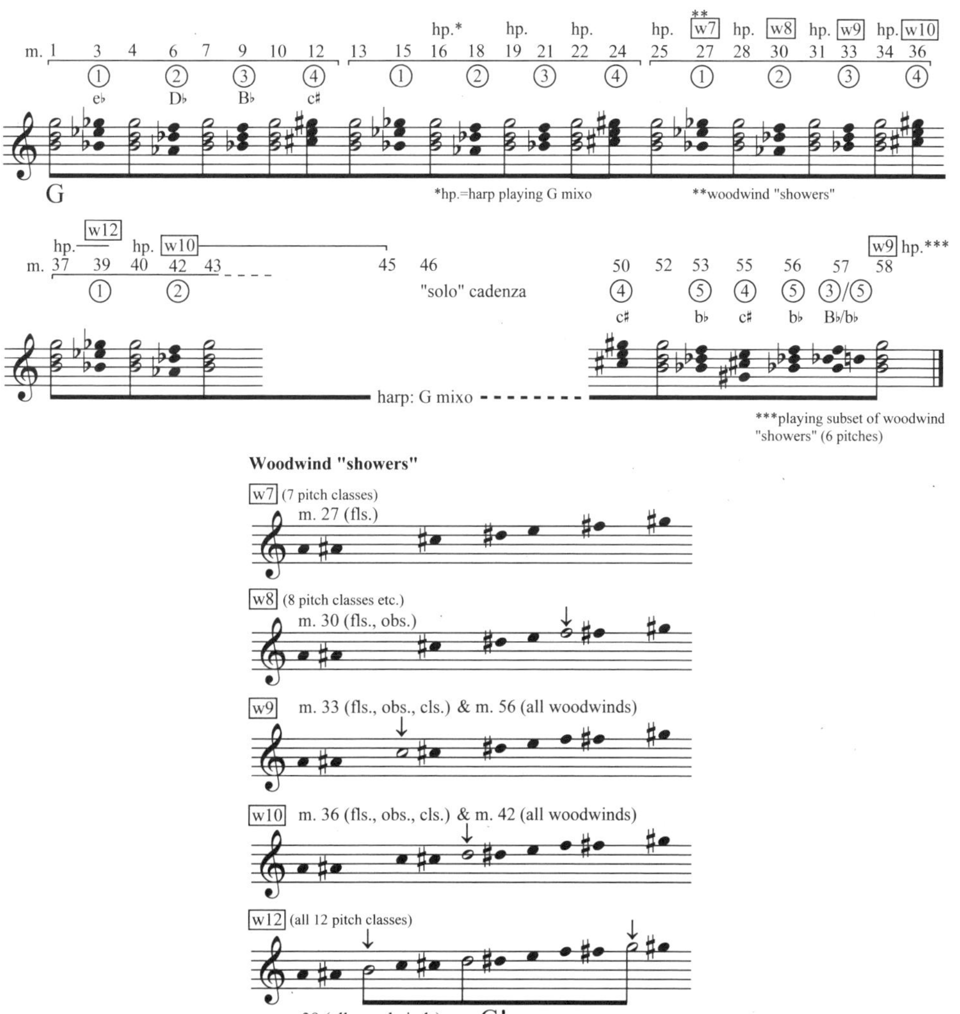

FIGURE 5.5a. Electra Rising, *mvt. 1. Reduction of orchestral chords and collections.*

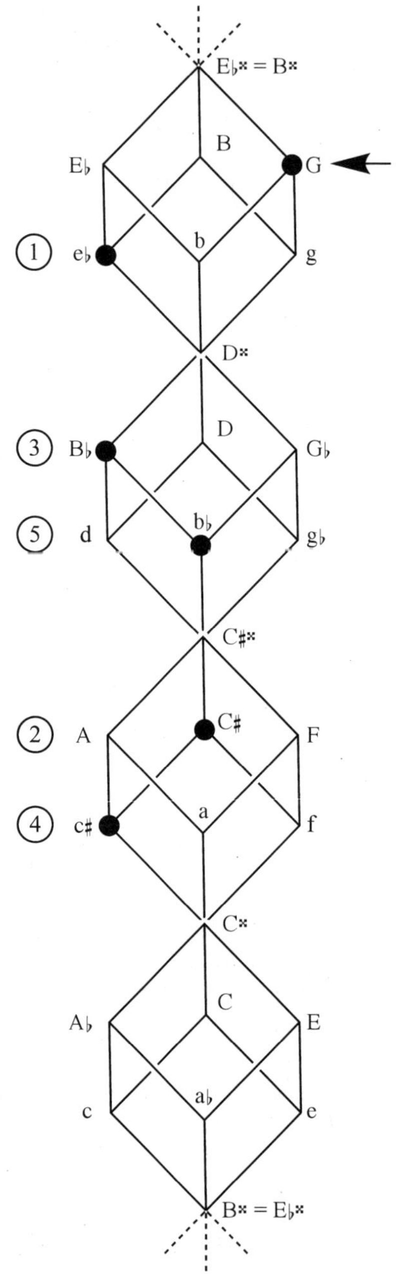

FIGURE 5.5b. Electra Rising, *mvt. 1. Orchestral triads plotted on a cubic lattice.*

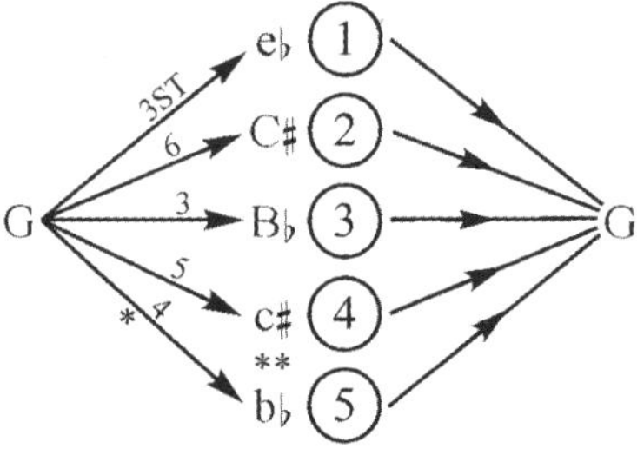

FIGURE 5.5C. Electra Rising, *mvt. 1. Voice-leading size between pairs of triads.*

nearness, in terms of voice leading, between G and the other triads to which it moves.[13] Each edge (line) represents a semitone in voice leading between triads (points). G major and G minor, for instance, differ by just one semitone (B→B♭) and are thus connected by a single edge. The shortest path between G major and E♭ minor, the first two orchestral triads, consists of three edges—that is, a total voice leading of three semitones (G, B, D)→(G♭, B♭, E♭).[14]

Another way to look at these voice-leading relationships is by compiling the total semitonal voice leading between pairs of triads (Figure 5.5c). G and e♭, for instance, have a total semitonal voice leading of 3, whereas G and C♯ (D♭) have a total voice leading of 6, the maximum possible between any two major or minor triads.

The figure also shows that the harmonic cycle has its own internal rhythm as measured by relative voice leading size. G to e♭ is relatively near (3 semitones); G to D♭ relatively far (6 semitones); G to B♭ (3 semitones) relatively near; G to c♯ relatively far (5 semitones). The resulting "voice-leading" rhythm—*near–far–near–far*—is a consequence of the changing distances between G and each of the secondary triads, the periodicity of the pattern suggesting a breathing-like effect.

Relative repose versus relative tension is further accentuated by the solo cello line. In mm. 1–2, the cello's descending figure (the movement's principal theme) produces, with the orchestra, a G mixolydian macroharmony (see Figure 5.4). But in m. 3 the cello lingers on A and G, pitches that clash with the underlying shift in the orchestra to E♭ minor, which, in turn, prompts the cello to subsequently inflect its immediately ensuing notes (B, F)→(B♭, F♯) at which point it (briefly) joins the world of E♭ minor.

The A and G therefore initially function like suspended notes that resolve to B♭ and F♯, the latter displaced by an octave. But the cello resists, hangs on to A, E, and G (all from G mixolydian) and introduces C♯, thereby shifting its scale to D harmonic major. In m. 4 the cello retains the F♯ as the orchestra returns to a G major triad, thereby shifting the macroharmony from G mixolydian (mm. 1–2) sharpwards to G major.[15] The subtle harmonic interplay between cello and orchestra in these first several bars establishes a dramatic relationship between the two entities that unfolds over the course of the movement, and indeed, the work as a whole.

The continual relaxation/tension in the harmony may be likened to exhaling/inhaling or muscles relaxing/contracting. Relaxation is associated with G: G *triads* in the orchestra and simpler, diatonic *scales* in the cello. Tension, on the other hand, takes the form of non-G triads in the orchestra and more dissonant macroharmonies: octatonic and "near"-octatonic, polychords, and other denser collections. The resulting macroharmony in m. 3, for instance, is a subset of E♭/E octatonic—more dissonant, and therefore tense, than the diatonic collections that surround it.[16] In other words, the relaxation/tension found in the alternation of G and non-G triads is echoed in the macroharmonies, understood at the scalar level and filled in by the solo cello.

The various harmonic strands in this movement are transparently differentiated in the orchestration. While the orchestral triads are relegated to the strings (the strings play nothing else), two other strands, the harp and woodwinds, reinforce the strings and solo cello, respectively. Beginning in m. 16, the harp augments the G triad in the strings with a fluttering figure that outlines G mixolydian (D, the fifth scale degree, is absent) thereby colouring the G triad with G mixolydian macroharmony (see Figure 5.4). Only once does the harp linger while the harmony changes to E♭ minor (m. 39, not shown), when, at m. 45

FIGURE 5.6. Electra Rising, *mvt. 1, mm. 49–58.*

(not shown), the harp replaces the strings entirely, providing the sole G foundation upon which the cello unfurls its "true" cadenza.

"Woodwind showers," as Forsyth calls them in his program notes, consist of pitches in the winds notated aleatorically: the pitches are specified but not their precise rhythms, and the notes within boxes are to be played with proportional duration and repeated until indicated (see m. 58, Figure 5.6). The showers begin at m. 27 (not shown), always in tandem with the non-G triads in the strings. Figure 5.5a catalogues the pitches contained in each entry (labelled w7, w8, w9, etc.) and shows where these entries occur in the music.

The harp thus stands on the side of relaxation; the winds, on that of relative tension, aligned with the more complex voice of the solo cello. Each successive wind entry brings in a new pair of instruments until all sound at m. 39 (not shown). Furthermore, each entry becomes progressively harmonically dense: initially consisting of just seven notes (w7), each subsequent entry adds another pitch to the "shower" (w8, w9, w10) until the aggregate (w12) sounds at m. 39, skipping an 11-note "shower." At m. 42 (not shown), a shower extends *over* a G triad for the first time, before evaporating, just as the cello takes up the "true" cadenza.

By this point the harmonic cycle in the orchestral strings has sounded three times (see Figure 5.5a). A fourth cycle, which begins at m. 37, is interrupted by the densest woodwind shower (m. 39), which in turn washes away the string accompaniment entirely. It is as if the solo cello, with the aid of the woodwinds, has finally shed the constraints that the orchestral accompaniment placed upon it. The cello now enjoys the relative freedom of an almost unaccompanied cadenza, which it pursues more or less in F♯ minor, encumbered by nothing more than a thin, passive sheen in the harp, whose figure is frozen in G mixolydian, its harmonic stasis rendering it impotent, lifeless, devoid of the breathing-like shifts to secondary triads. Something is amiss.

The orchestra is resuscitated in time for the movement's coda (m. 50ff., Figure 5.6). But the regimented chord progression that had so rigidly defined the movement's structure until its dissolution by the "solo" cadenza, is now disrupted (see Figure 5.5a). We now learn that the cycle was not just interrupted; it is broken. For the first time the principal theme is not accompanied by a G triad, instead by a C♯ minor triad (m. 50). At m. 53 a "new" triad sounds, B♭ minor, that unexpectedly moves *directly* to C♯ minor (and back again). G not only no longer mediates the secondary triads but also cedes primacy to the latter.

In the closing moments of the movement, even the harp, heretofore aligned with the G triad in the strings, is infused with the chromatic pitches of the last woodwind shower, abandoning G mixolydian for the first time. The harp, like the strings, has been brought under the spell of the solo cello.

The drama, as it unfolds over the first movement, may be summed up as follows. At first the solo cello gently pushes against the regimented harmonic progression in the strings. Eventually it breaks free ("solo" cadenza in F♯ minor), the "regime" reduced to a lifeless G mixolydian shimmer in the harp that no longer guides the cello's pitches via secondary triads. The orchestra never fully recovers, its strict progression disbanded in the coda. The cello (reinforced by the woodwinds), a restless force throughout, succeeds in disrupting the orchestra (strings and harp), a force of relative repose.

From the perspective of "abstract" instrumental drama, an interpretation along these lines suffices. In this case, however, it is hard to ignore the extra-musical facts. What of the work's title and all that its reference to Greek mythology implies? Kenneth Winters, in his CD liner notes, reports that "Forsyth has warned us against probing it for Graeco-Freudian connotations. He says he was invoking the Agamemnon/Electra, father/daughter relationship only as a symbol of the close musical relationship that has always existed between himself and Amanda."[17] We have been warned. But it may be too late: Forsyth let the genie out of the bottle.

Electra Rising was not only dedicated to the composer's daughter but written *for* her and, to some extent, with her collaboration (on the solo part). The work, at the time of this writing, has only ever been played by Ms. Forsyth, perhaps because of how closely—too closely?—it has been associated with the cellist, a connection that statements such as this one by the composer himself have only reinforced: "*Electra Rising is* Amanda. Amanda *is Electra Rising*. The work fits her like a glove."[18] Did Forsyth mean that the concerto *as a whole* reflected his daughter's character, that it was a portrait of her in music? Or did he mean that the solo cello part suited her strengths as a performer? We cannot know for sure, but it seems reasonable to assume that Forsyth meant both. As my purpose here is not biographical but rather to tease out musico-dramatic qualities evoked by this work, let us leave Amanda out of the picture in order to speak, more universally, about the mythical Electra. More to the point, where is Agamemnon?

If Electra's voice is represented by the solo cello/woodwinds, then the force with which it wrestles, the strings/harp, may be taken as Agamemnon's voice. Electra—young, impetuous—is the restless force; Agamemnon—old, rooted (in G), stable—the force of repose. Father extends a guiding hand, leads, but faces resistance; daughter (as youth are want to do) challenges and rebels as she searches for her own identity. They come together, they separate. Ultimately—in this movement, at least—the force of rebellion assumes the upper hand, disrupting the status quo. Youth, in its quest for self-discovery along the path to maturity, defies the symbol of maturity itself.

Third Movement: Brooding and Benevolent Visions

Contrast between harmonic relaxation and tension occurs in the third movement as well. But now the tables are turned. Instead of a general state of repose (G major triads and G diatonic collections) ceding to remote, secondary triads and denser macroharmonies, the reverse takes place: relative dissonance, reinforced by metrical freedom, dissolves into relative consonance and metrical regularity. It is the natural continuation of the first movement, which ended in a state of disquiet.

The solo cello continues its role as the force of harmonic restlessness, now in the form of relatively dissonant chords, while the orchestra occupies purely diatonic space (see Figure 5.7). The movement's initial [014] trichord "chime" {B♭, C♯, D} (m. 1) generates most of the solo cello's chords, many of which articulate [0148] (m. 2, m. 9). Diatonic interludes in the orchestral strings restore calm after each of the cello's tense chordal statements. One imagines visions of a benevolent

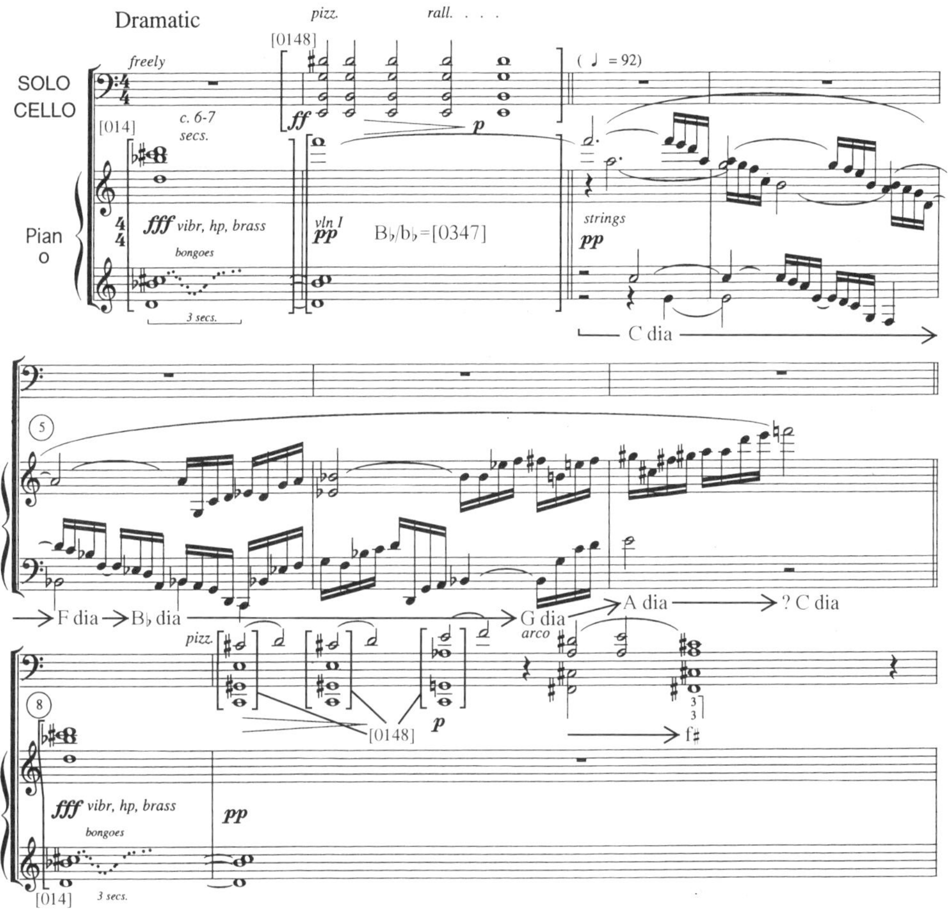

FIGURE 5.7. Electra Rising, *mvt. 3, mm. 1–9.*

Agamemnon intruding into the thoughts of an inwards-turned, brooding Electra. The first such interlude (mm. 3–7), for instance, begins in C diatonic then drifts flatwards around the circle of fifths (F diatonic, B♭ diatonic) before swinging back sharpwards (G diatonic, A diatonic) and finally settling back in what we may take as C diatonic on account of the F natural. This type of collection modulation recalls a procedure common in the music of Carl Nielsen.[19]

The movement ends with the {B♭, C♯ ,D} chime, a trichord with two tones in common with the G minor triad, ensuring efficient voice leading into the finale, which opens with a G major/minor chord (see Figure 5.8).

Fourth Movement: Unity

This G/g (major/minor) sonority with which the finale begins was foreshadowed at the end of the first movement (m. 57) by a B♭ major triad (the cello's low D natural) superimposed on the newly arrived B♭ minor triad (see Figure 5.6). Now G/g plays a decisive role in setting the harmonic tone of a movement awash in scales that fluctuate around G major (and G lydian) through efficient voice leading (Figure 5.8).

Figure 5.9a catalogues the voice leading between various collections in the first 28 bars. With G entrenched as tonic, and G major the mediating scale, semitonal inflections of scale degrees 3, 4, 6, and 7 gently shift the macroharmony to nearby scales. The G major *scale* assumes the dominant role played by the G major *triad* in the first movement.

Figure 5.9b graphs the scales identified in Figures 5.8 and 5.9a on a cubic lattice, extending the music under consideration to m. 71 (not shown in Figure 5.8). Points on the graph connected by an edge (line) represent scales separated by one semitone. Moving from G diatonic to C acoustic, for instance, involves B→B♭. The graph only shows a portion of seven-note space. Yet the scales present in mm. 1–71 are all bunched closely together illustrating the efficient voice leading among them.

A good deal of the movement is thus literally painted in broad brushstrokes of G diatonic (and nearby) scales (Figure 5.10). At the movement's climax (m. 152ff.) the hymn theme (see m. 9ff., Figure 5.8) is suddenly darkened by transposition to B♭ minor, recalling the intrusion of the B♭ minor triad in the coda of the first movement, which there served to disrupt the orderly harmonic cycle. Here, in the closing moments of the finale, B♭ minor dominates, eclipsing G major in 4+1 phrases: four bars of B♭ minor for every one bar of G lydian. Whereas the first movement concludes uncertainly, the B♭ minor triad having worked its dark magic, in the finale the storm clouds are temporary: G reasserts itself forcefully in the coda.

Hymn-like; radiant (♩ = 80)

FIGURE 5.8. Electra Rising*, mvt. 4, mm. 1–28.*

FIGURE 5.8. *Continued.*

FIGURE 5.9a. *Collection voice leading in* Electra Rising, *mvt. 4, mm. 1–28.*

Bar													*Collection*
1–8	G			B♭	B			D					G/g chord
9–11	G		A		B	C		D					*G major (subset)*
12–13	G		A		B		C♯	D					G lydian
13–14	G		A	B♭			C♯	D				F♯	D harmonic major (G mode)
15–17	G		A		B	C		D				F♯	*G major*
17–21	G		A	B♭		C		D	E♭		F		G natural minor
21–3	G	A♭			B	C		D	E♭		F		C harmonic minor (G mode)
24–7	G		A		B	C		D		E		F♯	*G major*
27	G		A	B♭		C		D	E♭			F♯	G harmonic minor
28	G		A		B	C		D	E♭			F♯	G harmonic major

Collection voice leading continues in this manner until mm. 71 with G major mediating between the following scales: G dorian, G acoustic, G mixolydian, G melodic minor, D harmonic minor, B♭ acoustic, G natural minor #4 (mm. 56–7).

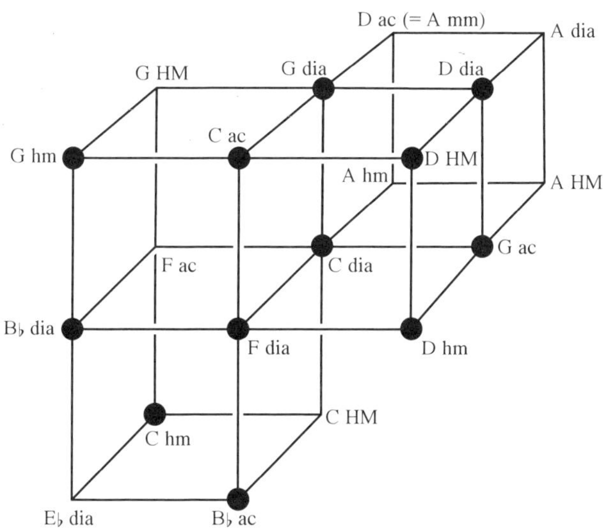

FIGURE 5.9b. *All scales (except one) in* Electra Rising, *mvt. 4, mm. 1–71, plotted on a portion of a cubic lattice.*

FIGURE 5.10. Electra Rising, *mvt. 4, mm. 142–68.*

FIGURE 5.10. *Continued.*

FIGURE 5.10. *Continued.*

A Father–Daughter Relationship Dramatized in Music

A tug of war on G occurs in both movements: in the first, at the level of the triad; in the last, at the level of the scale (or collection). The first features an alternation between the central G triad and secondary "flat" triads, coloured in the cello with chordal extensions. The finale, on the other hand, revolves around the G diatonic collection and substitutes, and despite frequent fluctuations in macroharmony, resounds with a great deal more *pure* G. In the first movement (and to a lesser degree in the third), the orchestra and solo cello are at odds with one another, operating in seemingly different worlds, a conflict that is largely resolved in the expression of common purpose in the finale where cello and orchestra contribute to the same, mostly consonant, macroharmonies.

Harmonically, then, the fourth movement not only extends the drama introduced in the first movement from the realm of triad to that of collection, but also provides a resolution. While in the first movement, the solo cello struggles against G and its associated harmonic regime (the G-centred harmonic cycle), in the finale, it wholly merges with G.

In terms of the father–daughter narrative, if the first and third movements document teenage rebellion, and a distancing between father and daughter, in the finale Agamemnon and Electra appear to have achieved a mutual understanding, a sense of common purpose.

Whether one reads *Electra Rising* in (auto)biographical terms, or in the more general psychological terms of a father–daughter coming-of-age story, or—perhaps most prudent of all—as an abstract drama involving opposing yet related entities that overcome their differences through protracted struggle, eventually expressing themselves in common voice, what seems clear is that by its conclusion, Electra, symbolically, has indeed risen.

NOTES

1. This is a revised version of a paper the author presented at the Canadian University Music Society Annual Conference, Waterloo, Ontario, June 2, 2012.
2. For another examination of Forsyth's single-minded treatment of a basic motive, see Edward Jurkowski's analysis of *Je répondrais...* in this volume.

3. I do not equate a general economy of *material*, expressed in various musical parameters, and which characterizes Forsyth's style, with *motivic* unity. The latter necessarily implies the former—but only with respect to *motive*. A composition may be highly unified via motive yet harmonically diffuse. What concerns me here is Forsyth's extension of the economical principle to the *harmonic* field.
4. Malcolm Forsyth, *Electra Rising*: Concerto for Violoncello and Chamber Orchestra, on *Electra Rising: Music of Malcolm Forsyth*, Amanda Forsyth (cello), Grzegorz Nowak (conductor), Edmonton Symphony Orchestra, CBC Records SMCD 5180, 1997.
5. Steven Mazey, "Making the Cello Sing: Calgary Cellist Amanda Forsyth Plays Father's Concerto at Two NAC Shows," *Ottawa Citizen*, April 29, 1997. Ms. Forsyth titled her next CD, a collection of works for cello and piano by her father, *Soaring with Agamemnon* (Peter Longworth [piano], Marquis Classics 81231, 1998). The album cover features a photo of a young Amanda pretending to fly on the shoulders of her father.
6. Eric Dawson, "Concerto's Premiere Promises Staying Power," *Calgary Herald*, November 10, 1995, D3.
7. "Ten Best," *Edmonton Journal*, January 10, 1997, F1.
8. John Sutherland, "Edmonton Symphony Orchestra / *Electra Rising*: Music of Malcolm Forsyth," *Performing Arts & Entertainment in Canada* 32, no. 1 (1998): 40.
9. Richard Whitehouse, "CD Review: *Electra Rising*," *Gramophone*, February 1998, 105.
10. Murray Dineen, "Bernardi Returns Light-Heartedness to NAC," *Ottawa Citizen*, May 1, 1997.
11. Dawson, "Staying Power."
12. All examples from *Electra Rising* are from the piano reduction.
13. Dmitri Tymoczko, *A Geometry of Music: Harmony and Counterpoint in the Extended Common Practice* (New York: Oxford, 2011).
14. The largest possible path between any two triads on the lattice is six semitones, for example, from G major to C♯ major (triads whose roots are a tritone apart). Note that by starting at the G major lattice point, one can approach C♯ major by moving downwards or upwards since the lattice itself is circular (the top point is the same as the bottom point).
15. The "relaxed" harmonies, consisting of various G-centred scales (G mixolydian, G major, D minor melodic [G mode]) are all connected by single semitonal voice leading, like different shades of the same colour.
16. The harmony in m. 3 may also be understood as a seven-note polychord: e♭ in the orchestra against A^7 in the cello. Polychords are often less complex, however, frequently formed by two triads that share a common pitch. Such is the case in m. 9 where B♭ and G♭ may be perceived as a B♭ triad with extensions ♯9 and ♭13—that is, a pentachord.

17. Kenneth Winters, liner notes for *Electra Rising*, CBC Records, 1997.
18. Malcolm Forsyth quoted in Winters, liner notes, *Electra Rising*.
19. See Robert Rival, "Flatwards Bound: Defining Harmonic Flavour in Late Nielsen," *Carl Nielsen Studies* 5 (2012): 258–79.

Allusion and Reflection in *Je répondrais…* for Solo Piano

EDWARD JURKOWSKI

ALTHOUGH KNOWN PRIMARILY as an orchestral composer, Malcolm Forsyth also amassed a sizeable and varied amount of chamber music throughout his long and celebrated career. Given his dual role as a composer and professional trombonist, it is perhaps not surprising that many of these works were written for various brass ensembles.[1] Yet instrumental compositions also feature prominently in Forsyth's oeuvre, and it is a work from this category to which I turn in this essay—specifically, his 1997 *Je répondrais...* for solo piano. Commissioned by Stéphane Lemelin through Radio-Canada, and premiered by the pianist on November 21, 1997, the three-movement work is a creative response to three composers Forsyth held in esteem throughout his life: Frédéric Chopin, Henry Purcell, and Robert Schumann.

Born in South Africa, Forsyth received critical attention for using aspects of his native country's music in some of his compositions.[2] In this essay, I add to this literature by presenting a descriptive analysis of some of the salient pitch and rhythmic elements in *Je répondrais...*, and specifically, how the composer integrates aspects of his South African heritage with Western art music in the work's three movements.

"à Purcell: Fantazia upon One Note"

The first movement, "à Purcell: Fantazia upon One Note," is a meditative, improvisatory-styled contemplation on Purcell's work by the same name. Tripartite in design (Part I encompasses mm. 1–56), it incorporates four motivic events. The first motive is the repetitive half note B (representing the allusion to Purcell's work in which a repeated whole note in the tenor serves as the stabilizing harmonic pitch for the various imitative lines running throughout the composition; see Figure 6.1 for this reference). The second motive is the upward arpeggiated grace-note gesture that is (predominantly) comprised of a major or minor harmony; in order to generalize the sonority for the ensuing discussion, I refer to its pitch-class set theory label, the [037] trichord. The third motive is the [016] trichord appearing in the bass; it is consistently comprised of the pitches B♭, A, and E♭, whose first complete instance begins at m. 28 (see Figure 6.2, in which this motive is beamed together for clarity). The fourth and final motive is the thirty-second-note gesture of an [0148] tetrachord.

One often noted feature of South African music is the use of additive, rather than divisive, processes to organize layers of rhythmic activity.[3] While I am not asserting a direct correlation with any one composition, the sophisticated layering and temporal organization of rhythmic events in Part I of "à Purcell" suggest an indebtedness to this type of music Forsyth would have known from his childhood. For instance, an omnipresent repeating B serves as the basis from which the [037] and [016] trichords are implemented in layers, always in consistent registral placements. Throughout Part I, additive rhythmic processes reposition the various statements of the [037] trichordal motive. There are three sections, each of which uses a different temporal relationship to organize these trichord appearances. For instance, the unifying element in Section I is eight half notes; from the outset of the piece, the pattern of trichord appearances (in terms of half notes; the double vertical lines indicate a unit of eight half notes)

FIGURE 6.1. *Purcell,* Fantazia upon One Note, *mm. 1–8.*

is || 8 || 4 4 || 1 7 || 4 4 || 1 7 || 8 ||. In Section II (mm. 24–45) the unifying rhythmic element is the pattern of [037] trichord appearances within 12 half-note groupings, an increase of duration by 50 per cent from Section I; here, the pattern is || 3 9 || 3 9 || 9 3 ||. Finally, Section III (mm. 46–56; mm. 50–6 are not shown) uses a third unifying element—four half notes, a reduction of 50 per cent from Section I; the pattern of trichord appearances is || 4 || 2 2 || 1 3 ||. A transitional pattern of || 1 9 || segues to Part II.

An additive rhythmic process also engenders the placement of the B♭, A, E♭ [016] trichord in Part I. For instance, the positioning of the low B♭ in m. 22 appears two half notes following the [037] arpeggio in m. 20; in m. 28 the B♭ appears three half notes following the arpeggiation in m. 26; in m. 39 four half notes following the arpeggio in m. 36; in m. 44 it is five half notes following the arpeggio in m. 41.[4] And the

FIGURE 6.2. *Forsyth,* Je répondrais..., *mvt. 1, mm. 1–49.*

FIGURE 6.2. *Continued.*

B♭ in m. 54—the transitional passage to Part II—appears three half notes following the final arpeggiation in m. 52 (not shown).

The final motive, the [0148] tetrachord, comprises the pitches C♯, F, A, and B♭. Although it plays a minor role in Part I (the sonority appears four times), an additive rhythmic process also determines its temporal placement. The first appearance of the tetrachord occurs in m. 13; its next appearance is 13 half notes later in m. 18; the third appearance of the harmony is 22 half notes later in m. 31—an additional nine half notes from the prior relationship; and the final statement in m. 47 is 31 half notes from the third appearance of the harmony—once again, an additional nine half-note duration.

Looking at the overall design of Part I, there are interesting relationships among the materials studied thus far. Initially, the appearances of the [016] trichord and [0148] tetrachord are more frequent when the organizational units of the [037] trichord are elongated (that is, eight and 12 half notes). However, as the movement progresses, the durational gap between appearances of the [016] and [0148] harmonies expands with a concomitant increase in the number of [037] trichord statements (engendered via the short organizational unit of four half notes) and elaboration of the ostinato B—the latter primarily through a variety of arpeggiated figures. The cumulative overall effect is a subtle increase in rhythmic motion throughout Part I, culminating with the extensive rhythmic activity beginning at the transitional passage in m. 54.

While additive rhythmic processes are the means by which Part I is organized, Parts II and III of "à Purcell" are freely designed, largely via improvisatory, cadenza-like flourishes. While the ostinato on the pitch B remains, the [0148] harmony, one that played a minimal decorative element in Part I, pervades throughout the music. Figure 6.3 illustrates the tetrachord's presence during the pinnacle of the work. Figure 6.4 identifies how the [0148] tetrachord is partnered with the omnipresent pitch B, creating the ostinato A, B♭, B, D♭, F pentachord, the harmony that pervades the calm Part III.[5] The brief coda, mm. 102–14 (not shown), recycles the motivic material from Part I, albeit without the earlier strict additive time point strategies. The absence of any rigid

FIGURE 6.3. *"à Purcell," mm. 69–83.*

FIGURE 6.4. *"à Purcell," mm. 84–96.*

organizational process by which these harmonies appear suggests that the coda functions more as a fleeting memory of earlier events, rather than a space for further developmental ideas.

One final observation of note is the shrewd harmonic integration Forsyth engenders from the particular pitch classes within the harmonies he has chosen. For instance, in Part I the three primary [037] sonorities include F♯, C♯, A; C♯, G♯, E♯; and G♯, D♯ (and a second G♯ an octave higher). The [016] harmony uses the pitches A, B♭, E♭. And the [0148] harmony uses the pitch classes C♯, F, A, B♭. Put simply, the first two [037] chords each have two invariant pitches with the [0148] tetrachord; the [016] also shares two invariant pitch classes with the tetrachord.

"à Schumann: Thumb-Piano"

The title of the second movement of *Je répondrais...* contains a double reference. On one hand, the title refers to the African thumb piano, or kalimba. Thumb pianos traditionally consist of a wooden board to which metal "tines" of varying lengths are affixed. Some have mechanisms for readily tuning the tines to different scales. The longest tines are typically in the centre, with shorter (and thus higher-pitched) tines arranged alternately in ascending order towards both sides of the instrument. The thumb piano is commonly held in both hands and both thumbs pluck the tines either simultaneously or in turn. Of particular significance is the layout of the various tines: unlike a Western percussion instrument such as a marimba or keyboard instrument such as a piano, where registral pitch space is correlated with either left or right motion, as seen in Figure 6.5, there is a parallel-directional motion when alternating hands play a scale pattern on a kalimba. The tuning of most kalimbas involves notes from a diatonic or non-diatonic scale ascending on the tines from the centre outward in an alternating left-right fashion (Figure 6.5 from Chapman, is a kalimba based upon the pentatonic scale G, A, B, D, E).[6] When any tine is plucked, the adjacent tines also vibrate and these harmonizing secondary vibrations serve a similar role to the harmonic overtones of a string or keyboard instrument—that is, they increase the harmonic complexity of an individual note.

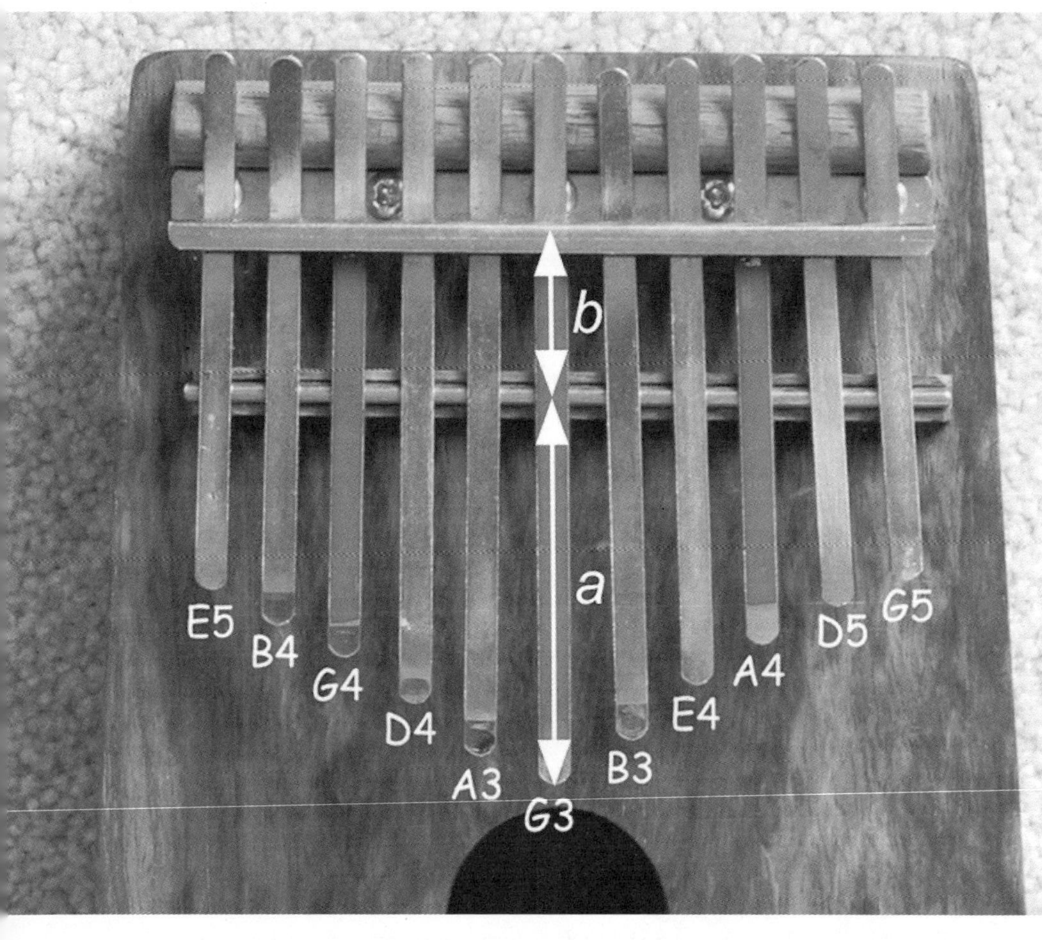

FIGURE 6.5. *Illustrating the 12-note tuning of a kalimba. [Chapman 2012]*

Along with the reference to the African thumb piano, Heather Schmidt suggests Forsyth's title also contains a veiled allusion to Robert Schumann's stylistic use of the thumbs to articulate the inner complexities of his piano pieces.[7] However, while the left and right hands participate in an ascending scalar structure in a kalimba, the design of the piano is such that analogous hand gestures—that is, mirrored hand motion beginning from a central axis point—engender either strict intervallic mirroring (for instance, articulating the white notes using the pitch D as a central axis point) or loose mirroring

Referential Statement of Motives 1 and 2

Senza fretta; come un sogno

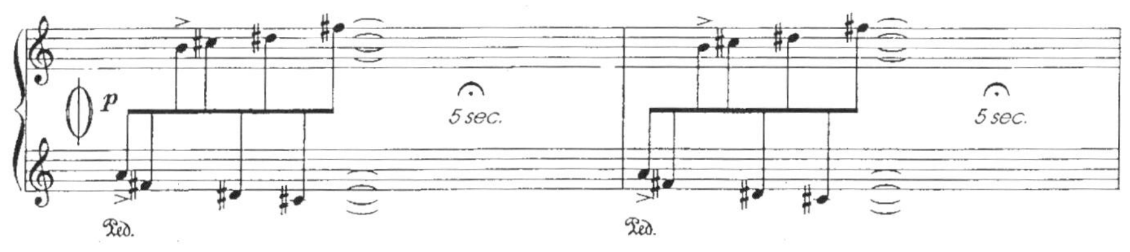

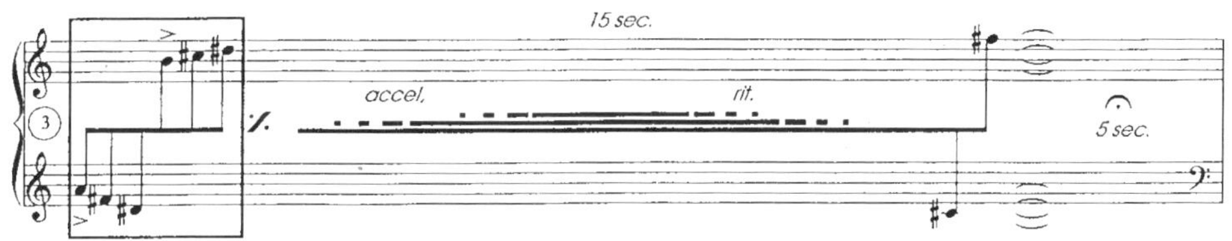

Variation I

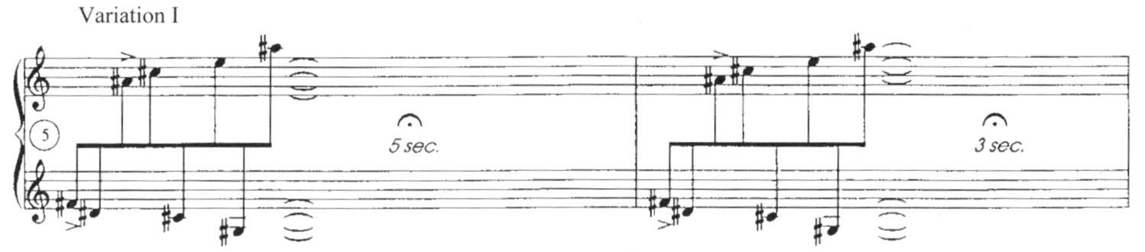

FIGURE 6.6. *"à Schumann," mm. 1–12.*

FIGURE 6.6. *Continued.*

(when articulating the white notes using the pitch C as a central point). As an illustration, consider the opening measures of "à Schumann": here (see Figure 6.6) the thumbs from both hands articulate the opening pitches of their respective arpeggiated gestures. Analogous with the pentatonic scale (in set theory parlance, [02579]) that is created by the cumulative attacks of the tines in Figure 6.5, the aggregate outcome from the inversional gestures generates a B dominant ninth chord.

In essence, "à Schumann" consists of a series of increasingly elaborated variations on three successive motivic ideas (mm. 1–4 contain the referential presentation of the first two motives; the variations begin at m. 5 [the first variation adds the third motive], m. 9, m. 11, m. 18, and m. 26; the fourth and fifth variations are not shown). The first motive is the inversional scalar idea (a motive where the thumb slightly accents the opening pitches of the inversional gesture played by each hand). The pitch material from each hand is played in alternating fashion—possibly a reference to the alternating hand motion when playing a kalimba. The second motive is the hexachordal cadential-like gesture (see m. 4 in Figure 6.6). Two inversionally related [026] trichords generate the harmony—that is, C, E, F♯ in the left hand and B, C♯, E♯ in the right. A fermata, as witnessed at the end of m. 4, regularly concludes this particular motive. While the harmonies represent different trichordal families, the motive's inversional relationship bears an association with the first motive. Specifically, in the opening measures, inversionally related [037] trichords are contained within the tetrachord of each hand (an F♯ minor triad played by the left hand and B major by the right hand). We will return to a comparable relationship towards the end of the movement.

The third motive is the [0148] tetrachord; the harmony is virtually always generated from the pitches C, D♯, E, and G♯. As noted above, the tetrachord initially appears in m. 8 of the first variation as an interpolated harmony between the repetitions of the cadential hexachord. However, in variation four this tetrachord takes on a more substantive role within the cadential gesture of each successive variation—to the point that on the final page of the score (mm. 31–51, see Figure 6.7)

FIGURE 6.7. *"à Schumann," mm. 31–51.*

we find simultaneous presentations of two transpositions of the [0148] tetrachord, each played by a different hand. The inversionally related [037] trichords in this passage (i.e., the subsets contained within these tetrachords)—an A major triad in the left hand and a B♭ minor in the right—reference the comparable major/minor relationship at the outset of the movement, providing a nice frame to the movement overall.

To summarize, the movement consists of a series of five variations on three distinct motives, each of which represents a different family of harmony: inversionally related [037]s, a hexachord derived from two inversionally related [026] trichords, and a [0148] tetrachord. The work is designed such that the primary focus of developmental activity at the outset rests upon the first of the three motives. However, through the course of the movement, more attention is placed upon the third motive—that is, on the [0148] harmony. The work's final variation contains the most extensive focus upon two forms of a [0148] harmony, with two inversionally related [037] trichords playing a vital role in expressing these transpositions of the sonority.

"à Chopin: White-Key Study in African Mode"

The final movement, "à Chopin: White-Key Study in African Mode," is a nod towards Chopin's famous piano etude, Op. 10, No. 5, commonly labelled the "Black-Key" etude. Here, the music exclusively uses the white keys (although there is an inexplicable appearance of a singular D♯ grace note in m. 63), and it is these seven pitches that possibly serve as the reference to "mode" in Forsyth's title. However, the kinship with Chopin is limited to the titles, for the pieces are otherwise quite different in formal design, pitch material, duration, and rhythmic energy. A dance-like ebullience permeates the eight-minute "à Chopin"—a trope perhaps suggestive of the fond childhood memories Forsyth has identified as an important part of his African heritage.[8]

The design of "à Chopin" is evocative of a common African instrumental form, termed by Simha Arom as ostinato-variation.[9] He writes that an ostinato engenders a thematic idea or series of ideas; repetitions of the pattern are varied, largely the result of ever changing contrapuntal and rhythmic devices. Arom asserts that the definition is

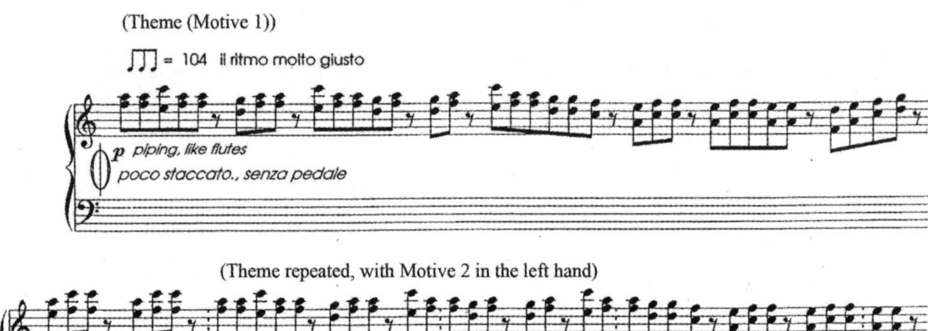

FIGURE 6.8a. *"à Chopin," mm. 1–11.*

not in conflict with Western musicological definitions of continuous variation.[10]

Figure 6.8a illustrates the movement's two primary motivic ideas: Motive 1, the right-hand series of dyads emphasizing intervals of thirds, fourths and fifths, frequently played with a staccato articulation; and Motive 2, a single-line melodic bass line, usually played legato. Variants of these motives appear in a number of ingenious ways, engendering a type of *fortspinnung* development. Figure 6.8b illustrates the diversity of interesting ways variants of these two motives materialize in this work.

In tandem with the ostinato-variation form of "à Chopin" is its overall tripartite design. For instance, with respect to rhythm and dynamics, the work's opening *piano* dynamic and consistent eighth-note rhythm in the right hand gradually alters at m. 77 to substantive use of sixteenth-note rhythms and frequent syncopated accents. Measure 152 demarcates the point of a continuous piano dynamic, combined with augmented or sustained rhythmic values, to close the work with a calm and gentle repose.

Although both harmonic and melodic intervals of the third, fourth, and fifth saturate the piece, suggesting a tonal basis for the movement, any perception of a tonal centre is achieved primarily through tonal

FIGURE 6.8b. *Tonal centres and motivic movement in "à Chopin."*

Measure nos.	*Tonal Centre*	*Comments*
Part I		
1–13	F, D	Motives 1 and 2 in referential presentation
14–35	A, D, and C	RH and LH interaction of Motive 2
36–51	C, D	Similar texture as mm. 1–14, with different melodic material played by LH
52–76	D, C	Three-part texture: upper and lower voices employ Motive 2; the middle voice utilizes Motive 1, ending with a transitional passage that segues to Part II
Part II		
77–107	C	Motive 1 punctuated with accents played by LH; gradual increase in dynamic to double forte at m. 102
108–21	A, C	Return to texture of mm. 15–35 using different pitch material; gradual increase in rhythmic activity
122–38	C	Motive 1 presented canonically by RH and LH
139–46	Ambiguous	Transition, Section (A): Motive 2 played by LH
147–51	C	Transition, Section (B): Motive 2 played by both hands, with significant rhythmic activity that segues to Part III
Part III		
152–79	A	Regular presentation of two-pitched eighth-motive, played by the LH; the RH plays variants of Motives 1 and 2
180–99	A	Culmination of texture in mm. 152–79, with gradual elongation of rhythmic values
200–12	A	Calm, chorale-like texture played in 3/2 rhythm

assertion, rather than functional grammar. The large-scale tonal areas also correlate with the tripartite design. For instance, following the opening's suggestive F tonal focus, the pitch material focuses upon different tonal centres, ultimately settling on C by m. 60. C represents the primary tonal area of interest throughout Part II, while A is asserted throughout Part III: the seventy-measure passage features a gradual decrease in rhythmic energy—both expansive rhythmic values and sustained pedal notes dominate the final portion of the piece. The work ends gently upon the piece's sole minor triad, A minor.

|| The preceding survey of Forsyth's three-movement *Je répondrais...* demonstrates how the composer deftly integrates stylistic attributes from two divergent musical cultures. On one hand, the means of association can be through direct musical practice. Consider, for instance, Forsyth's use of additive rhythms and layers of rhythmic activity that organize the opening part of "à Purcell" along rhythmic time points, a stylistic feature prevalent in African music. Yet, at the same time, the musical events associated with these time points use tertian harmonies (major and minor chords, or more broadly, an [037] trichord) or the atonal [016] and [0148] sonorities from Western art music grammar. However, the association may also be allusionary; two examples include the relationship in "à Schumann" between the nineteenth-century composer's stylistic use of the thumbs to articulate his idiomatic piano sonorities and the alternate hand gestures when playing an African kalimba (this gesture is especially relevant with the first of three motives from the theme and subsequent variations), or the "white note" pitch material in "à Chopin" and the "black note" G♭ major material used in the Polish composer's Op. 10, No. 5 piano etude.

The integration of elements from these two cultures should not be seen as a type of imperialistic appropriation of African culture—as, say, Puccini's use of Japanese melodic material in *Madame Butterfly* or Native American folk elements in some of Dvořák's American-period works. Rather, I would argue that Western and African cultural elements play an equal and integrative role in Forsyth's rich composition. One is not cast in a supportive role with the other; they are interdependent and vital elements whose sum is greater than their individual parts.

NOTES

1. See Dale Sorensen's survey of Forsyth's brass music in this volume.
2. See, for example, Kathy Primos "A Life Experience: The Orchestral Works of Malcolm Forsyth," *SoundNotes* 6 (Spring 1994): 12–21. An edited version of this article is reproduced in this volume.
3. Chapter 5 in Simha Arom, *African Polyphony and Polyrhythm: Musical Structure and Methodology* (Cambridge: Cambridge University Press, 1991) contains a useful outline of such additive processes in this music.
4. Alternatively, one can interpret the passage as three half notes following the extensive arpeggiated figure in mm. 42–3.
5. The ostinato initially contains a C♯; from m. 88 until the end of the piece, the harmony inexplicably is spelled with a D♭.
6. David M.F. Chapman, "The Tones of the *Kalimba* (African Thumb Piano)," *Journal of the Acoustical Society of America* 131, no. 1 (January 2012): 945–50.
7. Heather Schmidt, program notes for *Solus*, CBC Centrediscs CD-CMCCD 9603, 2003.
8. Forsyth reflects on his childhood musical influences in Eitan Cornfield, "Forsyth Documentary," on *Canadian Composers Portraits: Malcolm Forsyth*, Centrediscs CMCCD 8802, 2002.
9. Arom, *African Polyphony*.
10. For an introduction to ostinato-variation in African music, see Arom, *African Polyphony*, 39–41.

7

"Here, All Is a Beginning"

Reflections of Forsyth in A Ballad of Canada

MARY I. INGRAHAM

A BALLAD OF CANADA for Mixed Choir and Orchestra, Malcolm Forsyth's last large-scale composition, was completed in 2010 and premiered in June 2011, only months before he passed away.[1] When asked about his title in an interview with composer Trifon Heney in April 2011, Forsyth responded simply that *A Ballad of Canada* was an attempt to write music to texts that were "iconically Canadian...identifiably Canadian."[2] What this meant for Forsyth is not easy to determine, but in his selection, manipulation, and musical settings of the poems he chose, we find evidence of a profoundly poetic musical artist revelling in and reminiscing on the place he called home. "Canada is the land," he declared; "it's a vast, vast space and covers all kinds of topography...The history of Canada has been shaped by the land."[3] In addition to reflecting Canada's varied landscape and celebrating its history, *A Ballad* situates Canadians (including the composer himself) within the spaces described and across the stretches of time that comprise Canada's history. Specific regions and places within the country are suggested, as are historical events, but Forsyth's organization of the texts is not chronological. Thus, the subjects who speak and the spaces the texts describe acquire intertextual relationships that reveal their similarities as well as expose their differences.

There are five movements in *A Ballad*, each taking its title from its original source. These are grouped by Forsyth into three parts: Part I: The Land sets "In the Yukon" (poem by Ralph Gustafson); Part II: Canada in Time of Trial includes three poems, "In Flanders Fields" (John McCrae), "The Toll of the Bells" (E.J. Pratt), and "On the Waverley Road Bridge" (Carl Hare[4]); and Part III: The Land consists of "Newfoundland" (E.J. Pratt). Forsyth's title for the work as a whole implies a coherent narrative—*a* ballad—and the opening text, "Here, all is a beginning," suggests the beginning of a story that will lead through the events and experiences of the five poems towards the declaration at the end of the last movement,

> *And the story is told*
> *of human veins and pulses,*
> *of dreams that survive the night.*

Each of the movements in *A Ballad* echoes the unique evocations of Canada and Canadians in its text, style, and format, with Forsyth adding his own creative voice to reflect their specific geographical, historical, and personal references. As indicated earlier, the story across *A Ballad* is not linear, but rather circles backwards and forwards in time, juxtaposing reflections of the past with evocations of the present and future. The fluidity of time and place that results from this combination of textual and musical materials thus creates a dynamic record of human relationships that both starts and ends with "here." In the descriptive note in the printed score, Forsyth describes his vision for *A Ballad*:

> *The quiet and the vastness of Canada's far Northwest are celebrated in the opening setting, "In the Yukon." The Northern Lights arch gloriously over the scene. The last of the five movements, "Newfoundland," takes us to the eastern end of the country, where the Atlantic meets the lonely and grand shores of that province...In the finale ("Here the tides flow, and here they ebb...") the*

wildness of Canada's eastern shore is pictured. A final crashing wave, a flickering of the Northern Lights, and the music vanishes.[5]

Between these reflections on Canada's extreme geographical locations, Forsyth considers World War I as well as the war in Afghanistan, the former with one of the most iconic Canadian texts, "In Flanders Fields" and the latter by way of a poem from Carl Hare's *On the Waverley Bridge Road.*[6] Connecting these movements is the first of Forsyth's two settings of texts by E.J. Pratt, here a poem titled "The Toll of the Bells" that memorializes the lives lost in the sinking of the SS *Greenland* off the coast of Newfoundland in 1898, "a natural disaster all too common off the rocky crags in the frozen Atlantic" and a community response that Pratt himself witnessed.[7] The movement in time from World War I back to the SS *Greenland* disaster in the late nineteenth century and then to contemporary events in Afghanistan exemplifies the broad temporal gestures in Forsyth's narrative that require listeners to consider connections between poems without necessarily linking them chronologically or to specific human reminiscences.

The pull of differing perspectives obliges us instead to consider the relationships of such moments to each other and to ourselves. In doing so, commonalities arise across poems in their portrayal of human strengths and weaknesses embedded in beliefs about nature or religion, all of which remain immanently hopeful. Tensions between the diverse subject matter and formal attributes of the poems that establish as well as infer meaning on this theme are reflected in Forsyth's musical settings. Musical frameworks result from his representation of these tensions by way of contrasting musical sections that engage simultaneously melodic, timbral/textural, and rhythmic materials. Forsyth's compositional style here is derived from brief intervallic motives that are thoroughly embedded in vertical and horizontal textures and a harmonic language that, similar to his earlier orchestral work, moves fluidly "between tonal, atonal and ambivalent" sonorities.[8] The frequency with which contrasting materials are heard in each movement of *A Ballad* thus results in an audibly episodic style. In this way, *A Ballad* reveals the profoundly poetic quality of Forsyth's compositional voice that, like Gustafson's, reflects a "distinctively personal stance, which revises and reuses, rather than rejects, its romantic and modernist history."[9] In the pages below, I consider the poetic and musical gestures that reinforce what I perceive to be Forsyth's personal stance with respect to the texts and their potential meanings and how this translates into his music, for it is here, in the composer's conscious decision to "revise and reuse" textual and musical materials and in his concentration of expressive gestures across *A Ballad*, that the most illuminating evidence can be found of what Forsyth might have meant by this work as "iconically" and "identifiably" Canadian.[10]

Continuity and Discontinuity

Typical of Forsyth's style, the primary musical materials used to unify musical and textual materials in *A Ballad* are heard early in the first movement so that their recurrence encourages reminiscence and reflection.[11] The opening and closing gestures of *A Ballad* reflect one such motive, specifically in their allusion to another "iconically Canadian" work, his 1984 orchestral suite *Atayoskewin*. Forsyth describes his reuse of the "little wisp of the Northern Lights" in *A Ballad* as "a kind of leitmotif...because it's [one of the first and] the very last thing that happens; I bring it back at the very end of *Newfoundland*...just this wash of colour which reminisces about what you've heard in the first setting."[12] (See Figures 7.1a–c for a comparison of the original motive in *Atayoskewin* and presentation in the first and fifth movements of *A Ballad*. Note the similarities across these statements in gesture, metre, and [especially with Figure 7.1c] intervallic movement.)[13] This "perfect little wash of colour suggesting movement, the colours of the Northern Lights, the sort of vagueness,"[14] exposes Forsyth's desire also to portray the visual effect of the aurora borealis: the shimmering curtain of light evoked in the glissando scalar motive appended to the intervallic motive also becoming a recurring melodic motive across the movements of *A Ballad*. Reference to the Northern Lights in the first poem inspired the connection between these works: "At night, the northern lights played, great over country."[15]

FIGURE 7.1a. Atayoskewin*, m. 1. Flute, piccolo, and oboes. Northern Lights motive.*

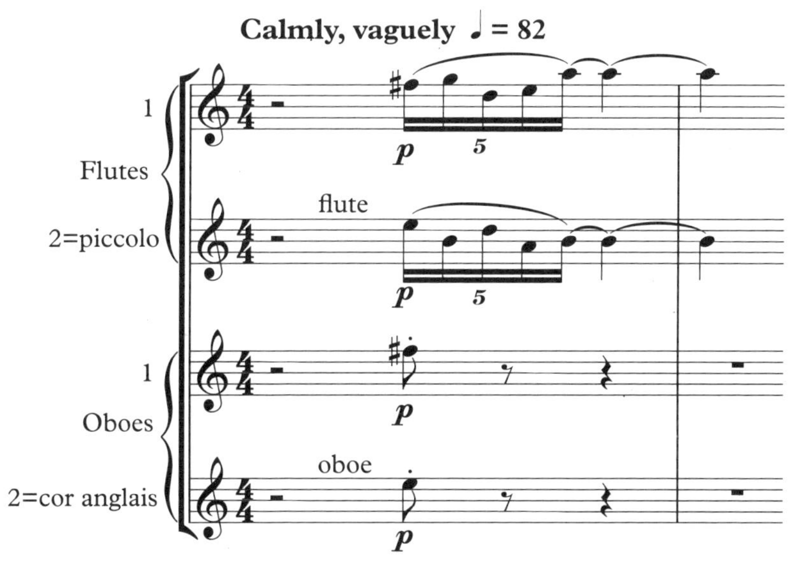

FIGURE 7.1b. A Ballad of Canada*, mvt. 1, mm. 2–3. Flutes and oboes. Northern Lights leitmotif.*

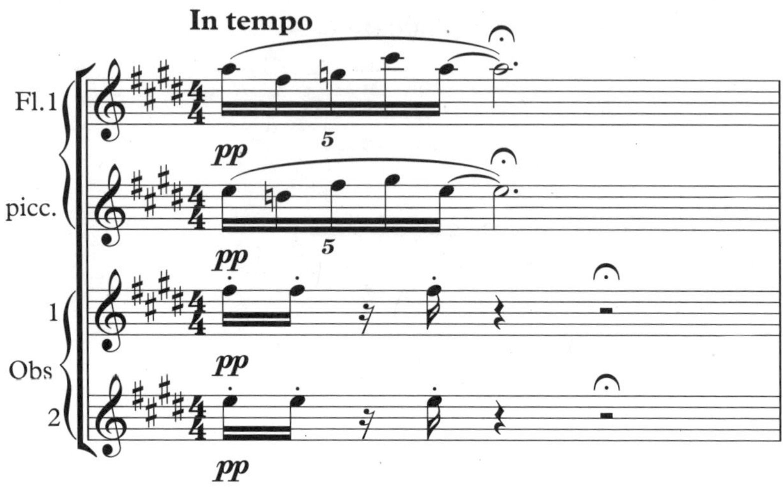

FIGURE 7.1c A Ballad, *mvt. 5, m. 132. Flute, piccolo, and oboes. Northern Lights leitmotif.*

Forsyth's predilection for constructing melodies from small intervals (here, fourths and semitones) is also evident in this leitmotif and reflects a compositional technique employed in his earliest orchestral works that ultimately—through an approach to voice leading that luxuriates in the dissonances of suspensions—impacts both melodic and harmonic domains.[16] Although each movement in *A Ballad* is written as a closed formal structure, Forsyth's flexible motivic play and attention to the contrasting moods, characters, and styles of his texts and music is heard through frequent changes in rhythmic figuration and gesture, vocal and instrumental textures, fluid harmonic language, and timbre, and results in a work that *sounds* spontaneous but in fact is intricately organized.

A Ballad is no less coherent for its episodic quality. Motivic activity across each movement returns to an opening gesture or melody, and from the beginning of the first movement to the final "wisp of the Northern Lights" leitmotif in the last measure, intervallic invention allows Forsyth to revise and reuse musical elements from one movement to the next, as a means of establishing links across the disparate physical and emotional landscapes of Canada and Canadians described in the texts. The musical score and its performance do not reveal such qualities readily or conventionally, but rather by way of seemingly discontinuous musical narrative as well as the sparse language of his texts. "Poetry," Ralph Gustafson writes, "becomes what it releases meaning from."[17] Given that all of the five poems used in *A Ballad* are subjected to some textual manipulation, we can also consider Forsyth as releasing further meaning beyond the original text versions, actually re-poeticizing and extracting additional connections within the poems by omission, repetition, and isolation of words. We might therefore speak of Forsyth's poetic intent for *A Ballad* in his music as well as in his reworking of texts, for its letting go of excessive textual language and musical technique in favour of gesture, allusion, and the images of Canada and of the composer as artist that these suggest.

This chapter considers each of the five movements of *A Ballad* separately, focusing on Forsyth's adaptations of the original poems: his recreation of time and place through encounters with sound and sensory experiences, and the continuities and discontinuities in form and motivic technique that remain within his musical settings. Discussions and examples provided here are not intended to provide a full analysis of the structure or motivic development of the work, but rather to serve as an overview of some of its more audible poetic representations. Listeners might reasonably hear additional similarities across musical examples as a result of Forsyth's continuously varied motive construction and the adaptable harmonic language described previously;[18] score readers will be rewarded with even more intricate connections.[19] Consideration of Forsyth's interpretative treatment of his poetic texts, I propose, suggests a perspective across *A Ballad* that focuses experiences on the present and diminishes thoughts of the past in order to increase the possibilities for the future.

Part I: The Land

Movement 1: "In the Yukon," by Ralph Gustafson (1909–1995)

The first movement of *A Ballad* is based on a 14-line poem by Ralph Gustafson titled "In the Yukon."[20] Forsyth omits nearly five lines of Gustafson's short poem in his setting, indicating that he "changed the emphasis of it a little bit" to "concentrate on the visual imagery of the Northern Lights and the salmon and the moose and the great glory of the green hangings."[21] Gustafson's full text, with the lines used by Forsyth set in roman type, is shown in Figure 7.2. Forsyth's change in emphasis is clearly evident when the texts are overlaid as shown in this figure. Gustafson's original poem begins with an evocation of the past that invokes a foreign (here, European) heritage ("Europe, you can't move without going down into history") before situating the reader in the New World with the contrary proclamation that "Here, all is a beginning." By omitting the first line, Forsyth places his story firmly in the present while still suggesting future opportunities that starts "Here" (in the New World) at the "beginning" (of what, we don't know). Both Gustafson's and Forsyth's texts are grounded in nature, and both describe the playful yet fateful upstream journey of salmon ("The leap for dying") and their natural, forested surroundings ("The timbered hills").

Forsyth, however, breaks the structural defences of the poem by interpolating and repeating lines of Gustafson's original poem in his version in order to establish a clear contrast between the landscape that his words describe and the movement of the salmon within it. The inherent tension within the movement of the salmon is both elegant ("the salmon turned silver arcs") and predictable ("The leap for dying"), and Forsyth's decision to omit the final lines of Gustafson's poem might be considered as a poetic gesture that allows for a more ambiguous future. There is, however, a glimpse of the future in Gustafson's close that leads Dermot McCarthy to suggest that this "is a poem of joy, of beholding, of yet another overwhelming of the self by a power beyond comprehension to which the imagination entrusts its regeneration."[22] In Gustafson's poem, Europe and the New World are entwined, governed by a history that appears to hold the poet to his past, against the freedom of his present. For Forsyth, without such overt references to the past, the present—while serious—offers beauty and possibility. And it is perhaps this idea of the regeneration of life and beauty within nature that connected Forsyth so intensely to Gustafson's words.

FIGURE 7.2. *"In the Yukon," poem by Ralph Gustafson. Text used by Forsyth in* A Ballad *in roman.*

Europe, you can't move without going down into history.
Here, all is a beginning. *[Forsyth's inserted text:* At night, the northern lights played, great over country/Without tapestry.../[...]/...They were green,/Green hangings and great grandeur.*]* I saw a salmon jump,
Again and again, against the current,
[Inserted text: Here, all is a beginning.*]* The timbered hills a background, wooded green
Unpushed through; the salmon jumped, silver.
This was news, was commerce, at the end of the summer
The leap for dying. *[Inserted text:* And the salmon turned silver arcs.*]*
Moose came down to the water edge
To drink and the salmon turned silver arcs.
At night, the northern lights played, great over country
Without tapestry and coronations, kings crowned
With weights of gold. They were green,
Green hangings and great grandeur, over the north
Going to what no man can hold hard in mind.
The dredge of that gravity, being without experience.

Many of Forsyth's changes to the poem evidence a desire to excise references to human interests in favour of nature's expression. For example, by omitting the first part of line 6 ("This was news, was commerce"), he maintains the focus on the movement of salmon "at the end of summer." Of the six final lines of Gustafson's poem, Forsyth chooses only two and a half, retaining this emphasis on the natural surroundings that now describe the shimmering dance of the Northern

Lights, without reference to the "coronations, kings crowned with weights of gold." In the lines Forsyth omits, Gustafson references Old World, historical perspectives; he portrays the grandeur of the Northern Lights as natural rather than human-made. Forsyth includes the words "without tapestry" in the text he interpolated into the first line of his setting but omits it in his last statement; without continuing with Gustafson's text, the reference remains oblique, heard perhaps specifically for its connection to the visual display of the Northern Lights rather than to the past.

Place is established somewhat vaguely in the poem and the presence of the poet/composer is integrated purely as an observer ("I saw a salmon jump") within it: the place is simply "against the current," within "the timbered hills," and beneath "the Northern Lights." By closing the movement with the text and musical depiction of the Northern Lights, Forsyth thus retains his focus and releases the story from the ambiguity of death and sentimentality that appear to close Gustafson's. Although Forsyth's closing text remains somewhat open, the concentration of words and emphasis on living beings allows for a resolution in which all future action is synthesized into the present—a specific moment of time and place that is "here" and "over the north." Forsyth underscores this sense of closure by framing the movement with the Northern Lights leitmotif (see Figures 7.1b and 7.1c).

The musical setting for "In the Yukon" is a closed rondo-like structure that is articulated in motivic, stylistic, textual, and textural domains. The A section includes an ascending and descending scalar melody that will be heard across the work (here ascending in C major and descending in G major and marked "calmly, vaguely") and the Northern Lights leitmotif shown in Figure 7.1b as well as the descriptions of place that open the poem. When the choir enters in m. 25 with the text "Here, all is a beginning," brass and voices intone a sombre mood that portrays the majestic setting homophonically while the unison voices and chordal brass in fourths underscore a somewhat static representation of the place (see Figure 7.3a). The A section returns for a third iteration in m. 86, resuming the homorhythmic texture to depict the scene in which the "Moose come down to the water edge."

A more fluid and imitative texture (marked "sprightly") arrives in the B section (beginning in m. 42, not shown) for "I saw a salmon jump, / Again and again, against the current" in response to the action and cyclical representation of life described in the text (see Figure 7.3b). References to the movement of salmon swimming upstream form the climax at the point of Forsyth's repetition of the text "The leap for dying" in the second B section (mm. 73–8, not shown). The imitative texture here, however, does not encourage listeners to dwell on the words disproportionately, but rather urges the forward movement of the salmon towards the final A section in which the Northern Lights are reflected timbrally and intervallically "over the north"—the "here" of which Forsyth's re-poeticized text speaks. A and B sections alternate three times in quick succession (often less than 20 measures apart) and the movement concludes with a final A section and a reiteration of the Northern Lights leitmotif. Forsyth's manipulation of this leitmotif across the movement involves internal variations of pitches, intervals, and changes in contour in its linear expression, evident in the brief A and B section excerpts included here in which the common interval of a semitone is highlighted in the A section vocal melody and perfect fourths in the B section. Instrumental gestures shown in Figure 7.3a pick up both of these intervals, as is particularly evident in the initial eighth-note to half-note figure across the brass instruments.

FIGURE 7.3a. A Ballad*, mvt. 1, mm. 25–7. AB voices with brass choir. Section A.*

FIGURE 7.3b. A Ballad, *mvt. 1, mm. 47–50. SA voices. Section B.*

Part II: Canada in Time of Trial

Movement 2: "In Flanders Fields," by John McCrae (1872–1918)

"In Flanders Fields" is arguably one of the most familiar Canadian poems.[23] Forsyth makes no changes to the original text or its strophic structure, save for repetition of the last line of each stanza and additional emphasis on the cautionary closing words through repetition of the first ("Take up our quarrel with the foe") and third ("The torch; be yours to hold high") lines in the last stanza. His most obvious modification to the simple strophic form of the original poem involves framing the movement with introductory and concluding instrumental sections and interpolating a contrasting musical refrain between each of its three stanzas. This has the effect of creating a more expansive and descriptive orchestral work capable of uncovering more of the surface nuances and inner tensions of the poem. The refrain serves as the A section in Forsyth's three-part modified rondo form (plus coda) for this movement. In it he alternates distinct musical styles and timbres: A sections (the refrain) are largely instrumental and utilize the full orchestra in expressing a strongly aggressive style, and B sections, which present the three stanzas of text and are introduced with a woodwind flourish, incorporate most of the vocal and textual material and are accompanied primarily by a smaller instrumental group comprised of strings, winds, and harp and a still, calm, distant, and spacious mood.

The contrasting musical moods of aggression and calm between the A and B sections underscore a text that suggests the humanity of death as experienced in the feeling of absence or loss of those who died and the presence of those who remain, making a place for nostalgia and memory in the present. Stanzas are further distinguished by Forsyth's use of vocal timbres: the first stanza is sung by women's voices only (until the repetition at the end of the stanza of the text "the guns below, the guns below"), the second stanza is for men only, and the final stanza is sung by the full choir. Sopranos and altos voice a reflection on the past through their reminiscence in stanza 1 ("In Flanders fields the poppies blow"); tenors and basses remind us of the gains and losses through war at the end of this stanza (as noted above) and in the second stanza's "We are the Dead"; and full choir combines in the final stanza, urging vigilance for the future ("Take up our quarrel with the foe"). A coda (beginning in m. 99, not shown), based on material from the B (textual) section, is set homorhythmically for full choir, uniting all voices and perspectives in a final musical climax on the text:

If ye break faith with us who die
We shall not sleep, though poppies grow
In Flanders fields.

This is accompanied by a crescendo to *fortissimo* on the text "We shall not sleep" (especially mm 102–3, not shown) and an instruction to the performers to sing "with more decisiveness / stronger consonants." The poem is set largely imitatively and Forsyth saves chordal textures for emphasis, such as occurs in his pairing of women's and men's voices in m. 64 (not shown) and this closing section. Reminiscence returns with a diminuendo to *pianissimo* on the last words, "In Flanders fields," as the music dissolves to niente.

The movement begins with an instrumental A section marked "Aggressive and Forceful" played by the full cohort of strings, brass, and percussion; accented sixteenth-note figuration sounding within this weighty texture prompted reviewer Christopher Moore to describe this refrain as "a musical depiction of live gunfire."[24] Although the

FIGURE 7.4a. A Ballad, *mvt. 2, mm. 1–4. Violins and violas. Section A motive.*

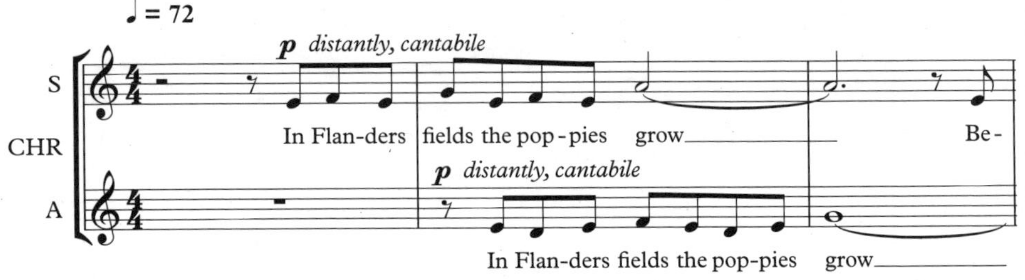

FIGURE 7.4b. A Ballad, *mvt. 2, mm. 17–19. SA. Section B motive.*

refrains are uniformly more militaristic and aggressive and they contrast conspicuously with the calm, cantabile mood, eighth-note movement, a narrow melodic range and the prominent woodwind timbre of the B sections, these sections are not motivically discrete (see Figures 7.4a and 7.4b for the primary A and B motives). As an example of their overlapping ideas, in mm. 31–2 of the first B section Forsyth interjects a brief motive with brass and percussion in fourths and fifths that resembles the A section mood and melody heard earlier, before the choir sings, "Scarce heard amid the guns below" (see Figure 7.4c. Consider especially the major and diminished thirds and parallel movement here, and in mm. 3–4 of Figure 7.4a). Moore attributes this moment to "the thud of a bomb exploding in the distance."[25]

Forsyth highlights further nuances of the text in the bass drum that insinuates itself into the full SATB chorus of the final B section; it begins in m. 85 (not shown), at first inaudibly, but increasingly insistent so that by m. 97 (not shown) it is played *forte* and with full choir for a final and insistent iteration of the text "Take up our quarrel with the foe." The movement closes with four measures that link the woodwind gesture that opened the B section (now descending rather than ascending) to the aggressive A section figuration shown in Figure 7.4a, played by muted brass.

FIGURE 7.4C. A Ballad, *mvt. 2, mm. 31–2. Brass and percussion.*

Movement 3: "The Toll of the Bells," by Edward John Pratt (1882–1964)

Written in 1923, E.J. Pratt's "The Toll of the Bells"[26] commemorates the public religious ceremony held to honour the loss of lives from the sinking of the SS *Greenland* off the coast of Newfoundland in 1898. Pratt was present at the event and recalls his experience:

> *The great memorial was held in the Anglican cathedral, with several representative clergymen speaking messages of consolation to the immense congregation of mourners. The words burned into our souls as they described the struggle of the men on the floes, the pitched battle with the elements at their worst, and the ironic enigma of Nature and its relation to the Christian view of the world.*[27]

The poem does not describe the event itself, rather its aftermath in these ceremonies, with Pratt focusing primarily on human responses to the disaster: the ritual of Christian death that promises comfort ("Sorrow has raked up faith"), faith in the afterlife ("Today the vaunt is with the grave"), and specifically the Christian belief in the Resurrection ("now swells the tidal triumph of Corinthians"). His concluding lines allude to the "ironic enigma" described in his recollection of the event, in which

> *Only the bells' slow ocean tones, that rose*
> *And hushed upon the air, knew how to tongue*
> *That Iliad of Death upon the floes.*

This is the second of two places in the poem where Pratt comments on the ineffectiveness of religious ritual to honour people or events, the previous statement appearing in the third stanza in which he dismisses the sounds of ritual as powerless to "find a language to salute / The frozen bodies." The reference to Homer in the final line ("That Iliad of Death upon the floes") might therefore signify a shared belief in the role of human error in such tragedies that is denied in rituals promoting such events as nature's, or even God's, will. In defence of Pratt's potentially pessimistic view of others' beliefs in salvation through external practices, Vincent Sharman writes that Pratt's poetry frequently suggests a change in perspective, that individuals "look in the wrong direction, away to the Deity, to systems, to Nature, rather than to themselves, the defiant heart."[28] If this is the case, then Forsyth's alterations and setting provides such a refocusing through its emphasis on the individuals within the text.

Forsyth describes choosing this poem for *A Ballad* not only for its link to an "iconic event in Canada, the cruelty of the sea," but also for its "musical imagery."[29] Pratt's poem is full of references to the sounds of bells and guns, a "band's low requiem," an "organ-prelude," a "trumpet-blast," and "voices anthemed." While Forsyth did not include all of these in his final version of the text, those that do occur are accompanied by obvious musical representation: the opening chimes (mm. 1–3, not shown) representing the tolling church bells, setting the text "dumb hearts unspoken" with a *pianissimo* dynamic and sparse texture in light string harmonics (m. 10, not shown), a homophonic choral section accompanying the text "the band's low requiem" (mm. 13–18, not shown), trumpet figuration for the reference to a "trumpet-blast" (mm. 20–4, not shown), rhythmic figuration in the timpani to repeat the reference to "the ritual of the guns" (mm. 1–3, for example), and so on.

Forsyth set only 11 lines of Pratt's 28-line poem;[30] by reducing the text so dramatically, he narrowed the already concentrated poetic description of the event to focus more clearly on the role of the human subjects in the story. Nearly all of Pratt's references to the Christian faith are removed, leaving Forsyth to highlight human witness to the event: "The flag half-mast," "the cortege," and "trumpet-blasts," and a gesture to the "final tribute...at altar-rails." Nonetheless, he retains the reference to these acts as rituals and thus preserves the essence of conflict between natural and human control and the illusions of power and faith in nature. In the end, for both Pratt and Forsyth the delusions of ritual vanish in favour of real-world experience. Figure 7.5 shows Pratt's full text, with the lines used by Forsyth in roman.

FIGURE 7.5. *"The Toll of the Bells," poem by E.J. Pratt. Text used by Forsyth in* A Ballad *in roman.*

We gave them at the harbour every token—
The ritual of the guns, and at the mast
The flag half-high, and as the cortege passed,
All that remained by our dumb hearts unspoken.
And what within the band's low requiem,
In footfall or in head uncovered fails
Of final tribute, shall at altar-rails
Around a chancel soon be offered them.

And now a throbbing organ-prelude dwells
On the eternal story of the sea;
Following in undertone, the Litany
Ends like a sobbing wave; and now begins
A tale of life's fore-shortened days; now swells
The tidal triumph of Corinthians.

II

But neither trumpet-blast, nor the hoarse din
Of guns, nor the drooped signals from those mute
Banners, could find a language to salute
The frozen bodies that the ship brought in.
To-day the vaunt is with the grave. Sorrow
Has raked up faith and burned it like a pile
Of driftwood, scattering the ashes while
Cathedral voices anthemed God's To-morrow.

Out from the belfries of the town there swung
Great notes that held the winds and the pagan roll
Of open seas within their measured toll,
Only the bells' slow ocean tones, that rose
And hushed upon the air, knew how to tongue
That Iliad of Death upon the floes.

With these 11 lines of text, Forsyth creates a short, through-composed movement of 40 measures that clearly distinguishes his interpretation from Pratt's formally structured "two sonnet" poem. Forsyth situates the moments of obvious musical representation noted above within an evocative musical background of instrumental timbres and foregrounded choral textures. The sparse chime and bass drum that open the movement followed by unison bass voices intoning the text "The ritual of the guns and the mast" thus express not only the ritual (chimes) and the guns (bass drum), but also the tension between spiritual and human conflict in the singing voices. The chimes cease in m. 19 (not shown) and return only for a final, single toll in m. 28 (not shown) with the text "the dropped signals from those mute banners." A muffled timpani rhythm plays in the space between, as background to the musical representations of "trumpet-blasts" and "the hoarse din of guns" noted above. And it is a variant of this *pianissimo* timpani rhythm crossed with a homorhythmic, dissonant flute, piccolo, and oboe choir that closes the movement. Against this backdrop, Forsyth interjects additional motivic gestures from string, brass, and woodwind groupings. Examples include the violins and violas that punctuate the homophonic bass choir in mm. 4–20 (not shown) and muted brass and timpani fanfares in mm. 20–6 (not shown).

Forsyth's treatment of vocal lines in this movement includes unison, imitative, and homorhythmic choral settings that sit largely in the foreground of the musical space. Recalling a similar use of voices to articulate structural divisions in the second movement, Forsyth allocates military references to men's voices in m. 2 (noted above) and in mm. 14–16 for the text "And what within the band's low requiem fails of final tribute." Figure 7.6a illustrates the instrumental accompaniment in this section in which trumpets and trombones evoke the sombre mood "with funereal tread" in a homophonic texture. In mm. 30–7, movement between vocal lines in fourths emphasize a text that describes the failure of words and sounds to "find a language to salute the frozen bodies" (see Figure 7.6b). Women's voices narrate the descriptions of reminiscence beginning with "and as the cortege passed / All that remained by our dumb hearts unspoken" in mm. 7–13 (not shown), and full choir is

FIGURE 7.6a. A Ballad, *mvt. 3, mm. 14–18. Trumpets and trombones.*

engaged for descriptions of human denial (beginning with "shall at the altar-rails / ...soon be offered them") and leading into a musical climax on the final reiteration of the text "The frozen bodies" (see Figure 7.6b).

Forsyth expressed a desire not to overwrite his middle movements.[31] Sparse orchestral textures and the brief yet intense instrumental interjections heard in this movement allow him to sustain the emotional tensions within the text while still providing the audible and visible representations of its detailed narrative.

Movement 4: "On the Waverley Road Bridge," by Carl Hare (b. 1932)

Forsyth described the poem "On the Waverley Road Bridge"[32] written by his friend and colleague Carl Hare as "very moving," and he explains his musical response as "very sparse...so that the words could be unobstructed."[33] Hare's text speaks to universal experience, with the timbre of the times (in this poem, a contemporary conflict in the Middle East) reflecting centuries of human conflict past, present, and future, while at the same time communicating a momentary but profound personal connection between two strangers. The empathy felt between the grief-stricken woman in the funeral cortège who has lost her son and the parent holding a son watching her is shared in an instant through their bodily gestures: the mother's hand that waves "absent-minded in its grief" and her "wondering eyes" that appear to look directly and probingly at the narrator. The difference in perspectives (both physical and

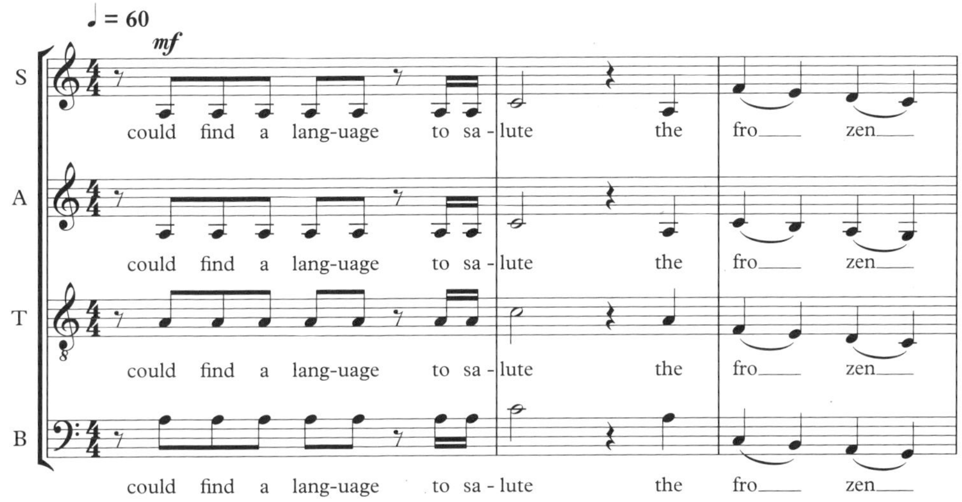

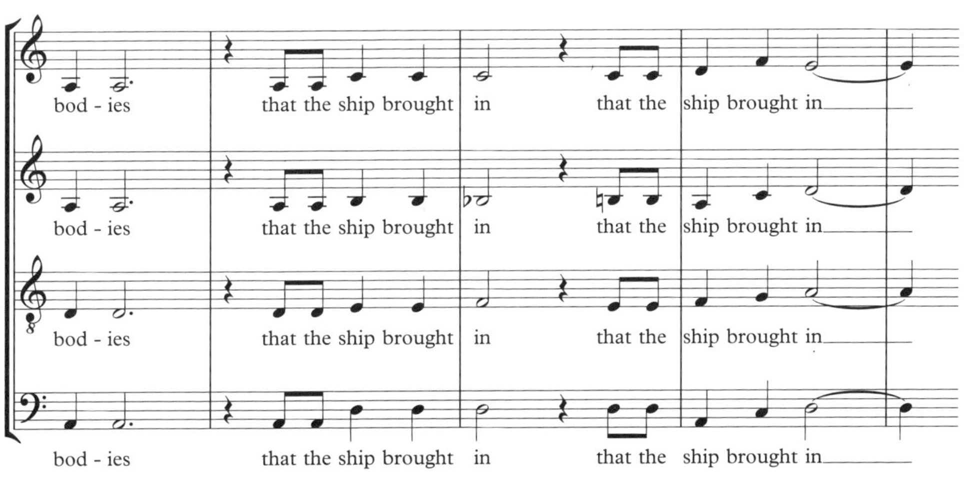

FIGURE 7.6b. A Ballad, *mvt. 3, mm. 30–7. SATB.*

emotional; felt and perceived grief) and the self-consciousness of their gestures is a tribute to the intense bond felt between observer and observed and to their shared fear and feelings of loss that responds with a desire for human contact. Where the mother in the cortège holds only a memory of her son and reaches out, the narrator clings to the child, urging him to "stay closer," understanding in that moment the sorrow of another's bereavement and wondering, "How could I bear such a loss?" It is an intensely beautiful poem and musical setting, so evocative and so painfully personal.

Forsyth makes no changes to Hare's 10-line poem, but where the poem is ambiguous on who is in the crowd watching the procession, Forsyth is clear: it is finally a communication between two mothers. Although he sets the opening five lines of the text for tenor voices, sopranos enter with "Her son no longer in her arms / As mine is now." The "us" of the tenor opening ("Waves up to us") reflects a deep connection to the event by all spectators. But continuing with sopranos, Forsyth makes clear that the mother in the procession is "gazing up" at the mother with her son and that the place of true empathy lies in their shared experiences.

Time appears to stand still in this poignant vignette, the unspoken bond between the mothers suspending time and transcending place. Forsyth recaptures this sensation musically in his delicate textures and simple melodic lines, but he also extends the space to include other spectators at the event by incorporating men's and women's voices and through brief instrumental gestures connected to individual words and thoughts in the poem. These gestures carry worlds of meaning beyond the individual texts they reinforce, plotting tensions within the event, and exposing feelings of loss and the power of memory that are unspecified in Hare's poem but revealed in the anonymous voices with whom they resonate.

A close reading of the poem and Forsyth's musical response reveals the power of these moments within moments. The movement, only 47 measures in length, is through-composed. Tenors sing the opening descriptive line, almost monotone to start and thinly orchestrated as an accompanied recitative in style and texture; women's voices enter in

FIGURE 7.7. A Ballad, *mvt. 4, mm. 44–7.*

m. 24 (not shown) as noted above. Fleeting instrumental timbres captivate us further, in the rapid flute motive in mm. 8–12 (not shown) that imitates the movement of the mother's hand "wav[ing] up to us as with delicate fingers," the plaintive oboe melody in mm. 18–24 (not shown) accompanying the words "The hand, absent-minded in its grief," and a toy piano heard first in mm. 28–9 (not shown) between "her son no longer in her arms" and "as mine is now." These seem to hold us within the instant of the encounter. Reflecting the close of the second movement, Forsyth distils the motivic material from across this short movement into a final four-measure statement (mm. 44–7, see Figure 7.7), in which the singing of the text "stay closer to me" (first as a soprano solo and then repeated with ATB choir) is followed by a rolled G–B♭–C♭ triad in the toy piano (recalling mm. 28–9), sustained D's in the oboes (recalling mm. 18–24), and a return of claves, not heard since m. 1, and marimba, not since m. 15.

Part III: The Land

Movement 5: "Newfoundland," by E.J. Pratt (1882–1964)

E.J. Pratt's "Newfoundland"[34] is the longest poem included in *A Ballad*, despite Forsyth excising more than half of it for his musical setting. Pratt's unique style in this long-form lyric poem holds neither a consistent rhyme pattern nor a regular structure and, similar to "The Toll of the Bells," personifies nature's acts of destruction and creation. Two voices are heard across six stanzas in Pratt's poem, with odd-numbered stanzas describing the place of nature's contact with the coast of Newfoundland, and even-numbered stanzas the evidence of its power in the debris that remains on the shore. Stanzas 1, 3, and 5 portray the waves, wind, and rocks, ascribing human qualities to the tide that flows with "a lusty stroke of life," winds that blow "with familiar breath" and cliffs "keeping watch" over the harbours. These evocations contrast with descriptions in stanzas 2 and 4 of the place of contact: the kelp, shells, and stones that collect on the shore, and a broken rudder that suggests a tragedy at sea or failure to navigate. In a sixth and final stanza, Pratt links all of these phenomena and places of contact in a succinct reiteration of the poem's key elements:

Tide and wind and crag
Sea-weed and sea-shell
And broken rudder—
And the story is told.

Some of Pratt's descriptions allude to the damage inflicted by the tides and winds (kelp "tangled around a spar / [that] covers a broken rudder"). In the poem as a whole, he does not linger on the sea's wrath or its capacity to destroy but rather underscores the manner in which the ocean surges and recedes in parallel with human experiences.[35] In structure and thematic content, Pratt's text expresses both personal and universal emotions in a manner that is neither confessional nor impersonal, describing through allusion and metaphor the emotional and physical impact of natural and human action. Unlike "The Toll of the Bells," however, "Newfoundland" does not relate a single event but rather "the accumulated ache of the human condition that always means broken rudders, tangled and crushed shells, and open doors."[36]

Most of Forsyth's changes to Pratt's poem involve omitting extended descriptive passages in nearly every stanza, including leaving out two of the three contact stanzas entirely (see Figure 7.8; Pratt's text with the lines used by Forsyth in roman), and thus retaining concise descriptions of "sea-weed and sea-shell / And broken rudder." By removing much of its excess, Forsyth rewrites Pratt's poem to situate the speaker/narrator more plainly in the present moment and he begins, as Pratt does, with the word "Here." Like his rewriting of Gustafson's poem in the first movement, Forsyth avoids potential allusions to the future, such as in his omission of text that describes "thresholds," "eternal pathways," and "doors" that imply future openings such as the possibility of life after death.

Figure 7.8. "Newfoundland," poem by E.J. Pratt. Text used by Forsyth in A Ballad *in roman.*

Here the tides flow,
And here they ebb;
Not with that dull, unsinewed tread of waters
Held under bonds to move
Around unpeopled shores—
Moon-driven through a timeless circuit
Of invasion and retreat;
But with a lusty stroke of life
Pounding at stubborn gates,
That they might run
Within the sluices of men's hearts,
Leap under throb of pulse and nerve,
And teach the sea's strong voice
To learn the harmonies of new floods,
The peal of cataract,
And the soft wash of currents
Against resilient banks,
Or the broken rhythms from old chords
Along dark passages
That once were pathways of authentic fires.

Red is the sea-kelp on the beach,
Red as the heart's blood,
Nor is there power in tide or sun
To bleach its stain. It lies there piled thick
Above the gulch-line.
It is rooted in the joints of rocks,
It is tangled around a spar,
It covers a broken rudder,
It is red as the heart's blood,
And salt as tears.

Here the winds blow,
And here they die,
Not with that wild, exotic rage
That vainly sweeps untrodden shores,
But with familiar breath
Holding a partnership with life,
Resonant with the hopes of spring,
Pungent with the airs of harvest.
They call with the silver fifes of the sea,
They breathe with the lungs of men,
They are one with the tides of the sea,
They are one with the tides of the heart,
They blow with the rising octaves of dawn,
They die with the largo of dusk,
Their hands are full to the overflow,
In their right is the bread of life,
In their left are the waters of death.

Scattered on boom
And rudder and weed
Are tangles of shells;
Some with backs of crusted bronze,
And faces of porcelain blue,
Some crushed by the beach stones
To chips of jade;
And some are spiral-cleft
Spreading their tracery on the sand
In the rich veining of an agate's heart;
And others remain unscarred,
To babble of the passing of the winds.

Here the crags
Meet with winds and tides—
Not with that blind interchange
Of blow for blow

That spills the thunder of insentient seas;
But with the mind that reads assault
In crouch and leap and the quick stealth,
Stiffening the muscles of the waves.
Here they flank the harbours,
Keeping watch
On thresholds, altars and the fires of home,
Or, like mastiffs, Over-zealous, Guard too well.

Tide and wind and crag,
Sea-weed and sea-shell
And broken rudder—
And the story is told
Of human veins and pulses,
Of eternal pathways of fire,
Of dreams that survive the night,
Of doors held ajar in storms.

Forsyth described Pratt's "Newfoundland" as "wonderfully evocative" in both style and language. Lines of different lengths are held together by Pratt's use of text repetition (anaphora) and echo the rhythmic movement of natural phenomena: the "ebb...and flow" of tides and winds that "blow...and die" as they meet the crags and shores of the Newfoundland coast. Forsyth retained this rhythm in his setting, remarking on "the beat of the refrain that [Pratt] uses first of all to describe the tides, then to describe the winds, then to describe the crags of Newfoundland. Everything is very much a refrain; it is almost strophic, but not strictly."[37]

Despite often incorporating broken rhythms and irregular phrase lengths, the flow of metrical stresses in Pratt's poem create a song-like quality; they move with a variable but natural rhythm of speech that recreates nature's gestures and reveals meaning in its unfolding. "The tides ebb and flow through the words of the first stanza," Edna Froese writes of Pratt's poem, "forc[ing] the voice to rise and fall but always within the tension ('held...to move') created by the lack of pauses where pauses would be expected because of the rhythm of the tide and the end of the line."[38] These musical processes obviously appealed to Forsyth, who modulated the dynamic movement of Pratt's poem to exploit the inherent tensions of what Froese describes as "conflicting expectations" in Pratt's text.

As with previous movements, Forsyth maintains the sequence of Pratt's stanzas. However, with the reduction of text from 78 to 34 lines, and from six stanzas to (essentially) four, the music does not follow the strophic structure and is, instead, set as a through-composed form (ABCD coda). Within each section, Forsyth retains Pratt's textual metre but alters rhythmic patterns, tempos, instrumental textures and timbres, and other stylistic elements to underscore the changing moods as the story unfolds. Nonetheless, Forsyth is able to recreate Pratt's textual use of anaphora in his rhythmic stresses on first and third beats (in 4/4; see Figure 7.9a) in the melodies of the first three sections on the words "Here," "tide/winds/crags" "flow/blow/meet" in dotted or tied half notes of three or four beats, and in the half-note emphasis of the words "not" and "but" later in the verse. Forsyth's overall design for this movement also does not allow him to recreate Pratt's refrains. Instead, the opening eight measures (marked "Brilliantly") form a brief introductory section featuring glissando thirty-second-note flourishes in strings and winds that recall the opening of the first movement (here as an E major ascending scale rather that the G major descending scale in the first measure of the first movement); as noted earlier, the close of this movement with the Northern Lights leitmotif also contributes a unifying musical element.

The "tides" of the first stanza of Pratt's poem are the focus of the A section in mm. 9–54 (not shown). Forsyth reduces the dynamics and texture of the instrumental accompaniment in this section, marked "Solemnly," to winds, strings, and harp, with glockenspiel and discreet percussion, so that the voices can dominate the musical expression. The word "Life" is celebrated as the melodic and harmonic climax of this section at m. 40 (see Figure 7.9b). At this moment, Forsyth uses a homophonic SATB vocal texture and a modulation to F♯ major with a crescendo to *fortissimo*; the major ninth is added by the orchestra

(G♯ in the first clarinet and second violins, and within the figuration of the glockenspiel, vibraphone, and harp).

A further modulation in m. 55 (not shown) introduces the new B section (marked "Jubilantly, moving forward slightly") that musically reflects the winds (Forsyth's second stanza) as an imitative texture, and includes a change to women's voices (sopranos and altos). The imitative motive first heard in the full orchestra is passed to the women in m. 66 with a modification in the performance description to "Lightly and slightly faster" and a reduction in the orchestral texture that assists also in reflecting the agility of the blowing winds through a sixteenth-note rhythm that seems to whirl around the notes G and C (see Figure 7.9c).

The C section, beginning in m. 86 (not shown), Forsyth's third stanza, describes the rugged cliffs against which the wind and waves collide. A change in vocal timbre to men only (tenors and basses) is accompanied here by trombones, and the mood is described in the score as "More ponderous." The winds continue to blow with thirty-second-note figuration while the weighty, homorhythmic sound of a full trombone choir depicts the power of the sea, of tides, thunder, and waves, focusing not on the violence of these natural events, but on the heaviness of the "mind that reads assault / stiffening the muscles of the waves."

A new section begins in m. 97 (not shown) with imitative SATB entries on Pratt's final (sixth) verse "Tide and wind and crag." Imitative and homophonic choral writing alternate in this D section, dividing its six lines into further, shorter phrases. "And the story is told / Of human veins" is homophonic; the continuation of this line, "and pulses," is imitative, as is the repeat of the second line. Homophonic emphasis returns for the final line of Forsyth's text, "Of dreams that survive the night" (see Figure 7.9d), the fourths and semitones of its final iteration in m. 122 (not shown; particularly the B–C♯ dyad in the sopranos, and F♯–B in the basses) closing the section with a familiar intervallic dissonance founded on the semitone and fourths of the Northern Lights leitmotif described previously. But this dissonance is resolved to consonance in the coda that begins in m. 123 (not shown),

FIGURE 7.9a. A Ballad, *mvt. 5, mm. 16–20. SATB.*

as the movement and the work as a whole conclude with full choir, a repeat of the scalar flourishes from the beginning of the movement (and, as noted earlier, of the work as a whole), and a final expression of the Northern Lights leitmotif also heard at the beginning of the first movement. Forsyth omits the final line of Pratt's text, "Of doors held ajar in storms," but with the return of the now-familiar leitmotif, he closes musically what might be considered an open-ended text and a diverse collection of poetry.

A Lived, Musical Life

Forsyth's attention to detail in his settings of these five poems in *A Ballad* is a distinguishing feature of his compositional style that can be heard across many of his vocal and instrumental works.[39] The manner with which he manipulates texts and orchestrates their potential for creating meaning remains an impassioned acknowledgement of his tremendous gift for storytelling. Through such details he is able to focus on highly nuanced changes in mood evident in the poems, creating an experience of naturalness and freedom within otherwise stable formal structures. But more than this, the changes he makes to

FIGURE 7.9b. A Ballad, *mvt. 5, mm. 39–40. SATB with full orchestra.*

FIGURE 7.9c. A Ballad, *mvt. 5, mm. 67–9. SA.*

FIGURE 7.9d. A Ballad, *mvt. 5, mm. 115–7. SATB.*

his chosen texts—whether through omission or repetition or through choices of voicing and performance textures and timbres—reveal an artist profoundly responsive to the expressive potential of contemporary poetry. A sense of local landscapes, of country, and of connection to place are exposed without name in the poetry, but are understood to exist within the context of Canadian history that has been "shaped by the land" as well as by the people who live within it.

All of the poems Forsyth chose for *A Ballad* are narrated by an observer, yet each describes a space in which we might find ourselves looking outward as well as inward. In the first movement, contrasting perspectives reveal a distant grandeur of the landscape and the intimate gesture of salmon leaping up stream; in the second, third, and fourth movements the casualties of human actions draw our focus to individual response and responsibility; and in the fifth the scale of nature's power forces our awareness of our own humanity and mortality. Throughout *A Ballad*, the descriptive imagery, poetic rhyme, and metre of the texts suggested to Forsyth the sounds and styles to use as well as the inherent tensions of what is, and is not, spoken. Across all five poems, Forsyth also finds reasons to omit overt expressions of the past and future, allowing his final texts to explore personal expressions of humanity and to portray what it means to be human in this moment.

Perhaps because of the continuities and discontinuities between his texts and their original poems and the episodic nature of his musical setting, *A Ballad* occupies a unique place in Forsyth's output that might not have been possible earlier in his career, but that is neither innocent nor the confessional work of an artist aware of his mortality. *A Ballad* resonates deeply with Forsyth's life and work, echoing through evidence of self-quotation from earlier compositions, generating a sense of belonging to a place that is mediated through a poetic approach to musical language and that ultimately exposes an unrestrained self-awareness. This is clearly evidenced in the texts selected for *A Ballad*, revealing the human side of Canada in nature, war, and death, cutting through the idealism and cynicism of events, places, and individuals to illuminate the unfolding of their human relationships. Poetry and music blend in Forsyth's settings in an evocative balance of the tensions of life and death and in contrasts of playful seriousness and glorious grandeur that suggests, alternately, present and past, and proximity and distance. Ultimately, these gesture to Forsyth's evocations of Canada's physical landscapes and to an expression of the depths of his own humanity and of a musical soul striving for a place as

> *the story is told*
> *of human veins and pulses,*
> *of dreams that survive the night.*[40]

What lies between and beyond Forsyth's choices of text and responses in music illuminate the images of a lived, musical life, that focused deliberately on the present in order to encourage possibilities for the future.

NOTES

1. *A Ballad of Canada* lasts approximately 23 minutes. It was co-commissioned by the National Arts Centre Orchestra and the Edmonton Symphony Orchestra, and had its premieres with the National Arts Centre Orchestra and the combined choirs of the Ottawa Choral Society, Ottawa Festival Chorus, Cantata Singers of Ottawa, and the Ewashko Singers in Ottawa in June 2011 and the Edmonton Symphony Orchestra with the Richard Eaton Singers in November of the same year. Forsyth died on July 5, 2011, and thus did not live to hear the performance in his hometown of Edmonton in a concert celebration of (what would have been) his 75th birthday. *A Ballad of Canada* is also discussed briefly by Leonard Ratzlaff in this volume.
2. Trifon Heney, "*A Ballad of Canada*: Interview with Malcolm Forsyth," *sound + noise*, April 10, 2011, http://soundnnoise.com/2011/04/10/a-ballad-of-canada.
3. Heney, "*A Ballad of Canada.*"
4. Hare's poem is actually titled "A Young Mother" and is from an unpublished collection of poems titled *On the Waverley Bridge Road*. Forsyth altered the title to name his movement "On the Waverley Road Bridge."
5. Malcolm Forsyth, *A Ballad of Canada*, score (Toronto: Counterpoint, 2011).
6. "On the Waverley Road Bridge" (Forsyth's title) commemorates the Highway of Heroes, a stretch of road between Trenton and Toronto, Ontario, "where the coffins of the deceased soldiers from Afghanistan are paraded" (Forsyth, quoted in Heney, "*A Ballad of Canada*"); the Waverley Bridge is along this road.
7. Forsyth, *A Ballad of Canada*.

8. Kathy Primos, "A Life Experience: The Orchestral Works of Malcolm Forsyth," *SoundNotes* (Spring/Summer 1994): 20. See also Primos in this volume.
9. Dermot McCarthy, *A Poetics of Place: The Poetry of Ralph Gustafson* (Montreal and Kingston: McGill-Queen's University Press, 1991), 130.
10. Although associations with personal circumstances might be an intriguing place to consider Forsyth's own circumstances, *A Ballad* is not merely an autobiographical work. Forsyth knew he was gravely ill while composing this piece and understood that this might be his last completed work; when Heney asked him in April 2011 what he was contemplating next, Forsyth simply replied, "At the moment, I'm just clearing my head" (*"A Ballad of Canada"*).
11. See also McClelland, Rival, and Primos in this volume.
12. Heney, "*A Ballad of Canada*."
13. Forsyth describes his inspiration for *Atayoskewin* as "something of a mood, a feeling that I had when I made my first-ever trip to northern Alberta during the winter. It was very cold, and I saw this barren land where the tar sands are being developed. It's a very forbidding land, but it has a kind of majesty which is unmistakable. It's a very quiet place." Cited in Robert Markow, "Programme Notes: Malcolm Forsyth, Atayoskewin," NAC Canadian Orchestral Composers: Landscape and Soundscape, 2010, http://www.virtualmuseum.ca/edu/ViewLoitDa.do?method=preview&lang=EN&id=17348.
14. Markow, "Programme Notes."
15. Forsyth moves two and a half lines from near the end of Gustafson's poem to the beginning of his text in order to make this connection to the Northern Lights more explicit. This further allows him to separate the two distinct ideas in the first line of the original poem: "Here, all is a beginning" and "I saw a salmon jump." These two ideas then form the basis of the contrasting musical sections discussed here.
16. Primos, "A Life Experience," 20.
17. Ralph Gustafson, "New World Northern: Of Poetry and Identity," *University of Toronto Quarterly* 50 (Fall 1980): 55.
18. In her 1994 article "A Life Experience," musicologist Kathleen (Kathy) M. Primos describes this approach to motivic construction as "serv[ing] as a catalyst for Forsyth's developing harmonic language and hence for his handling of tonality, which fluctuates between tonal, atonal and ambivalent" (20).
19. Forsyth's score is in C and is available through Counterpoint Music Library Services.
20. "In the Yukon" is the last of 21 poems that Gustafson published in 1960 in a collection titled *Rocky Mountain Poems*. The complete text of "In the Yukon" is from *Selected Poems* (2001) by Ralph Gustafson, and is used by permission of Véhicule Press.
21. Heney, "*A Ballad of Canada*."

22. McCarthy, *A Poetics of Place*, 125.

23. "In Flanders Fields" was first published in December 1915 in *Punch* magazine. Several versions now exist. Forsyth uses this poem in its entirety.

24. Christopher Moore, "At the NAC, Feel-Good Beethoven and a Composer's Lyrical Ode to Canada," *Globe and Mail*, June 10, 2011, updated May 3, 2018, www.theglobeandmail.com/arts/music/at-the-nac-feel-good-beethoven-and-a-composers-lyrical-ode-to-canada/article629095/.

25. Moore, "At the NAC."

26. "Toll of the Bells" is assumed to have been written in 1921. Of the original poem's 28 lines, Forsyth uses 11. The poem was published as part of the collection *Newfoundland Verse* (Toronto: Ryerson Press, 1923), 15–16, and was sourced by Forsyth from *E.J. Pratt: Complete Poems*, vol. 1, ed. R.G. Moyes and Sandra Djwa (Toronto: University of Toronto Press, 1989).

27. E.J. Pratt, *E.J. Pratt on His Life and Poetry*, ed. Susan Gingell (Toronto: University of Toronto Press, 1983), 8.

28. Vincent Sharman, "Illusion and Atonement: E.J. Pratt and Christianity," *Canadian Literature* 19 (Winter 1964): 22.

29. Heney, "*A Ballad of Canada*."

30. In *E.J. Pratt on His Life and Poetry*, Pratt introduces this poem as "a couple of sonnets which, though written long after the event of course, yet commemorates, however inadequately, a great church service held here in St. John's when the *Greenland* came in with her survivors and her dead. Some of the older people will remember the event. I was only a boy at the time but it is an ineffaceable memory. No part of the whole ritual that made up the formal side of the service seemed able to the same degree to bring home to our hearts as the bells did the solemnity and desolation of the tragedy" (60).

31. Heney, "*A Ballad of Canada*."

32. As noted above, Forsyth's "On the Waverley Road Bridge" is based on a poem titled "A Young Mother" from an unpublished collection originally titled *On the Waverley Bridge Road* by Carl Hare. The poem was commissioned by Forsyth for *A Ballad of Canada* in 2010, and inclusion of its text in this chapter is with the permission of the author. In his interview with composer Trifon Heney in April 2011, Forsyth indicates that Hare "wrote several things and sent them to me for my approval, and I chose this one called *On the Waverley Road Bridge* [sic]. It commemorates the Highway of Heroes from Trenton to Toronto where the coffins of the deceased soldiers from Afghanistan are paraded down the highway on the Waverley Road Bridge. It's now a tradition. People will gather on the days the cortège passes through, and they bedeck the bridge with Canadian flags and other sorts of mementos. And it's a very moving little poem."

33. Heney, "*A Ballad of Canada*."

34. "Newfoundland" was written by Pratt in the fall of 1922 and included in the collection titled *Newfoundland Verse* (Toronto: Ryerson Press, 1923), 87–90, and was sourced by Forsyth from *E.J. Pratt: Complete Poems*, vol. 1, ed. R.G. Moyes and Sandra Djwa (Toronto: University of Toronto Press, 1989).
35. Angela T. McAuliffe, *Between the Temple and the Cave: The Religious Dimensions of the Poetry of E.J. Pratt* (Montreal and Kingston: McGill-Queen's University Press, 2000), 82.
36. Edna Froese, "E.J. Pratt as Lyricist," *Canadian Poetry* 30 (Spring/Summer 1992): n.p.
37. Heney, "*A Ballad of Canada.*"
38. Froese, "E.J. Pratt as Lyricist," n.p.
39. See also Leonard Ratzlaff in this volume.
40. Pratt, "Newfoundland," lines 75, 76, 78.

8
Interlude
Reminiscences

CARL HARE

Professor, author, poet

MALCOLM FORSYTH

Music was his breath
He inhaled atmospheres around him
exhaled landscapes across oceans
bright with African and prairie sun
white with blizzards
dark with rattled gales

Within his countries
he discovered the ululations of winds
snares' thickets
by percussion's reverberating hills
the sonorous blasts of brass
against the deep bass throbbing
throughout his sounding forests
the dark-throated cello's cry
and the rustled sighing of the strings

Rhythm nestled and surged in his blood
crept nervously under the strings' conversations
skittered mischievously through their whisperings
beat against the crowding words of choruses
at home in dark foliage-hidden beats
or with the calculated stresses
of a distant century's cavalier
toying with his golden nymphs

Word and meaning sang to him
and he sang back
lifting their two voices in the sentient air

enveloping both in a vibrant stream of notes
or teasing them with sly arrangement

Sudden discoveries mark his terrain
vistas open miraculously
or wrench without warning
in perilous curves
and abrupt changes
perspectives expand before us
or fade and disappear
logic and surprise teasing each other

Challenges attracted and exhilarated him
to collect for his own world
the humble wheezing of an instrument
animals in childish rhythms
the vastness of a continent
the glory of a daughter's bow

Humour tinged his utterance
shone in his eye and his sharp ear
his passions lay deep
his enthusiasms rich and multifarious
his teaching lucid and inspiring

Complex himself and the routes he carved
yet his maps remain precise and clear
unfolding revelations
to those who explore them
and translate luminously to us
as do his person and his music echo
vivid in our memory.

August 14, 2011

TOMMY BANKS (1936–2018)

Musician, television personality, senator

MY HAPPY AND TUNEFUL ACQUAINTANCE with Malcolm began shortly following his arrival in Edmonton from South Africa. At the time, my band, which was chiefly involved in television performances in those years, had a vacancy in one of our three trombone chairs. Malcolm fit the bill perfectly and became our colleague at about the same time he joined the Edmonton Symphony Orchestra (ESO). The times and days of these respective engagements did not, fortunately for us, conflict. He immediately became "one of the guys." His humour and some of his wonderful eccentricities became evident and much appreciated.

At about the same time, he became a member of the Goliard Brass, a quintet with Don Harris, Harry Pinchin, Gloria Ratcliffe, and Dave Otto. There was no formal hierarchy, but Harry says that Malcolm was the de facto leader of the quintet, which was involved mostly in recording for the CBC. Malcolm once conducted the ESO in the performance of a wretched piece of music I wrote for the ballet, keeping a straight face, and managing to somehow make a creditable performance of it.

When I was producing the music for the ceremonies of the 1988 Winter Olympic Games in Calgary, a few fanfares were in order. I asked Malcolm to write three of them. He was a terrific orchestrator, of course, in all respects; but his writing for brass (these fanfares had to be pretty brassy) was extraordinarily good, and they all came off beautifully.

He brought great pride to our city and our country with his music. His compositions marked, in my mind, the point at which audiences who, like me, didn't want to work too hard, began to look forward to new music that was immediately, upon first hearing, enjoyable. Because Malcolm wrote accessible music, there were tunes and understandable harmonies.

We'll always have the genius of his music, of course, but we all greatly miss his wide knowledge of practically everything, his often outrageous opinions, and the sometimes dour outward visage—a character creation cleverly contrived to mask the mischievous and good-natured imp within.

NORA BUMANIS & JULIA SHAW

Harpists

WE WERE DELIGHTED in 1990 when Malcolm Forsyth agreed to accept the commission from CBC to compose a piece for our first CD. We had been acquainted with him for many years and each of us had struggled with the harp parts to many of his orchestral works. While these parts were challenging (to say the least) they were also always well written, audible (a rarity), rhythmically complex, and rewarding to play. Knowing that we were in capable hands, we really looked forward to performing and recording *The Kora Dances* that he was writing for this commission. In those days, we naively thought that we shouldn't tinker with the composer's intentions and we worked diligently to learn each and every note of this piece as it came to us page by page by unrelenting page.

Eventually (about two weeks before the scheduled recording), the pages stopped coming and the piece was complete—or so we thought. In our naiveté, we decided that it would be a good idea to invite Malcolm to the recording session to oversee what was not the most rehearsed cut on our CD. This is where Malcolm taught us the first of many valuable lessons: never, ever, let the composer in on a recording session of his own music unless you have unlimited time to make huge changes!

Amazingly, we all survived this ordeal and went on to become friends. We discovered that, besides music, we all shared an affection for Marx Brothers' movies, puns, poodles, and good food—combined with generous amounts of good wine. He entertained and educated us with his recall of all things historical. He was extremely well read and well spoken. His passion for proper use of the English language was legendary and we learned never to split an infinitive or to end a sentence with a preposition—at least in his presence.

Having shed the ridiculous notion that we should never interfere with artistic genius, we endeavoured to teach Malcolm some of the finer points of writing for the harp. An eager student, he quickly learned the effectiveness of enharmonic equivalents while continuing to delight us with the clever use of hemiola and syncopation. The culmination of his compositional skills, harp-writing knowledge, and humour was *Hesperides*. What an absolute joy for all involved—singers, harpists, and listeners!

On a professional level, we are grateful that Malcolm did so much to expand the repertoire of our instrument with intelligent and effective compositions in virtually every musical genre. On a personal level, we are honoured to have had him as a friend as he truly enriched our lives.

ALLAN GILLILAND

Composer, professor

I HAVE SO MANY fond memories of Malcolm Forsyth. He was a consummate professional and one of my most influential teachers. Malcolm never did anything in a small way and when I started copying music for him he was vehemently opposed to computer notation programs. But, as time passed, he could see the writing on the wall and I ended up copying a number of his later works on a program called Finale. Rather than accepting the program's shortcomings, we spent weeks refining Finale's basic template. He insisted that I find a way to change the thickness of slurs, the position of ties, the distance of the dot on a dotted note, the spacing of music when it first appears after a clef or barline, and even the angle of beamed notes. By the time we were done, his computer scores looked better than even Finale programmers thought they could.

Malcolm was also an incredible teacher. I studied with him for two years and afterwards went to him for advice on many pieces. He taught me a cellular approach to composition that I still use today. This method allows one to generate a large amount of material from a three- or four-note cluster. It also pointed the way to freeing me from tonal harmony while still being firmly rooted in a harmonic and melodic world. Malcolm Forsyth was a musician of unwavering standards and I feel honoured to have had him in my life.

JOHN MCPHERSON

Trombonist, composer

I WAS 13 when Malcolm Forsyth accepted me as a private trombone student and little did I know at the time that this would be *the* life-changing moment that shaped my future and career as a musician. What I did know is that his presence was powerful and intimidating, and that I had never experienced anyone even remotely like this.

As I look back on the early years with Malcolm, I realize that we had a traditional master/apprentice relationship: I did exactly what he asked for and he took on the responsibility of educating me in not only the technical but also the broader and deeper aspects of music.

A master teacher, he challenged, pushed, and cajoled his students to become their best. His excitement and full engagement in music was constant and a sense of responsibility to honour, sustain, and contribute to the furtherance of high art was his primary goal.

Having Malcolm as a mentor in my formative years meant I grew up recognizing that simply playing the trombone, no matter how well, would not represent a full musical life, and when I began to compose and arrange and lead ensembles I realized he had already opened those paths in me.

It's impossible to express how incredibly privileged I feel to have had Malcolm Forsyth as my teacher, mentor, colleague, and friend, and I'm extremely honoured and proud to, in some small way, carry on his lineage.

FORDYCE C. (DUKE) PIER

Trumpeter, professor

BRASS PLAYING—its artistry, repertoire, pedagogy, execution, and culture—formed an essential strand of Malcolm's musical, educational, and personal life. He and I met in 1973 during my interview for a position as "trumpet teacher/performer" at the University of Alberta, where he was already a faculty member. Being a trombone player, he was of course on the interview committee. Our mutual enthusiasm for and dedication to all things brass immediately drew us together and led to a friendship and collegial liaison that spanned 38 years, until his death in 2011.

Malcolm's brass persona was rooted in his studies at Cape Town University and professional work in the Cape Town Symphony in his native South Africa, where many of the musicians had Dutch and English backgrounds. Although he had been in Canada five years by the time we met, he was still keenly interested to learn more about the North American brass-playing style, and many were the discussions and energetic arguments about its merits and shortcomings. While admiring the rich, burnished tone of the best North American players, he could be quite scathing about a tone that had followed this ideal to the point where the tone had become so dark that it "had no colour at all." As in all subjects for Malcolm, the unthinkingly doctrinaire was anathema.

As high-flyingly cerebral a person as he was, he nevertheless submitted to the pedestrian demands of maintaining instrumental artistry. I remember the year the Edmonton Symphony Orchestra, in which we both played, performed Ravel's *Bolero*. The preceding summer Malcolm literally chained himself to his trombone, not only practicing the famous solo (the *bête noire* of many a trombonist) dozens of times a day, but engaging in a strict general regimen of endurance and range studies. He would often challenge himself to walk into his studio, pick up the instrument cold, and play through the extremely high and taxing solo. Perhaps not physically the healthiest of strategies, but certainly one that developed a toughness of mind for the artistic test which lay ahead. As I sat immediately in front of him on the stage of the Northern Alberta Jubilee Auditorium for the concerts, I was in a good position to admire the masterful result.

Finally, with regard to Malcolm's musical legacy, it should be noted that there are a number of professional trombonists performing in Canada today who learned their art in whole or in part due to his strict and demanding pedagogical guidance and from the artistic model he provided.

In the last four or five years of his life, before he became sick, but long since he had performed professionally, Malcolm bought a new trombone, and reveled privately in the gorgeous tone of the instrument on simple, mid-range melodies. Yes, Malcolm was a brass person.

TANYA PROCHAZKA (1952–2015)

Cellist, professor

THANK GOODNESS he washed his hands!

Malcolm was a great friend and musical colleague. He was a man of uncompromising integrity and honesty with a firm belief in the value of total musical scholarship. Malcolm also had a wonderful sense of humour.

In 2006, Malcolm was composer-in-residence at the Prince Edward County Chamber Music Festival in Picton, Ontario. I was one of the musicians who played his masterpiece *The Tempest: Duets and Choruses* for oboe and string quartet. Malcolm introduced this work with great gusto to the packed audience prior to our performance and left the stage heading straight for the bathroom. As we entered the hall we were met by strange watery noises and puzzled looks on the faces of the audience. Then, the penny dropped. Malcolm's lapel microphone was still on and broadcasting to the audience! Stéphane Lemelin leapt over a row of chairs and sprinted to the bathroom. Suddenly, the sounds ceased but not before the whole audience had burst into enthusiastic laughter and applause. The performance of *The Tempest* was inspired and Malcolm took all the laughter and humour in his generous stride.

RAYFIELD RIDEOUT

CBC Radio producer, woodworker

MALCOLM AND I ENJOYED spending time together, especially when collaborating on projects. It was even better if we could put the other to the test. Here are two examples.

When Malcolm composed *umGcomo*, a piece for slit drums and pianos, he asked me if I would build two drums for him. I had never done any woodworking like this before. I built a bass drum with two tongues and a small drum with six tongues. I used exotic woods—padauk and wenge—and Malcolm was present at every stage. He was very demanding in not just the sound but also the appearance of these drums. We spent a lot of time "tuning" each tongue, and it seems that with changes in weather, the drums would go out of tune in just a day. When he gave the nod of approval for the musical properties, he then insisted on some decorative touches. Nothing could be left simply plain and functional. In the end, it was a success. The drums were used in the premiere of the piece in Poland by the Hammerhead Consort, and it was later recorded live at the Winspear for broadcast on CBC Radio.

Another project we collaborated on was one in which Malcolm ended up doing most of the work. I came up with a tune that I thought would be a pretty good replacement for the "Hockey Night in Canada" theme. There was a contest on, and the prize for the winner was a good amount of cash. Over lunch I hummed the tune for him. Malcolm thought it worthy enough to work on, so he orchestrated it on his software program, and kept playing it back for me and altering it to suit my sensibilities. I was the one to give the final nod of approval. We entered it into the contest, and I thought it should have won, but it drew no attention. Although I was proud of my composition, he did not speak of it again. It was not a resounding success, but it was a lot of fun.

CHRISTOPHER TAYLOR

Bass trombonist

MALCOLM WAS A FORMIDABLE PERSONALITY in the Edmonton and Canadian music communities. As professor of composition in the University of Alberta Music Department, he was known to expect only the best from his students. He was an excellent teacher, demanding but fair. During the time that I was his bass trombone student, he built an excellent student trombone ensemble that led to the formation of his own professional group, the Malcolm Forsyth Trombone Ensemble. Working with Malcolm in this group, and also in the Edmonton Symphony Orchestra as a colleague, was always a learning experience for me, as Malcolm was ever the teacher.

Malcolm's personality was multifaceted and his interests numerous. Naturally, many of these are expressed in his compositions: rigorous intellect, theatre, humour, tonal colour offered by orchestral instruments and African indigenous musical instruments, rhythmic complexity, poetry, and a love for both his homeland as well as adopted country. Many works are well composed and just plain fun, but, for Malcolm, I think his serious works express his deepest thoughts on the human condition, the natural world, love, and beauty. Malcolm once told me had he not become a musician he would have become an artist. I think he would have been a good one.

The premieres of many of Malcolm's works, small and large, I have been involved in have always been musically challenging and exhilarating, not to mention the numerous and raucous after-concert parties. His music is not always easy to perform or to understand upon first hearing, but it is, for me, some of the best contemporary Canadian music.

I am very fortunate to have known Malcolm for these many years as a teacher, colleague, friend, and mentor.

9

A Life Experience

The Early Orchestral Works

KATHY PRIMOS

OVER THE PAST THIRTY YEARS OR SO, Malcolm Forsyth has established himself as one of Canada's most widely performed composers, with a substantial body of works to his credit in many different genres. In 1986 he won the JUNO Award for the best recording of a classical work,[1] and he was named Composer of the Year by the Canadian Music Council in 1989 after enjoying more than one hundred performances of his works within a period of three years. In addition to brass and wind music, there are choral and vocal works as well as various solo instrumental works. The real core of his output, though, lies in his

---

This chapter is reprinted, lightly edited, from the now-defunct Toronto journal *Sound-Notes* (vol. 6, spring/summer, 1994). At the time of writing Primos was a senior lecturer at the University of Witwatersrand, Johannesburg, South Africa. For this survey she drew upon material from her master's dissertation "The Compositional Style of Malcolm Forsyth's Orchestral Works: 1968–1982" (University of the Witwatersrand, 1988). The article's scope is thus limited to orchestral works composed before 1994. We have therefore added "early" to its original title. See Rival and Ingraham for detailed discussions of two important orchestral works that postdate this article's publication. The article is reprinted with both the author's and the journal's permission. —*Eds.*

works for orchestra, which include three symphonies, three concerti grossi (two for brass quintet and orchestra and one for string quartet and orchestra), concertos for piano, trumpet, and saxophone, overtures, and several other works.

Forsyth has been commissioned to write works for many well-known Canadian artists, including songs for Maureen Forrester and two concerti grossi for the Canadian Brass. *Atayoskewin*, a three-movement suite for orchestra was commissioned by the Edmonton Symphony Orchestra. Commissions for special occasions have included the orchestrally accompanied vocalise *Canzona*, set as the prescribed work per finalist in the Concours internationale de musique de Montréal; a fanfare, *Novum Spatium*, for the opening of the Jack Singer Concert Hall in Calgary; and *ukuZalwa*, an overture for the inaugural concert of the Natal Philharmonic Orchestra in South Africa.

Malcolm Forsyth's music is, from start to finish, a testimony a testimony to his particular blend of lived musical experiences, drawing its chief inspiration from his diverse activities as a practising musician. These include many years as a trombonist in the Cape Town and Edmonton Symphony Orchestras, playing a wide repertoire of classical and big band styles, also in jazz and chamber groups such as the Malcolm Forsyth Trombone Ensemble, as well as numerous conducting engagements. He has thus not only absorbed an intimate and wide-ranging knowledge of the orchestral repertoire but has had a long-term opportunity to assimilate, firsthand, the limitations and potentials of orchestral instruments and orchestration techniques.

But beyond the musical influences, there is an intensity of mood ranging from the angry and vehement to the serene and dreamy, the serious and solemn to the carefree and mischievously funny, which are all recognizable aspects of Forsyth's complex personality for those who know him well. In addition, his music usually has some programmatic connotation, sometimes obvious, sometimes not. Some of his poetic titles bear witness to the composer's vivid and fertile imagination. *The Salpinx*, for example, is derived from the name of the ancient Greek trumpet used for signalling in battle, the significance of which, according to Forsyth's program note, "is the spirit of battle suggested by pitting the string quartet against a full orchestra." *Sagittarius*, according to Forsyth, "derives from the sporty, outdoor mood of the zodiacal sign." His Symphony No. 2 is subtitled "a host of nomads," a phrase from James Joyce's *Portrait of the Artist as a Young Man*: "They were voyaging across the deserts of the sky, a host of nomads on the march." As further explanation, Forsyth has said, "I think the Symphony is about cloud-forms, as the Joyce quotation is, and the investiture of some sort of 'being' in clouds."

Other works contain more subtle and hidden extra-musical references. The themes of the Piano Concerto, for example, represent the opposing forces of good and evil, seen alternately as light and dark, or black and white.[2] The opening twelve-tone row depicts the entirety of creation; a specific harmonic progression centring around an F♯ tonality is a "God" theme, and pounding fifths in the bass represent an antithesis to the "God" theme. There is also embedded into the work a vicarious expression of the injustices of the racially segregated society of South Africa, Forsyth's native country. These connotations mirror aspects of his life experiences. While the associations are of interest, they are tenuous in their application by the listener throughout the concerto.

He is, then, a romantic eclectic. Of course, to be designated thus would have been anathema to most modernist composers, to whom innovation and esotericism have been the chief virtues. This innovation and esotericism has been a necessary and intriguing journey for musicians: composers' exploration of the uncharted musical spaces has profitably exploited musical experience. Forsyth was always open to that widened experience but selected from it only those aspects that helped him to communicate within his personalized idiom. Thus it is not true to say that his style is untouched by the inventive sounds of the time, but rather that innovation for its own sake has no particular appeal. Forsyth's music emerged more from a historically and experientially founded interplay of personal interests and influences.

What emerged, then, was a romantic and eclectic style firmly entrenched in a historically rooted twentieth-century sound, combining a high level of compositional craft with his mission to write player- and listener-friendly music. In his early orchestral works, Forsyth was already laying a foundation for the development of this personal style, which he further consolidated in his more mature works of the 1970s. A closer look at this process reveals the subtle incorporation of some of these features and their continuance into his later output.

The Orchestral Composer in Context

Not many composers get the opportunity to cut their compositional teeth on orchestral works, not to mention having them performed and broadcast, but that was how it was for Malcolm Forsyth. His Overture "Erewhon," a first foray into orchestral writing, was premiered in 1963 by the Cape Town Symphony Orchestra and led to a commission to write another overture to celebrate that same orchestra's golden jubilee. The following year, Arthur Fiedler conducted this *Jubilee Overture* and the National Orchestra of the South African Broadcasting Corporation broadcast Overture "Erewhon" twice. Forsyth's career as an orchestral composer was launched.

Meanwhile, he was gaining considerable experience in orchestral playing as a trombonist and, occasionally, as a conductor. In this way he gained firsthand knowledge of a wide orchestral repertoire and played under the baton of many international conductors, most notably Igor Stravinsky, who in 1962 conducted performances of *L'oiseau de feu*, *Scherzo fantastique*, *Apollon musagète*, and *Le baiser de la fée*. The initial flair for orchestral writing in his juvenilia was in no small part due to this firsthand seasoning in instrumental sound and colour.

Essay for Orchestra '67, written and performed in Cape Town shortly before Forsyth's emigration to Canada, was the first of his orchestral works to be performed in Canada. Shortly after this he received his first Canadian commission from the Canadian Broadcasting Corporation for a work to be played by the Alberta Chamber Players, conducted by Lawrence Leonard. This work, *Sketches from Natal*, was completed and premiered the following year in a live CBC broadcast. Forsyth considers all works prior to this as juvenilia, so *Sketches* may be viewed as the first of the early works that, I feel, typify his initial consolidation of a personal idiom.

Although the choice of medium and genres in Forsyth's early orchestral works marks his commitment to tradition, it is in the following works that he established an individual style and developed his flair for orchestration into a polished craft: *Sketches from Natal* (1970), Symphony No. 1 (1972), Piano Concerto (1975), *Sagittarius*: Concerto Grosso No. 1 for brass quintet and orchestra (1975), Symphony No. 2, *"...a host of nomads..."* (1976). Later works stand more as an affirmation of an already established individual style. These include *Quinquefid*: Concerto Grosso No. 2 for brass quintet and orchestra (1976–77), Symphony No. 3, "African Ode" (1981), *The Salpinx*: Concerto Grosso No. 3 for string quartet and orchestra, *Images of Night* (1981–82), *Rhapsody for 14 Strings* (1982), *Atayoskewin* (1984), Serenade for Strings (1986), Trumpet Concerto (1987), and *Tre Vie*: Concerto for Saxophone and Orchestra (1992).[3]

Ethnic Influences

Sketches from Natal draws upon Forsyth's African roots. He was born in Pietermaritzburg in Kwa Zulu Natal, a South African province noted for its soft undulating green hills as well as the craggy grandeur of the Drakensberg mountain range. The two movements of *Sketches from Natal* abound in imagery and atmosphere, the opening movement evoking the massive, towering edifice of Mont-aux-Sources, before an *allegro con brio* with its simulation of a Zulu boy's cheerful call and response song, a movement titled "Umfaan in the Hills" (see Figure 9.1). It is written for modest resources, requiring only two oboes and two horns plus strings. Surprisingly, though, it is not lacking in depth of colour, and clearly displays a youthful flair for imaginative orchestration.

African idioms and rhythms can frequently be recognized in Forsyth's music. Nowadays it is fashionable to incorporate such influences—often with some arbitrariness—but Forsyth's Africanism lies deep in his psyche and, in common with most people who have lived in Africa, will always remain a haunting part of his cultural identity. But the African sounds he carries in his memory, so frequently heard

FIGURE 9.1. Sketches from Natal, *mvt. 2, mm. 1–15. [Reproduced with the permission of G. Ricordi & Company (Canada) Ltd.]*

amongst workers in the streets and fields even as late as the 1960s when Forsyth emigrated to Canada, are now seldom heard. The advent of the transistor radio, together with the increased mechanization of labour, has taken its musical toll. Also, to hear Malcolm reminisce over the vibe of Cape Town's District Six jazz haunts where he sometimes played before it was cruelly demolished by the fanatics of the apartheid era is to know a little more of both the anger and sadness bound into his musical memory store.[4]

Thus, inspiration has undoubtedly been drawn from long-term, firsthand absorption of Southern African music. In addition to *Sketches*, the last movements of his first and second symphonies and certain parts of the Piano Concerto reflect this experience. In many instances it is the rhythmic aspect that brings out the association most clearly. Of these, the pounding bass notes on a reiterated pitch that recur frequently in the Piano Concerto and the simulated Zulu work song in the last movement of Symphony No. 1, following an introduction based on the sounds of a Chopi xylophone orchestra from Mozambique, come readily to mind.

Clear evidence of Forsyth's continued bond with Zulu music has emerged with some regularity in his subsequent writing. In his orchestral works, this would include his Symphony No. 3: "African Ode," the

FIGURE 9.2. *Symphony No. 1, mvt. 4, m. 6.*

movements bearing the evocative titles "Trees of Life," "African Dawn," and "Dance-Song," as well as his Overture *ukuZalwa,* a Zulu word meaning rebirth. Outside the orchestral works, the "Chopi" movement of his *Tre Toccate per Pianoforte* is his most intricate and sophisticated working of African polyphonic textures up to that date.

Canadian influences are also strong, but subtle and not so easy to define. However, the most overt link in the orchestral output appears in the vocalise *Canzona,* which emulates a North American Indian style of incantation; another would be the orchestral suite *Atayoskewin,* which was inspired by an aerial trip over the Canadian north, where Forsyth was deeply moved by the vastness and grandeur of the land. He wrote this music as an evocation of "its brilliant sunshine and crystalline air." The title is a Cree word meaning "sacred legend."

Forsyth's Rhythmic Idiom

The output is consistently shot through with textures built around or supported by persistent and frequently layered ostinatos characteristic of the intricate interplay of African polyphony. He generally notates his music within a stable metrical organization with a standard time signature, but clarifies any irregular rhythmic patterns across that metre by careful use of accent markings, as in the following measure from Symphony No. 1 (see Figure 9.2).

Rhythm involves the interflow of all parameters of music but, for me, the durational aspects of Forsyth's faster movements emerge as the most immediately foregrounded facet for the listener. These durational patterns mirror the breadth of his practical experience covering different performance practices, as they embody African, jazz, and big band rhythmic attributes, together with polyrhythms and polymetric groupings characteristic of many twentieth-century composers. Out of this mix Forsyth fashions a very personal rhythmic idiom. Performances of his works that fail to pick up the swing and vibe of these patterns do an injustice to that idiom.

Listener- and Player-Friendly Music

There are moments when certain musical memories seem to surface in a kind of celebratory manner, almost as if the composer is giving honour and acclaim to his most valued musical experiences. Usually they remain hidden in the fabric of the music, but occasionally Forsyth will indicate particular instances in interviews or in program notes, such as the inspiration drawn from Sibelius's Symphony No. 5 in the second movement of *Atayoskewin*. Sometimes these references are filled with exuberance and a touch of humour. This is especially so in *Sagittarius*, where the syncopated rhythm in the last movement simulates the rhythmic backing of Paul Desmond's *Take Five* and is later combined with an exhilarating waltz reminiscent of George Gershwin.

As such experiences are widely shared by audiences, listeners are easily admitted into that aspect of the musical discourse. The Mexican style of the second movement has similar connotations. There can be little doubt that Forsyth has enjoyed so many performances of his works—some of them repeated many times—because he wrote in a discourse in which his listeners could participate.

Having spent many hours discussing these works with Forsyth, what became most apparent to me was his desire to write player-friendly music—music that both suited and challenged the instrument, as well as the individual performer. After his appointment to the University of Alberta in 1968, Forsyth settled in Edmonton, where he became increasingly involved as a trombonist in the Edmonton Symphony Orchestra and in ensemble playing. This extensive experience created an awareness of the psychological and economic concerns involved in orchestral performance. He became very conscious of the need to avoid long periods of inactivity for the players; he also aspired to write idiomatic and satisfying parts for them to play. His choice of instrumentation almost always reflects the prevailing performance conditions and resources, since most of his works have been commissioned for specific orchestras and artists. Here it is interesting to note the difference between these early Canadian works and the juvenilia written in South Africa, where state and municipal support for orchestras at that time managed to absorb the cost of hiring extras to play non-standard instruments more readily than the community-owned counterparts in Canada. Thus, the Canadian works tended to be written for more standard instrumentation. On the other hand, the actual parts written for Canadian performers often tend to be more demanding, with a decidedly virtuosic flair noticeable in some of the writing.

Some of the orchestral parts have been written with certain players expressly in mind, giving them something both challenging and fulfilling to play. The virtuosic clarinet solo in the second movement of *Images of Night* and the first violin part of *Rhapsody for 14 Strings* are cases in point.

Forsyth's sympathy with the players of his music has caused him to avoid awkward or unidiomatic parts in his writing. On this subject he remarked, "As an orchestral player, I don't like playing things which I feel could have been written for any instrument or ought to be played on the cello, not the trombone...That's the kind of thing I won't do. I feel very strongly about that." Nowhere are these personal experiences and convictions more aptly applied than in *Sagittarius*.

Sagittarius and also *Quinquefid* were written on commission for the Canadian Brass, following a recording of Forsyth's *Golyarde's Grounde* on their disc *Canadian Brass in Paris*. Forsyth's firsthand experience of brass-playing influences his skilful writing for those instruments, highly suited to the superb technique and vibrant flair of all the members of Canadian Brass. There is an attractive feeling of spontaneity in *Sagittarius*, with its catchy melodies and jazzy rhythms, but the easy accessibility is founded upon an assured technique of orchestral writing. This is particularly evident in some of the teasingly interweaving textures such as the "hocketing" imitative entries in the concertante, creating a "bell-ringing" effect (mvt. 1, mm. 114–26, not shown).

Colouration

Even in his most heavily scored work, Symphony No. 1, Forsyth employs a traditional symphony orchestra, using resources that seem modest when compared to the requirements of many other twentieth-century works. But despite their modesty, the resources are manipulated with finesse and solid craftsmanship.

The creation of colourful and evocative effects with standard orchestral resources is a marked characteristic of Forsyth's style. His penchant for creating arresting foreground/background textures would appear to be connected to his affinity with painting, a talent that he in fact sidelined in favour of a musical career. He often seems to use orchestral timbres as a painter would use his palette, demonstrating a close bond between visual and aural colour. The atmospheric opening movement "Mont-aux-Sources" of *Sketches from Natal*, for example, conjures up the awesome majesty of that Drakensberg peak. A less overtly representational example occurs in the slow movement of the Piano Concerto, in which a clarinet solo is accompanied by a sustained pianissimo sonority in muted strings.

Forsyth created similar textures in several of his later works, filling in the foregrounded sounds with a background wash of colour, although the type of background is varied from work to work. This technique spawned those very memorable, dreamlike evocations in the slow movements of *Quinquefid*, *The Salpinx*, and *Atayoskewin*. In the latter work, this movement is in fact entitled "The Dream." The word also occurs in his chamber work *Dreams, Drones and Drolleries* for horn and piano. More recently, the Trumpet Concerto, which consolidates

Forsyth's unique stylistic stamps in so many ways, contains similar "dream" passages.

When Forsyth ventures to expand his orchestral colour, he typically uses the vivid and often glittering colours of the percussion section to good effect. Symphony No. 1 calls for cabaca and shell wind chimes. For the first performance these instruments were not available, so Forsyth actually made these instruments himself, the chimes built on a scissor-actioned wooden frame, the delicate shells suspended with bookmaker's twine, and the cabaca fashioned from a gourd commandeered from a friend's kitchen! A similar combination is featured in Symphony No. 3, where glass chimes with harp and celesta create one of those characteristic background textures, sustained throughout the entire movement. At the end of *Images of Night*, the percussion is instructed to dominate. The score at this point indicates, "Percussion should drown the orchestra."

Harmonic Resources

Harmonic colour is also an essential ingredient in these musical canvases. All kinds of harmonic idioms are harnessed into service, some very structured, others freely mixed from the palette. Discussing the genesis of *Images of Night*, Forsyth told me that the literature of the night had been very much on his mind, and the colours of Art Nouveau Arabian Nights—purple, green, magenta—are represented in the chords of the first movement.

In the orchestral works, beginning with Symphony No. 1, Forsyth developed an intervallic cellular technique that was to provide the ground roots for many of his subsequent orchestral works.[5] This work utilizes varied cells of perfect fourths, interlocked by a semitone. The cells, complete or incomplete, are freely worked into the texture of the music both melodically and harmonically. The work opens with a monophonic solo for violas, consisting of two phrases, each ending on a sustained note (see Figure 9.3), which is decorated by a secondary theme in the rest of the string section and percussion. Both themes contain strong references to Forsyth's cellular core material.

FIGURE 9.3. *Symphony No. 1, mvt. 1, mm. 1–21. Violas.*

These cellular constructions, extended in later works to include other intervallic combinations, served as a catalyst for Forsyth's developing harmonic language and hence for his handling of tonality, which fluctuates between tonal, atonal, and ambivalent. Different combinations of intervals have varied harmonic connotations, so combined cells contain a diversity of tonal, bitonal, and polytonal potentials.

It could be presumed that tonal implications would widen with extended cellular constructions. In practice, however, the cells turn in upon each other with a nullifying effect, so the more complex the extension, the more neutralized the tonal implications become. Forsyth, in fact, extended the interlocking technique into sonorities in which the presence of a definable tonality becomes elusive.

This intervallic cellular technique—arising out of Forsyth's study of the increased colourations of tonal chords through the nineteenth and twentieth centuries—is not applied rigidly and intensively, but serves as a freely utilized core in a composition. It is also used with more concentration in some works than others. Nevertheless, this technique became a central, formative factor in Forsyth's personal compositional style, and the manner in which he developed it and wove it into the musical texture became complex and, for me, most intriguing. Moving ambivalently between varied tonal and atonal frameworks, Forsyth worked this technique into a personalized harmonic idiom, also drawing upon triadic extensions, mirror constructions, clusters, sound masses, pedal points, and harmonic ostinatos.

Form

The structural fountainhead of the music springs from traditional syntax, motivic development, and metamorphosis. Out of this there often emerge melodies, sometimes very memorable and lyrical. It is therefore not surprising to find a fundamental alignment in Forsyth's works with macro-designs such as sonata, rondo, ritornello, variations, arch-form, and fantasia. His harmonic vocabulary, however, introduces a further dimension, where areas of stability and instability become an added part of the form-creating process.

Conclusion

Forsyth has thus been a consolidator rather than an innovator, selectively incorporating twentieth-century idioms and techniques into the network of a traditional musical canvas, in so doing, creating an eclectic output that undoubtedly radiates his own individuality. His creativity shows no sign of abating; he has just finished his 100th opus, *Sketches from Natal*: Suite No. 2, and a subsequent work, *Evangeline*, for soprano, trumpet, and chamber orchestra. There has never been an alignment with any particular "ism," nor any rigid attitudes of musical thought; he has simply remained free and true to himself, his performers, and his audience.

Writing music that allows concert audiences to participate in its discourse and providing aptly idiomatic and challenging scores for performers—while fulfilling his own aspirations as a musical craftsman, poet, and artist—seems to have been the recipe for Forsyth's considerable success. Above all, his music mirrors his insatiable zest for life experience and his strong desire to communicate it. In his own words, "I simply want to take a straight line between me and whoever is listening."

NOTES

1. Actually, Forsyth won this JUNO Award, his first of three for Best Classical Composition, in 1987, for the orchestral suite *Atayoskewin*. Two subsequent JUNO Awards were likewise for orchestral works: *Sketches from Natal* (in 1995) and *Electra Rising* (1998). —*Eds.*
2. In 2017 Jane Coop reissued her CBC Records recording of the Piano Concerto, with Mario Bernardi and the Calgary Philharmonic Orchestra, on the Skylark label (Sky1703). —*Eds.*
3. Two other works are *Valley of a Thousand Hills* (1989) and *These Cloud-Capp'd Towers* (1990), the latter for trombone and orchestra. In addition to revisions and arrangements of earlier pieces, orchestral works completed since 1992 include the following (in alphabetical order): *A Ballad of Canada* (2010); Concerto for Accordion and Orchestra (1998); Double Concerto for Viola and Cello (2004; rev. 2008); *Electra Rising* (1995); *Morning's Minion* (2000); *Requiem for the Victims in a Wartorn World* (2002); and *Trickster Coyote-Lightning Elk* (2006–08). —*Eds.*
4. District Six, an area in Cape Town, was peopled by those classified under apartheid as "Coloured" (i.e., Malay or of mixed-blood descent). Forsyth, classified as white, ran the risk of arrest for this activity. —*K.P.*
5. For a fascinating and detailed discussion of the role of intervals and harmony in Forsyth's early music, see chapter 3, "The Role and Use of Intervallic Cells," and chapter 4, "Forsyth's Harmonic Idiom and Tonal Organisation," in Primos's "The Compositional Style of Malcolm Forsyth's Orchestral Works: 1968–1982" (MA thesis, University of Witwatersand, 1988). —*Eds.*

10
Splendour in the Brass
A Legacy of Brass Music

DALE SORENSEN

MALCOLM FORSYTH'S BRASS MUSIC accounts for over 25 per cent of his entire compositional output and represents a significant contribution to brass solo and chamber music repertoire. Beginning with his *Quartet '61* (1961) for trombones, and ending with *Rondino & Tiddly Pom* (2008) for solo soprano cornet and tenor horn with brass band, Forsyth's extensive catalogue of brass music exemplifies the full stylistic range of his compositional career, from abstract compositional exercises to full-scale expressive explorations, and consists of utilitarian fanfares, music for students and amateurs, recital pieces, and large-scale concert works. Covering the gamut of expression, from introspective to extroverted, solemn to theatrical, tongue-in-cheek to serious, some have become standards in the repertoire. In this annotated list of several of Forsyth's works for brass, I include discussions of the circumstances surrounding their creation, a few of their musical and performance characteristics, and comments on their reception, with the aim of providing an introduction to Forsyth's compositional style and a glimpse into the variety of musical and extra-musical sources that inspired him.

Early Brass Music, 1961–1966

Forsyth taught himself to play the trombone at the age of 19. Three years later, after deciding to pursue an orchestral career as a trombonist, he enrolled in the music program at the University of Cape Town and there took composition lessons with Stanley Glasser, who taught his students how to compose by imitating the works of other composers—a method Forsyth later embraced as a teacher of composition himself.[1] Indeed, several of Forsyth's brass works reflect this historical approach to varying degrees, using material derived from, or modelled after, distinct musical or compositional styles from the past. Forsyth's three earliest brass works, the *Quartet '61, Poem for Brass* (1964–1966), and *Bachianas Capensis* (1966) reveal influences such as ostinato patterns, dance and song stylistic devices, and variation techniques.

Quartet '61 was written for trombone quartet, although the score allows for performances by bassoons, cellos, or horns. The first movement, "Ostinato: Andantino," uses a four-note ostinato pattern that is played by two trombones in parallel (mostly major) thirds. In the light-hearted third movement, *Vivace, alla Burlesca*, a 3–3–2 accent pattern is reminiscent of a tango. *Poem for Brass* exists in two versions, one for 12-piece brass ensemble (3 trumpets, 3 horns, 4 trombones, 1 euphonium, and 1 tuba) first performed by the University of Alberta Brass Ensemble on February 20, 1973, and another arranged in 1975 for symphonic brass section (2 trumpets, 4 horns, 3 trombones, and tuba). This three-movement work consists of original material presented as a series of variations that explore multiple styles and devices: a lyrical intermezzo, an elegy with cadenza, a fugue, and a waltz. *Bachianas Capensis* was written for alto, tenor, and bass trombones (or any three instruments of suitable range). Although the title appears to have been inspired by Villa-Lobos's *Bachianas Brasileiras*, it is, however, simply a short compositional exercise modelled after a Bach three-part invention. Forsyth's choice of the alto trombone in this piece is interesting. At this time, the South African style of trombone playing—a hybrid of British and Dutch styles—was characterized by a brighter tone quality than the North American style of playing, and favoured the use of small bore instruments, including the alto trombone.[2]

Brass Ensemble Music, 1968–1987

After arriving in Edmonton in 1968, Forsyth formed a trombone quartet, the Malcolm Forsyth Trombone Ensemble, which performed frequently in the region. The ensemble's self-titled album was released in 1982 at a time when few recordings for this combination of instruments existed.[3] In addition to works by composers such as Bruckner, Gabrieli, Marini, and Speer, the recording included one of Forsyth's own works, *Quartet '74* (1974), discussed below. Two of Forsyth's colleagues in this ensemble, John McPherson and Christopher Taylor (both former students and current Edmonton Symphony Orchestra [ESO] members) remember Forsyth as an excellent trombonist and musician who adapted well to the North American style of playing by acquiring large bore instruments, listening to recordings (classical and jazz) and working to develop the bigger, darker sound expected in the orchestra.[4] Taylor writes, "Malcolm...[played] well all three trombones, bass, tenor and alto, and could easily hit a top F5, even on the bass trombone, and could play very loud, particularly in the high register when needed."[5] McPherson adds, "He always stressed clean articulations, and had an energetic and even aggressive approach to his playing (when appropriate), which could be very exciting. Nothing irritated him more than a monotonous and boring approach to trombone playing."[6] McPherson describes his performances with Forsyth as "always exciting and exceedingly musical. He was a true leader, and was exacting in rehearsals, but it produced excellent results and I have yet to equal some of the fine ensemble experiences we had in the Malcolm Forsyth Trombone Ensemble."[7] Taylor concurs, "Playing alongside Malcolm...was always a learning and exciting experience. Always the teacher, Malcolm admonished us to strive for musical phrasing, good sound, balanced ensemble where required, solos with individuality, and proper expression of style."[8] These musical qualities would be essential in performing Forsyth's subsequent trombone ensemble works, a varied collection notable for individual and distinctive characteristics.

In addition to this ensemble, Forsyth formed the Goliard Brass Quintet with some of his colleagues in Edmonton. Some of his first Canadian compositions were written for this group, among them *Aphorisms* (1969–1971) and *Triangles* (1972), whose titles are also his first to suggest extra-musical associations.[9]

The Golyardes' Grounde (1972), one of Forsyth's best-known works for brass quintet, consists of variations on a ground bass. The work is named after "a group of thirteenth-century renegade French monks who had taken to 'carousing and obscene versifying,' according to Forsyth."[10] Beginning with a descending four-note ground in the tuba, each instrument enters in turn with motives of increasingly complex rhythmic material. After all five instruments have entered, the ground and the other motivic material are developed melodically and rhythmically, with mixed metres and accented cross-rhythms creating a complex counterpoint.[11] Although *The Golyardes' Grounde* is a challenging work to perform, all of the parts are written idiomatically for their instruments and within a practical range. It is a fun piece that is rewarding both for performers and audiences that demonstrates Forsyth's emerging abilities as a composer who could create an engaging and complex work out of fairly simple melodic material. *The Golyardes' Grounde* is not only one of Forsyth's most frequently performed brass works, but has also become a standard in the brass quintet repertoire. At least in part, it owes this status to the Canadian Brass, the ensemble that championed the work all over the world.[12]

Quartet '74 is a three-movement work that explores the full expressive and dynamic potential of the trombone. Colourful and rhythmically complex (the second movement and most of the third are in 11/8 metre), the work features lyrical, melodic writing for all parts, alternating with passages demanding technical agility. The intricate interplay between parts (staggered entries and bell chords, for example) would become a hallmark of Forsyth's writing for the trombone ensemble and is found throughout the trombone section writing in his orchestral music as well. Christopher Taylor recalls working on Forsyth's *Quartet '74* as

> *a truly thrilling time for the players involved. We rehearsed in the basement of his house initially, and I remember it took forever to get through the first movement, but especially the third movement because of the 11/8 time signature. We'd be cursing Malcolm at how hard it was to play, and praising him at the same time for how marvellous his new quartet was. It is, in my opinion, one of the better advanced works for trombone quartet, displaying an obvious maturity of compositional invention and development, setting it apart from other works in the repertoire.*[13]

Sagittarius (1975), composed for the Canadian Brass on commission from the Banff Centre and the Canada Council for the Arts, is a concerto grosso for brass quintet and orchestra.[14] The work was premiered by the Canadian Brass in Banff on August 16, 1975, with the Canadian Chamber Orchestra conducted by Mario Bernardi. The title for the work was inspired by the astrological sign of Sagittarius under which Forsyth (and also Ronald Romm, then trumpeter with the Canadian Brass) was born. The work reflects the personality traits of Sagittarians, which the composer describes as "cheerful, forward, driving, confident and sometimes blustery."[15] *Sagittarius* uses all members of the quintet individually as soloists and together as an ensemble, both unaccompanied and with orchestral accompaniment. In the program notes to the score, Forsyth describes the work as an "extrovert piece in an accessible style," with contrasting moods and "rhythmic twists."[16] The diversity of Forsyth's musical inspirations are likewise evident in this work, with a second movement that "gently parodies the *Mariachi* style of Mexican popular music," and a third movement that, alternating 5/4 and 6/4 metres, is directly attributed to the jazz waltz style of Paul Desmond's famous *Take Five*.[17] Soon after the premiere of *Sagittarius*, the CBC commissioned Forsyth to write a second concerto grosso for the Canadian Brass, *Quinquefid* (1977), which was premiered on April 6, 1977, at the CBC Alberta Festival with the ESO.[18]

Canadian Brass tuba player Chuck Daellenbach recalls the excitement of becoming acquainted with Forsyth's music:

> *Remembering back to the early days when brass quintets had no music that could support a professional career, we were delighted to have a fine composer write for us who was intimately knowledgeable about brass. His works certainly raised the musical bar, equalling the finest string quartet and other established chamber music repertoire. Importantly, these works have indeed lasted the test of time—every brass player should be acquainted with Malcolm's fine writing for brass.*[19]

Two Gentil Knyghtes (1979), a substantial four-movement work for bass trombone and tuba, utilizes the full technical capabilities of the instruments, requiring from the performers a large registral range, dexterous slide/finger technique, and the ability to negotiate wide interval leaps. The third movement, whimsically titled "L'après-midi d'un hippo," calls for multiphonics—an effect produced by playing one pitch while simultaneously singing another—a technique found nowhere else in the composer's oeuvre. These characteristic pieces display several stylistic influences, including the music of Forsyth's native South Africa as exemplified in a section reminiscent of African drumming.

Solemn Intrada (1980) is a beautiful eight-part chorale written for two each of soprano, alto, tenor, and bass trombones. In one section, the overlapping parts effectively mimic the sound of pealing bells. This work was written for the Moravian Trombone Choir of Downey, which recorded the work on *Music for All Seasons.*[20] Although a common instrument in the Moravian trombone ensemble tradition, the soprano trombone is otherwise a rarity in North American brass music; accordingly, these parts may be played on flugelhorn or cornet (and French horn may substitute for alto trombone).

Eclectic Altos with Pokerbass (1982) for three alto trombones and a G-bass trombone is as much a theatre piece as it is a musical work, incorporating costumes, props, and staging instructions. Unabashedly humorous, the work contrasts the agility of the alto trombones against the ungainly G-bass trombone, an instrument whose slide length requires a handle to reach the lower positions. This work provides a rare example of the composer's use of the glissando in a stereotypically comical way.

Forsyth composed six more brass quintet works between 1979 and 1989: Four Pieces for Brass Quintet (1979), the third of which is "Renaissance Dance," in 7/8 metre; *Saltarello* (1982), a four-movement work with some creative staging instructions; *Pfeifferfanfar für Pfeiffers* (1985), a short fanfare; Toccata for Brass Quintet & Organ (1986), a serious concert work commissioned by the Great Lakes Brass Quintet; *Farinelli's Folly* (1986, revised 1988); and *Zephyrus* (1989), a short, lyrical work commissioned by a German brass group.

Of these works, *Farinelli's Folly*, perhaps the best known due to its recording by True North Brass, is subtitled "A Parody for Brass Quintet" and begins in a Renaissance vocal style with simple harmonies.[21] Gradually, the melody becomes more ornamented and the work transitions into a Renaissance dance, alternating between 3/4 and 6/8 metres. Then the "folly" begins in earnest, with the material treated in various styles (mariachi, calypso, baroque) complete with a quote from Richard Strauss's *Also Sprach Zarathustra* before concluding with a simple restatement of the melody. Some of the score indications, such as *Andante rubato mexicano* and *Nietzschioso e Pesante*, reflect Forsyth's wry sense of humour. According to Forsyth, *Farinelli's Folly* uses the

> *anonymous Portuguese melody commonly known as La Folia, [which] was known in England in the eighteenth century as* Farinelli's Tune, *since the celebrated castrato, Farinelli, had written Folia variations. In all probability the original title indicated that it was a "fool's dance," giving rise to the habit of treating it as an opportunity for musical parody (folly) and similar craziness. This particular lapse into musical folly is a companion piece to its composer's earlier work,* The Golyardes' Grounde.[22]

Solo Brass Compositions, 1978–2008

Surprisingly few of Forsyth's solo brass works were written for his own instrument, perhaps not coincidentally because his solo trombone works were all written on commission, whereas without such funding he appeared to gravitate toward writing for trombone ensembles rather than the solo trombone. A few early works for other solo brass instruments do exist, however, including *Mirrors* (1978), *Four Dice = 40* (1979), *Fanfare and Three Masquerades* (1979), and *Dreams, Drones and Drolleries* (1981). Between 1987 and 1995 he composed Concerto for Trumpet and Orchestra (1987), *Songs from the Qu'Appelle Valley* (1987), *Soliloquy, Epitaph and Allegro* (1988), *These Cloud-Capp'd Towers* (1990), *Evangeline* (1993–1994), Sonata for Trumpet and Piano (1994–1995), and finally, *Rondino & Tiddly Pom.*

Mirrors for horn and marimba was premiered by ESO members David Hoyt (principal horn) and Brian Jones (principal percussion), and choreographed for solo female dancer.[23] As the title suggests, the horn and marimba mirror each other's material at times, alternately engaging in a dialogue of contrasting material that is at times polyrhythmic. Forsyth uses extended techniques for the horn, including flutter-tonguing, a tremolo effect involving alternate fingerings (which effectively simulates a roll on the marimba), and muted and stopped colours.[24]

Forsyth's solo trumpet music encompasses an interesting variety of styles, and accounts for three of the four solo brass works written in the 1990s. *Four Dice = 40* for solo trumpet is a musical pun written for Fordyce Pier, a colleague of Forsyth's at the University of Alberta, on the occasion of his 40th birthday. Lasting exactly 40 seconds, the work is built on a tone row using the date 4/23/79 (corresponding to the 4th, 2nd, 3rd, 7th, and 9th degrees of the scale) and uses the dorian and phrygian modes whose initials correspond to those of Duke Pier (the trumpeter's more familiar name).[25] Despite its brevity, *Four Dice = 40* showcases Forsyth's creativity and wit.

Fanfare and Three Masquerades for horn and wind nonet was commissioned by the German double woodwind quintet Bläser Ensemble Mainz to feature their principal hornist John Ellis (a former student of Forsyth). The group's conductor, Klaus Rainer Schöll, requested a piece of "heitere blasmusik" (cheerful wind music) suitable for outdoor performances.[26] The premiere on June 22, 1980, at Weilburg Castle was praised as the "highlight of the evening" in the *Giessener Allgemeine* newspaper.[27] Each of the three masquerades consists of variations on themes by composers whose names are indicated in the score only by initials (J.B. for Johannes Brahms, N.M. for Nikolai Myaskovsky, and R.S. for Robert Schumann). The themes come from Brahms's Symphony No. 2, Myaskovsky's Cello Concerto, and Schumann's Piano Concerto.[28] This work exemplifies Forsyth's ability to create a pastiche modelled after other composers' work that bursts with originality.[29]

Dreams, Drones and Drolleries, a dramatic three-movement work for horn and piano, was commissioned by Margaret Bunkall (now St. Cyr), who premiered the work with pianist Janet Scott Hoyt on August 13, 1981, at the Banff Centre. Although more expansive than *Mirrors*, it includes some of the same techniques and adds rips and pedal notes, a nearly four-octave range, and a free unmetred section with ostinato patterns in the piano.[30] While attending the Banff School, St. Cyr had won a competition to commission a Canadian composer of her choice. She remembers that "it was a lot of fun working with Malcolm...I admired his trombone playing as well as his compositions, and am very glad that I chose him to write the piece. It is a wonderful addition to any horn player's library."[31]

Concerto for Trumpet and Orchestra was written on commission from the CBC for the Montreal Symphony and its principal trumpet, James Thompson, who premiered the work on January 12, 1988, with conductor Charles Dutoit. This expressive, colouristic work in four movements, attacca, explores the full range of the trumpet's character using descriptive score markings such as "languourous" and "fanfarish."[32] Utilizing a range up to high E♯, the trumpet's full capabilities are exploited through fast, technical passages, including the use of flutter-tonguing, multiple-tonguing, unmeasured tonguing patterns that gradually accelerate or decelerate, and rips. Various mutes provide colour, while rhythmic interest is provided through shifting accents, jazz-influenced material, and a brief homage to Stravinsky.

The percussionist is also featured prominently as an "obbligato or subsidiary soloist."[33] Trumpeter James Thompson worked closely with Forsyth throughout the composition of the concerto, corresponding by email and telephone. He remembers,

> *We discussed my style of playing, and he asked me what I liked. I would also sometimes play for him over the telephone snippets of some of the piece as he sent them to me, and also things that I thought of concerning articulation, dynamics, etc. It was very easy to work with Malcolm. He had an easygoing way about him that made it easy to exchange ideas. In fact, when we recorded the piece, I asked Malcolm if I could take the last note up to an E♭, which was not written. He thought that was a great idea, and to go right ahead. It's on the recording. I think the piece is unique, as it tends to be more lyrical than most other concertos, which suits my playing style. It was very well received by the audience; I received several comments about how beautiful the piece was, and the reviews were very, very good. I thought it was a very well-written and very interesting piece to play. I still think so today. In fact, I notice that it is played often, which is a great compliment to Malcolm.*[34]

The first works that Forsyth considered as bearing a "distinct Canadian identity" are not the works of his homeland, but those that reveal his interest in his new home: the *Three Métis Folk Songs from Saskatchewan* (1975).[35] Arranged for mezzo-soprano and piano with subsequent versions for full orchestra and chamber orchestra, the songs underwent an additional arrangement for brass band and percussion commissioned by the Hannaford Street Silver Band through the Ontario Arts Council. The arrangement was premiered on October 25, 1987, with the composer conducting. For this version, retitled *Songs from the Qu'Appelle Valley*, Forsyth admits to rewriting the entire first movement, subjecting the melody to several variations, including a rhythmically intricate section in 9/16 subdivided as 3/16 + 3/8.[36] In all three movements the melody is passed among several instrumentalists with varying degrees of development.

In 1990 Forsyth created another adaptation of these songs, commissioned by trumpeter Stuart Laughton (a member of the Hannaford

Band) and soprano Wendy Humphreys. *Métis Songs from the Qu'Appelle Valley* for soprano, trumpet (doubling flugelhorn and cornet), and organ, is an arrangement personalized to exploit Humphreys's additional abilities on the Celtic harp, as well as Laughton's on the bodhran. It contains expressive and virtuosic writing for the trumpet.

Soliloquy, Epitaph and Allegro for trombone and organ was commissioned by James Montgomery, then professor of brass at the University of Prince Edward Island. He premiered the work with organist Willis Noble on July 7, 1989, at the International Trombone Festival in Windsor, UK, and subsequently performed the work several times on various recital tours. The work is one of only three existing Canadian works for trombone and organ. The first movement, "Soliloquy," showcases the expressive qualities of the trombone over the colouristic accompaniment of the organ; "Epitaph" is a chorale dedicated to the memory of Alan Paton (1903–1988), a South African writer, teacher, and anti-apartheid activist; and the *Allegro* is a technical tour de force for both the trombone and organ.

These Cloud-Capp'd Towers was commissioned by the Prince George Symphony Orchestra with funding from the Canada Council for the Arts; Canadian virtuoso trombonist Alain Trudel gave the première on May 4, 1991, with John Unsworth conducting. The title comes from Prospero's speech in Shakespeare's *The Tempest*, and was chosen by Forsyth for whom the word *tower* evoked an atmosphere of "signaling and authority."[37] *These Cloud-Capp'd Towers* was subsequently performed in September 1992 at the International Trombone Festival in Detmold, Germany, where, according to Trudel, it "stole the show" on a gala concert of outstanding concertos performed by several of the world's premier trombonists.[38] Indeed, the audience's overwhelmingly enthusiastic response is evident on a live recording of this performance selected for inclusion on a limited-edition CD produced to commemorate the Festival.[39] *These Cloud-Capp'd Towers* was the product of a close collaboration between Trudel and Forsyth, who had known each other for some time and had previously discussed the possibility of a new work for solo trombone. Forsyth wanted to create an exciting work that would exploit the beauty of the trombone's tone, both lyrically and dramatically, and together they discussed expanding the registral range. Early on it became apparent that percussion would feature prominently in the orchestral texture, with a resulting cadenza for trombone and tom-toms. The work was intended to be shorter than a full concerto as Trudel's performance with the Prince George Symphony was to include Forsyth's new piece along with another standard work for trombone. Out of consideration for increasing the prospects of future performances Forsyth chose a modest instrumentation for the orchestral accompaniment and made the work easy enough for an orchestra to prepare with limited rehearsal time. In Trudel's mind, to accomplish this goal while also creating a meaningful work of substance is a fine balance that could only have been achieved by a true master.[40] Tailor-made to suit Alain Trudel's considerable technical and musical abilities, and with a range encompassing four octaves (from pedal F♯ to high F), *These Cloud-Capp'd Towers* is the pinnacle of Forsyth's trombone writing.

Laughton and Humphreys's collaboration with Forsyth continued with another piece of Canadiana, an adaptation of Henry Wadsworth Longfellow's epic poem *Evangeline*. Commissioned by a consortium of three orchestras with funding from the Canada Council, this cantata for soprano, solo trumpet, and chamber orchestra was written using Laughton's own abridged version of Longfellow's poem.[41] Originally conceived as a 20-minute work, *Evangeline* ultimately grew to double this length, which deterred two of the commissioning orchestras from programming it. Without sufficient rehearsal time to prepare the complete work, the Manitoba Chamber Orchestra (conducted by Simon Streatfeild, with soloists Laughton and Humphreys) included only the "Introduction," "Part the First," and the "Epilogue" in their premiere on April 6, 1994. "Part the Second" was not performed until April 8, 1997, in a complete performance of the work by the orchestra with soprano Heidi Klassen.[42]

Despite Forsyth's early expression of his cultural heritage in his orchestral compositions, the most overt manifestation of African influence to be found in his brass music occurs much later, in his Sonata for Trumpet and Piano from 1994–1995, commissioned by

Fordyce Pier with funding from the Alberta Foundation for the Arts. The second movement features "the small cross-rhythms of African music": a relaxed, improvisatory, syncopated "vocal" line contrasted with a more angular sixteenth-note pattern meant to evoke the sound of an African talking drum.[43] To make this effect more apparent, Forsyth indicates that the piano part can be played using a synthesizer with a log drum sound using a "marimba-style tremolo" for the syncopated lines. Likewise, the trumpet, "when using the bucket mute, may also be processed for some percussive sort of sound."[44] Cross-rhythms abound in the outer movements as well, although not with such an overt reference to African music. The first movement features polymetrical writing that places the trumpet and piano in conflicting time signatures, 12/8 against 6/4, while the third movement, a lively Vivace, features shifting accents, syncopated rhythms, and sixteenth-note flourishes.

As principal conductor of Edmonton's Mill Creek Colliery Band from 2002 to 2004, and again from 2006 to 2010, Forsyth wrote his final original brass work: *Rondino & Tiddly Pom* for solo soprano cornet and tenor horn with brass band. It was premiered on November 8, 2008, conducted by the composer and later performed by the Hannaford Street Silver Band in January 2010. The middle section of the work, "Lilting and ineffably simple," is based on a brief cue Forsyth had written for a film score, and within which Winnie-the-Pooh, and possibly Piglet too, are represented ("Tiddly Pom" is a Pooh poem written by A.A. Milne). Forsyth noted that "the brass band repertoire appears to lack a piece featuring its two important E♭ members as duo soloists, so this is a possible filler for that lack."[45]

Occasional Music, 2000–2008

Throughout his career, Forsyth composed several short utilitarian works (such as fanfares) for specific occasions. The new millennium marked a return to such *Gebrauchsmusik* for Forsyth, whose final brass works were exclusively written either for specific occasions and/or for amateurs, including *Blow! Bugle, Blow!* (2000), *Sonic Mobile* (2003), and *Arcadian Panoply* (2007).

Blow! Bugle, Blow! for mixed chorus and brass ensemble (3 trumpets, 4 horns, 3 trombones, and tuba) is a setting of Alfred Lord Tennyson's poem. It was commissioned for the International Society for Music Education Conference (2000) in Edmonton, and premiered on July 18, 2000, by the National Youth Choir of Canada and the brass of the Edmonton Wind Sinfonia (a community group), conducted by Leonard Ratzlaff. At 13 minutes in length, it is a substantial work suitable for students and amateurs.

Sonic Mobile for trombone choir and *Arcadian Panoply* for solo trombone and trombone choir (or trombone quartet) were both commissioned privately for wedding anniversary celebrations of members of the Ritchie Trombone Choir, a community ensemble in Edmonton made up of professionals, amateurs, and students. Both of these works display Forsyth's penchant for clever titles, and serve as fine examples of his skilful mastery of trombone ensemble writing.

|| Forsyth's use of brass instruments reflects a deep understanding of their capabilities: technique is exploited as a means to a musical end and not for the sake of virtuosic display. The writing is always idiomatic and natural in a way perhaps only a brass player themself could achieve. As a result, Forsyth's catalogue of brass music is remarkable for its consistently high quality and originality, and as an extraordinary legacy of work that continues to be performed and enjoyed by musicians and audiences around the world.

NOTES

1. Eitan Cornfield, "Forsyth Documentary," on *Canadian Composers Portraits: Malcolm Forsyth*, Centrediscs CMCCD 8802, 2002.
2. John McPherson, personal communication (email), July 23, 2013; Christopher Taylor, personal communication (email), July 27, 2013. When he came to Canada in January 1968, Forsyth's first performance work was on alto trombone, for the CBC in Toronto. According to Forsyth, he was "the only such player" at the time. Quoted in Jane Champagne, "Malcolm Forsyth: How to Get High on Your Own Music," *Canadian Composer*, March 1975, 18, http://www.musiccentre.ca/node/38062.

3. Malcolm Forsyth Trombone Ensemble, *Malcolm Forsyth Trombone Ensemble*, Crystal Records S224, 1982, vinyl.
4. McPherson, pers. comm.; Taylor, pers. comm.
5. Taylor, pers. comm.
6. McPherson, pers. comm.
7. McPherson, pers. comm.
8. Taylor, pers. comm.
9. *Aphorisms*, written between 1969 and 1972, comprises three movements: "Short and Pithy," "Slow and Wistful," and "Fast and Fluent," and was recorded by the Budapest Brass Quintet on *Rhapsody in Brass* (Koch Schwann 3-6708-2). The music of *Triangles* was incorporated later into his *Four Pieces for Brass Quintet* (1979).
10. Champagne, "Malcolm Forsyth," 16.
11. A detailed analysis and performance guide to this work can be found in Stephen Klingbeil, "A Performer's Guide to Selected Music for Brass Quintet, 1968–1990" (DMA diss., Southern Baptist Theological Seminary, 1993), ProQuest ATT 9428251.
12. Cornfield, "Forsyth Documentary." In 1974 Forsyth was hired to teach trombone at the Banff Summer Festival of the Arts, where he met members of the Canadian Brass. After reading through Forsyth's existing brass quintet music, the Canadian Brass decided to include *The Golyardes' Grounde* on their next recording, *The Canadian Brass in Paris* (Vanguard VMD-71253). According to Champagne, this was the first commercial recording of any of Forsyth's works, and it was revived on several subsequent Canadian Brass recordings over the years. It was also featured prominently during the Canadian Brass's ground-breaking concert tour of China in 1977. More recently, *The Golyardes' Grounde* has been rerecorded for *Canadian Brass Takes Flight* (Opening Day ODR 7416, 2012), which, according to founding member and tubist Chuck Daellenbach, "virtually sums up the music important to the career of the Canadian Brass" (personal communication, July 10, 2013).
13. Taylor, pers. comm.
14. This was Forsyth's first Canada Council commissioning grant.
15. John Gray, "Episode 3: Malcolm Forsyth," *The Composer's Chair* (podcast), Canadian Music Centre, 2008, http://musiccentre.ca/node/65921.
16. Malcolm Forsyth, *Sagittarius* (Concerto Grosso No.1) (Toronto: Counterpoint, 1975).
17. *Sagittarius* was performed frequently by the Canadian Brass throughout North America, and recorded with the National Arts Centre Orchestra and conductor Mario Bernardi. It is now available on *Canadian Composers Portraits: Malcolm Forsyth* (Centrediscs CMCCD 8802, 2002). The second movement, *Andante*, has proven to be especially popular, and has been arranged by the composer in three versions: for cello and piano (written for his daughter, Amanda); for two solo harps and string orchestra; and in a version arranged for two horns and piano in 2009.

18. According to Jean-Marie Barker, owner and president of Counterpoint Music Library Services Inc., which handles the distribution of Forsyth's catalogue, *Quinquefid* has not been performed since 1991. *Sagittarius* was last performed in 2001 (Barker, personal communication, July 24, 2013).
19. Daellenbach, pers. comm.
20. Los Angeles Philharmonic Trombone Ensemble, *Moravian Trombones Music for All Seasons*, Crystal Records CD220, 1993.
21. True North Brass, *Strong & Free*, Opening Day ODR 9320, 2000, CD.
22. Malcolm Forsyth, *Farinelli's Folly: A Parody for Brass Quintet* (Toronto: Counterpoint, 1988).
23. David Hoyt, personal communication, August 13, 2013.
24. A pedagogical guide to this work can be found in Eleanor Stubley, *A Guide to Solo French Horn Music by Canadian Composers* (Toronto: Canadian Music Centre, 1990).
25. Fordyce Pier, personal communication, August 13, 2013.
26. Gray, "Episode 3: Malcolm Forsyth."
27. John Ellis, personal communication, August 21, 2013.
28. Catherine Gerhart, "Annotated Bibliography of Double Wind Quintet Music," last modified February 20, 2013, http://faculty.washington.edu/gerhart/dwqbibliography/.
29. *Fanfare and Three Masquerades* was recorded by hornist Carol Lavell with the Canadian Chamber Ensemble conducted by Raffi Armenian, and is available on two separate recordings (Centrediscs CMCCD 3488, 1988, and CBC Records PSCD 2027-5, 2002) as well as a CMC sampler CD.
30. A pedagogical guide to this work can be found in Stubley, *Guide to Solo French Horn Music*.
31. Margaret St. Cyr (Bunkall), personal communication, August 15, 2013.
32. Malcolm Forsyth, Concerto for Trumpet and Orchestra (Toronto: Counterpoint, 1987).
33. Forsyth, Concerto for Trumpet and Orchestra.
34. James Thompson, personal communication, July 9, 2013. Thompson's recording with the Kitchener-Waterloo Symphony, conducted by Raffi Armenian, was released on two recordings: *Canadian Composers Portraits: Malcolm Forsyth* (Centrediscs CMCCD 8802, 2002) and *Canadian Trumpet Concerti: Hétu, Forsyth, Nimmons* (CBC Records SMCD 5130, 1993).
35. See Roxane Prevost's study of this work in this volume.
36. Keith Horner, liner notes in *Canadian Impressions*, Hannaford Street Silver Band, Stephen Chenette, CBC Records SMCD 5136, 1994.
37. A detailed description of this work can be found in Jennifer Raine, "Alain Trudel's Legacy: Selected Canadian Trombone Repertoire, 1984–2001" (DMA diss., Manhattan School of Music, 2002).

38. Alain Trudel, personal communication (phone call), August 5, 2013. At the occasion of the premiere, Trudel discovered that the bass trombonist in the orchestra was quite a fine player. Together, they schemed to locate an extra trombone and a suitable trombone trio piece, which was then sprung on an unsuspecting Forsyth, who gamely joined in for an encore. It probably took little persuasion, for according to Christopher Taylor (pers. comm.), Forsyth loved being in the limelight.
39. *21st International Trombone Workshop* (Hochschule für Musik Detmold HSD 003, 1992) is no longer available.
40. Trudel, pers. comm.
41. Stuart Laughton, personal communication, August 10, 2013.
42. Laughton, pers. comm.
43. Malcolm Forsyth, Sonata for Trumpet and Piano (Toronto: Counterpoint, 1994).
44. Forsyth, Sonata for Trumpet and Piano.
45. Malcolm Forsyth, *Rondino & Tiddly Pom* (Toronto: Counterpoint, 2008).

11
The Choral Music

LEONARD RATZLAFF

WHILE MALCOLM FORSYTH'S STATURE as a composer is based principally on his contributions to instrumental music, a substantial part of his compositional output is dedicated to choral and solo vocal music, a circumstance that is all the more remarkable because Forsyth had no formal singing training and viewed his own abilities as a singer with equal parts merriment and disdain. In fact, my most vivid personal recollections of Forsyth's singing are from the legendary parties he would hold at his home where, with pianist colleague Ernesto Lejano, his favourite party "trick" was to launch lustily into Tatiana's letter scene from Tchaikovsky's *Eugene Onegin*, complete with high, tremulous, and slightly out of tune falsetto, much to the delight of his guests. More to the point, on numerous occasions Forsyth solicited my advice and that of other choral conductors on questions of vocal range, appropriateness of text setting and tessitura, and other matters where he clearly felt his limited knowledge of the vocal instrument could present practical performance problems for singers in his choral and vocal works.[1]

The goal of this chapter is to provide a general overview of Forsyth's choral compositions, providing some details relevant to the inception of each work as well as commentary on his choice of texts and their most salient compositional elements. Bearing in mind some challenging aspects his choral music presents especially for the amateur choral singer, Forsyth was able to develop an expressive and compelling musical language in this medium that is ultimately quite gratifying to experience both as performer and listener.

Despite his lack of vocal experience or refinement in his own singing, the vocal music, especially the unique language, songs, and rhythms of the indigenous Bantu people he heard in his native South Africa, had always been a source of fascination for Forsyth, and a creative well from which he drew much in his own writing. In recalling his first encounters with music as a young boy, Forsyth credits his experience of hearing the sounds of Zulu singing in the town of Pietermaritzburg, where he grew up, as a major influence in his compositional language:

> *The house I grew up in in Pietermaritzburg—my street—was the major arterial street for all the buses at the end of the work day for all the black people who lived in the township of Edendale—a vast slum...at the end of the work day all the buses would come one after the other, packed with people; but all day long there would be black people wandering up and down the street singing, Zulus playing little home-made guitars, maybe playing repetitive ostinato figures and singing in Zulu (and of course I learnt to speak Zulu long before I learnt to speak Afrikaans). So I listened to them—I would play out in the front garden in the flowerbeds...and hear Zulu people singing their music and playing their little ostinato rhythmic figures, from my very earliest recollection, long before my father got me to listen to Johann Strauss waltzes. I heard this music and I knew it, without ever really thinking about it.*[2]

Forsyth wrote seventeen choral works beginning with *Music for Mouths, Marimba, Mbira and Roto-Toms* in 1973 and ending with the five-movement cantata *A Ballad of Canada* for chorus and full orchestra in 2010, co-commissioned by the National Arts Centre and the Edmonton Symphony Orchestras in celebration of Forsyth's 75th birthday. With the exception of *A Ballad of Canada* and one work scored for chorus and brass ensemble, *Blow! Bugle, Blow!*, the remaining works are either for unaccompanied chorus or for chorus with one or two instruments. Despite the smaller scoring, however, many of these works fall within the eight- to fifteen-minute range, a reflection of Forsyth's intent to make a substantial contribution in his choral settings by ensuring that the works were accessible and programmable in various concert situations. It is regrettable that his choral music has not gained as much traction in the choral community as his instrumental music for orchestras, bands, and chamber ensembles, as this repertoire features many finely crafted and uniquely expressive text settings. This circumstance may in large part be explained by the fact that Forsyth was not afraid to present singers with challenges both in his part writing as well as in the harmonic language that resulted. I have occasionally encountered comments from fellow conductors and singers who suggest that his choral writing is often "instrumental" rather than "vocal" in conception, and that the learning curve for singers is in some cases quite steep. Acknowledging that this is sometimes the case with his more demanding works, careful score study on the part of conductors and dedicated rehearsal on the part of singers can result in very compelling and rewarding experiences of this music.

A review of the chronology of his choral catalogue shows a fairly sporadic output at the beginning of his career (four separate pieces between 1973 and 1983, of which three are quite short), a subsequent break of six years, followed by a highly prolific period with an impressive output of eight choral works, many of them quite extended multi-movement works, between 1989 and 2001. Many of these were written in response to commissions from either the CBC, the Canada Council, or from leading professional and amateur Canadian choirs of various ages and voicings, a reflection of his increasing stature as a composer. Curiously, this prolific period was followed by another break of eight years before two works appeared: *Nursery Rhymes*, a short set of settings for unison voices, written for the Edmonton Children's Choir, and *A Ballad of Canada*. A more detailed study of this substantial oeuvre in Forsyth's catalogue could well be the subject for further research; my purpose here is to highlight the majority of these works briefly, focusing more on those that I have had the opportunity to perform or record, with a view to revealing interesting aspects of his style in writing for chorus.

Forsyth's initial foray into composing for chorus came not long after he immigrated to Canada, with *Music for Mouths, Marimba, Mbira and Roto-Toms* in 1973, a three-movement work for SATB chorus and one percussionist. The Da Camera Singers of Edmonton commissioned it, but the first performance was actually given in November 1973 by the University of Alberta Concert Choir under Professor Larry Cook's direction, as part of the Department of Music's Exploration concert series.[3] As Forsyth himself stated, this first attempt at choral writing turned out to be one of the seminal works in enabling him to integrate his experience of native South African melodies and rhythms into his early writing:

> *It didn't come to the surface until I came to Canada; suddenly being removed from all of that, I said, "I know that I am from Africa; I'm from a different place—I'm not from here." Suddenly, all of this music came to the surface, and I started writing African-sounding music for the very first time, in 1968...I then wrote a choral piece with percussionist called* Music for Mouths, Marimba, Mbira and Roto-Toms, *using a lot of Zulu phonic sounds—no actual Zulu text, but Zulu phonics, the syllables of which to me are so rhythmic and so musical.*[4]

Music for Mouths is a remarkably sophisticated work for an initial composition in this medium. In its three movements, the titles of which ("Iculenya," "Iculabili," "Iculathathu") are Zulu for "First song," "Second song," "Third song," Forsyth introduces a wide palette of vocal effects (singing, humming, whispering, speaking, shouting, tongue-clicking, and other percussive consonant effects such as "ksh" and "psh") to reflect the unique sounds of the native South African Bantu language. The outer two movements are highly rhythmic, with vocal lines that freely utilize all the vocal techniques described above, augmented by ostinato patterns in the marimba and especially the roto-toms, as well as the mbira, or African thumb piano.

The second movement features predominantly sustained humming tones interspersed with Zulu syllables in which the chorus uses glissandos at various stages to create a series of dominant seventh chords above a constant G dominant seventh chord tremolo in the marimba. On the final page of this movement the chorus resolves to a C minor chord, against the backdrop of the continuing marimba chord, finally giving way with a group glissando to the same chord as the marimba, which itself gives way to a final repeated mbira figure. The highly expressive writing for the chorus provides a mesmerizing contrast to the outer dramatic movements.

Although Forsyth composed several works for solo voice in the 1970s (most notably *Three Métis Songs* in 1975, a CBC commission for the Canadian contralto Maureen Forrester),[5] he wrote no other choral music until March 1980, when he was on a sabbatical leave and residing in London. Here, in a span of just two weeks, he wrote two non-commissioned short works, "The Sea" (poem by American Dorothy Parker) for eight-part female voices, and "Sudden Light" (British Raphaelite poet Dante Gabriel Rossetti) for mixed chorus in 16 parts.[6] In "The Sea," Parker portrays an idyllic existence by the sea:

Who lay against the sea, and fled,
Who lightly loved the wave,
Shall never know, when he is dead,
A cool and murmurous grave.[7]

Forsyth sets this text with an almost ethereal lightness, beginning with a simple major third interval, from which he expands the texture in both soprano and alto voice parts, eventually reaching a high B natural in the soprano. The key alternates between F and the relative minor D, albeit without the use of any accidentals. Through the gradual expansion of repeated intervallic patterns of seconds, thirds, fourths, and fifths (sopranos moving upward, altos downward in contrary motion), both in the introductory "Ah" section and in the verses that follow, Forsyth creates a buoyancy alternating with periods of repose that is descriptive of the inexorable rise and fall of rolling sea waves. This is a hauntingly beautiful setting that deserves more exposure in the equal voice repertoire of female ensembles.

"Sudden Light," with a text by Dante Gabriel Rossetti and completed only two weeks after "The Sea," could not be more contrasting in tone, ambience, and resultant difficulty. Rossetti's poem is a melancholic recollection of love at a chance meeting with a beautiful woman from whom the poet had been parted for years.[8] In this work, tenors and basses, frequently set in dissonant four-part chords in predominantly lower tessitura, presumably play the part of the troubled poet, while the sopranos and altos, also frequently divided in dissonant clusters, mostly sing "Ah," often in distantly higher registers (with several soprano solos requiring high D♭s). The prolonged dissonances in registers that are vocally difficult to sustain contribute to the demands of this part-song, which to this author's knowledge has yet to receive its first performance.

Three years later Forsyth returned to the choral medium with "In the Dying of Anything" (1983) for mixed chorus. At the time, he was in Johannesburg on a short guest lecturing assignment at Witwatersrand University (also referred to as Wits University) that involved work with their university choir; the piece was premiered by the Wits Chamber Choir on June 6, 1994, and received several more performances over the course of his term there that winter.[9] The text is an excerpt from a poem by Brian Patten, one of the so-called Liverpool poets who flourished in that city in the 1960s around the same time that The Beatles emerged from Liverpool's vibrant pop music culture. The excerpt is powerful in its brevity:

In the dying of anything there walks a creature looking for its song;
huge, it bends down planets that it might ask them
the ways back to life again.

But we lie quieter now, older...
In the dying of anything...[10]

Barely a minute in duration and the most accessible of the three part-songs, this setting begins and ends with a lyrical descending line repeated several times in the alto voice, accompanied by a constant A major chord in second inversion in the tenors and basses, with D♯ in the soprano. The middle of this short part-song is the second line ("huge, it bends down planets") that is sung by tenors and basses, while the sopranos and altos contribute a simple duet on "But we lie quieter now, older." Like "The Sea," this miniature is a true gem that deserves wider popularity.[11]

Another six years passed before Forsyth turned his attention again to choral writing. Increasing demands for instrumental works through commissions from the CBC, the Canada Council for the Arts, various orchestras as well as instrumental and vocal soloists marked the interim period, with high points including a compulsory work for solo voice and orchestra for the Concours internationale de musique de Montréal (*Canzona*, 1985), the Edmonton Symphony Orchestra (ESO)'s commission and subsequent recording of his suite for orchestra, *Atayoskewin*, for which he received his first of three JUNO Awards in 1987, and the CBC Radio–commissioned *Sun Songs* (1987) for mezzo-soprano Judith Forst and the CBC Vancouver Orchestra conducted by Mario Bernardi.

In 1988 Forsyth composed *Three Zulu Songs* (SSA, flute, oboe) commissioned from the Canada Council for the Arts for the Toronto Children's Chorus, Jean Ashworth Bartle, conductor. The work premiered May 14, 1988, in Toronto. As with *Music for Mouths*, Forsyth here utilizes many characteristic sounds of the Zulu language, but the main text is a set of three poems by the early twentieth-century South African poet Benedict Wallet Vilakazi. These attractive songs are very straightforward in their tonal design, albeit with some rhythmic complexities, with the main challenge for singers being the Zulu text and combining their singing with various other rhythmic activities (snapping fingers, clapping, etc.)

Endymion's Dream (SSAATTBB, unaccompanied) was written in 1993, commissioned by the CBC for the Vancouver Chamber Choir, Jon Washburn conductor, for performance at the 1993 World Symposium on Choral Music. It premiered in Vancouver on August 2, 1993. Forsyth drew upon a wide range of English poets from the Renaissance through the twentieth century for many of his solo and choral works. A passage from *Endymion* (1818) by the English Romantic John Keats (1795–1821) was the source for this commission. The opening of this 12-minute work, describing the poem's protagonist Endymion's rather troubling and grotesque dream, contains some of Forsyth's most challenging writing for chorus, with extensive chromaticism, use of chord clusters, and wide ranges requiring well-trained singers. The final section, subtitled "Thou Art as a Dove," (Endymion's awakening, fully rested and calm), which Forsyth indicates could be performed as a separate piece, is markedly more diatonic in conception and contains some serenely expressive moments. In contrast with the opening section, no accidentals are used for the first 47 measures of "Thou Art as a Dove," and only toward the end is there a supple movement away from C major, bringing the piece to a restful close in A major.

In 1994–1995 Forsyth completed *Three Love Poems of John Donne* (SATB divisi), on a commission from Pro Coro Canada with funds from the Alberta Foundation for the Arts. The premiere took place in Edmonton on October 6, 1995, with guest conductor Frieder Bernius. For this cycle, Forsyth turned to the poetry of seventeenth-century mystic poet John Donne, choosing three views of love. The first, "The Sunne Rising," chides the sun for waking lovers from their night's reverie ("Busie old foole"); the second, simply titled "Song," laments the inconstancy of women; the third, "Holy Sonnet XVII," expresses the mourner's jealousy that God has taken his beloved too early: "Since she whom I lov'd hath payd her last debt to nature." Although there are definite challenges in this cycle as well, Forsyth utilizes less divided parts and the vocal ranges are less demanding than those in *Endymion's Dream*. The elegiac third song is without question one of Forsyth's most expressive works for chorus.[12]

In 1997 Forsyth composed *Northern Journey: Three Songs for Women's Chorus* (SSSSAAAA unaccompanied). Commissioned by Elektra Women's Choir, Vancouver (Diane Loomer and Morna Edmundson, conductors), this work premiered in Vancouver on May 15, 1999. The poems for these three settings for female chorus were all selected from *Unmarked Doors*, a collection of poems published in 1992 by Edmonton poet Inge Israel.[13] All three are highly evocative settings of poems describing distinctly different northern locales: "Auyuittuq" (Canada's first national park north of the Arctic Circle, on Baffin Island); "Kluane Glaciers" (Yukon Territory); and "Winter Sky" (Northern Lights in Alberta). These settings employ the full range of colours possible for women's chorus, as well as, in the first, loon calls, and in the third, aleatoric staccato pitches on "Ah" to depict the flickering of Northern Lights. They exhibit Forsyth's increasing confidence in setting music for the voice: what initially may seem like quite difficult sounds to absorb are frequently approached from unison beginnings to create brilliant sonorities that call to mind some of Forsyth's writing for brass and wind choirs in his orchestral music.

Forsyth composed three works in 2000: *Glasnost*, for five voices (SSATB) and tape, commissioned by the Cantilena Consort and director Alexander Tumanov, that premiered May 26, 2000, in Edmonton; *Snug the Joiner as Lion Fell: A Jest for Male Voice Choir*, commissioned by Chor Leoni Men's Choir, Vancouver, with Diane Loomer, conductor, that premiered July 13, 2000, at the Association of Canadian Choral Conductors Podium 2000 Conference in Edmonton; and *Blow! Bugle, Blow!* (SATB divisi, brass ensemble), commissioned by the International Symposium for Music Education (ISME) for the National Youth Choir of Canada with myself conducting. This last work was premiered at the ISME 2000 conference by the National Youth Choir of Canada and the Edmonton Wind Sinfonia on July 16, 2000, in Edmonton.

Glasnost, a setting of another poem by Inge Israel, is unique in Forsyth's choral writing in its use of electronic tape and its scoring for a five-voice solo ensemble. The poem recalls an experience of entering a church in Moscow shortly after the fall of Soviet rule, where a service with Slavonic singing (here represented by the Russian sixteenth-century hymn *Edinorodnyi Syne* ["O Only-begotten Son and Word of God!"]) is interspersed with the narrative of the poet, and accompanied by taped street sounds as well as the interruptions of a tour guide inside the sanctuary.

Snug the Joiner as Lion Fell: A Jest for Male Voice Choir is Forsyth's only writing for male chorus. This short but demanding work falls into the category of choral theatre, a genre that the Chor Leoni ensemble had developed over the years with its highly entertaining Bard on the Beach summer concert series in Vancouver. The text is excerpted from Shakespeare's play within a play, "Pyramus and Thisby" from *A Midsummer Night's Dream*.

In his setting of Alfred Lord Tennyson's well-known poem, *Blow! Bugle, Blow!*, Forsyth was able to mix his legendary talent for writing distinctive sonorities for brass instruments with an effective setting for the choral ensemble. This work features a wide range of stunning effects: the choir delivers the text with a harmonic clarity and beautifully shaped lyricism, accompanied by rich low brass chords, a wide range of horn calls, and quick scale-like flourishes in the trumpets (occasionally playing with mutes), all combining in the final section to create the "echoes that roll from soul to soul."

In 2001 Forsyth completed *Hesperides: A Song Cycle of Poems* by Robert Herrick (SATB chorus and two harps). Commissioned by the Canada Council for the Arts and Renaissance Arts Enterprises for the Elora Festival, *Hesperides* was premiered in Elora, Ontario, on July 25, 2001, by the Elora Festival Singers and the Paragon Harp Duo (Nora Bumanis and Julia Shaw) under Noel Edison, conductor. *Hesperides* can rightly be considered one of Forsyth's most ambitious and artistically satisfying choral works. At nearly 20 minutes in duration and in 12 movements, this choral cycle presents settings of a selection of poems from a large 1,200-poem collection, *Hesperides: Or the Works Both Human and Divine*, by English Restoration poet Robert Herrick (1591–1674). Born in London and educated as a cleric at Cambridge, Herrick was ordained in 1623 and appointed the Vicar of Dean Prior in Devonshire. He was deposed from this position by Cromwell during the English Civil War in 1648, which coincidentally was the publication year of this volume of poems, but in 1660 he successfully petitioned King Charles II, newly restored to the throne, to have his vicarage appointment returned to him.[14] The title of this volume of poetry is in direct reference to the three nymph-like daughters of

Hesperus in Greek mythology who tended his garden and guarded a tree that produced golden apples. Often referred to as "Daughters of the Evening" or "Sunset Goddesses," they apparently loved to sing, and came to be regarded especially in the Renaissance and post-Renaissance as symbols of earthly beauty and pleasure.[15]

This voluminous collection provides evidence of a cleric who, although never married, advocated a well-rounded appreciation for experiencing life at its fullest, both sensually and spiritually. Needless to say, Forsyth's choice of poems clearly favours the sensual and earthy side of Herrick's writing. In the opening song Forsyth sets Herrick's "The Argument of the Book":

I Sing of Brooks, of Blossomes, Birds and Bowers:
Of April, May, of June, and July-Flowers.
I write of Youth, of Love, and have Accesse
By these, to sing of cleanly-Wantonnesse
I sing of Times trans-shifting; and I write
How Roses first came Red, and Lillies White.
I write of hell; I sing (and ever shall)
Of Heaven, and hope to have it after all.

A sense of lyricism pervades this cycle, with melodic writing that is often playful, sometimes melancholic, but always full of invention. It features frequent pairings of women and men's voices in apparent dialogue, occasionally interspersed with full four-part writing, usually to draw home the point of a particular movement. Most notable is the role played by the harp duo in setting the mood for each movement, as well as in providing a commentary on many aspects of the text; one is reminded of the artful manner in which writers of German art song used the piano to heighten the emotive qualities and nuances of the texts they were setting.

By this time in his career Forsyth was a mature orchestrator and had a strong command of the capabilities of the instruments he was using; nevertheless, harpist Nora Bumanis relates how he frequently consulted with her on the possibilities of the instrument for special effects during the writing of this cycle. The result is a chamber music cycle that fully weaves harps and voices in the fabric of each movement.[16]

The first poem is set in a sprightly 6/8 metre, and features the harps playing simultaneously in C and E♭ major, with the chorus alternating in unison between SA and TB triadic lines, based on these two chords.

Before proceeding to the main themes implied in this opening verse, Forsyth chose a short poem, "(To His Book): Another," in which Herrick clearly references his anticipated critics, by referring to their "hinder parts...where swelling Piles do breed." It is set for bass solo, to be sung "with malevolence, half spoken," while the harps provide not only a highly dissonant low-range accompaniment and *sforzando* chords, but also use a grotesque-sounding pedal slide device at the very end for effect.

In the two songs that follow, Forsyth sets two of Herrick's poems devoted to the rose as a symbol of transitory beauty: "To the Virgins, to Make Much of Time (Gather ye rosebuds while ye may)" and "How Roses came red." In the first, the harps alternate between two dominant seventh chords (F♯7 and A7; D7 and F7; etc.) in what is essentially a waltz, accompanying unison singing by all four voice parts. By contrast, in "How Roses came red" (for SA alone), Forsyth adopts a more narrative approach in telling the story of how roses blushed when first being compared to the whiteness of Sappho's breasts.

This latter song, with its reference to Sappho, introduces one of the main themes in the cycle: the poet's fascination with various parts of the female body. The three songs and their main thematic focuses are "The Kisse: A Dialogue" (focusing on lips); "The shooe-tying" (on instep and knees); and "On Julia's Breath/Cherrie-Ripe/To Anthea/On Julie's Lips" (again, on the lips). The first of these, "The Kisse," also in a quick 6/8 metre, makes prominent use of dialogue between SA and TB voices, and only on the final line does the full chorus sing together for the first time on the text "Love, honie yields, but never stings." As if to highlight the irony of this line, Forsyth employs a full *sforzando* chord cluster in both harps. Love stings indeed.

"The shooe-tying," set for full-throated divisi male chorus, relates the male lover's excitable response to the woman's invitation to tie her shoes, only to be rebuked by her blushes. Here again, the harps use a special effect at the end, lightly stroking the strings with a "whistle-sound" to illustrate the blush.

The final setting in this three-song sequence is, as the title implies, actually a melded setting of four separate poems. In this movement Forsyth has incorporated an SSA trio arrangement of the well-known English setting, attributed to the composer Charles Edward Horn (1786–1849), of Herrick's poem "Cherrie-Ripe" that describes an attractive maiden selling cherries at market. The other poems are presented, alternating with Horn's melody, in quasi-recitative style by the remaining voices, as if to represent Julia's many suitors. Forsyth sets the final poem in the sequence in imitative style as a double canon closing with a brilliant homophonic phrase: "Sweet are my Julia's lips and cleane as if o'erwasht with Hippocrene." The harps' accompaniments to this movement highlight the qualities of playfulness suggested in the poetry, with use of arpeggios, glissandos, ostinatos and harmonics, to be played "Lightly" and "Dancingly."

In the two movements that follow, "How Violets came blew" and "Upon Julia's breasts," Forsyth utilizes the full chorus in five- to eight-part divisi. In the first, a somewhat subdued setting (in B♭ major), Love, represented by Venus, is jealous of the violets for offering a sweeter scent than she, so she beats the flowers until "Her blowes did make ye blew." As if to emphasize the violets' sadness at such treatment, Forsyth introduces some quasi-blues effects in the final chorus phrase. The second movement, brilliantly set in the key of C major, is introduced with rising *fortissimo* arpeggio figures in both harps, following which the chorus sings, in full voice, "Display thy breasts, Julia! There, let me behold that circummortal purity."

These latter two movements can be heard as a pivotal chorus moment in the cycle: they provide a natural progression from the three earlier settings relating to a woman's feet, knees, and lips, but they also mark the beginning of a distinct thematic shift from the more outwardly graphic elements of Herrick's poems to the more intimate, reflective, and ultimately melancholic mood portrayed in the next movement "To His Mistresses." Beginning in this movement, Herrick pleads, "Helpe me, now I call to my pretty Witchcrafts all, Old I am and cannot do that I was accustomed to." Forsyth emphasizes this shift by having the chorus sing in very low register, in the distant key of B♭ minor, accompanied by sombre low-register chords in the harps.

As if to conjure up as quickly as possible a return to the energies of youth, Forsyth sets the next text, "Bring your Majicks, Spels and Charmes to enflesh my thighs, and arms; is there no way to beget in my limbs their former heat?," in a quick scherzo in F major, with the harps becoming progressively more frenetic in their arpeggios, first in eighths and then in sixteenths. The ultimate goal, of course, is to find renewed strength "to pleasure you," and here his setting achieves some translucent and tender moments, finishing with a B♭ major chord, to be sung "almost whispered."

The final two movements of the cycle, "To Silvia to wed" and "On himself," complete the transformation from feelings of playfulness and outright lust to an actual quest for permanence ("Let us, though late, at last, my Silvia, wed and loving lie in one devoted bed") and, finally, to an almost philosophical acknowledgement that love and pleasure do in fact meet "in womankind." As if to confirm this acknowledgement, Forsyth gradually moves from setting the voices in imitative dialogue in each of these final two movements to strong homophonic statements. The final page features a sequence of phrases on the text "All pleasures meet in Womankind," alternating antiphonally between chorus and harps, that quickly move from the key of C major through E major, C♯ major, A major, F♯ major, E major again, and finally back to C major, the key with which the entire cycle began.

The *Hesperides* cycle is one of Forsyth's most successful works for chorus—musically interesting and entertaining both for singers and listeners. The vocal and musical challenges in a number of his previous works from this productive period are not as present here, and Forsyth's gift for expressive and imaginative portrayal of these delightful poems is more readily apparent and accessible to the average vocal musician.[17]

The last major opus in Forsyth's writing for chorus, *A Ballad of Canada*, was to occupy his energies over the last two years of his life.[18] In five movements and nearly 25 minutes in duration, this work can be seen as a drawing together of Forsyth's vision of the country he was to adopt and live in for over 40 years, his highly expressive orchestral and choral writing, and his reverence for the emotive power of poetic expression in the texts he set. *A Ballad* was premiered in June 2011 by the National Arts Centre Orchestra in Ottawa and a 200-voice chorus was assembled from several choirs in the Ottawa area and prepared by the National Arts Centre Orchestra chorus master Duain Wolfe, under the direction of Music Director Pinchas Zuckerman. This was the final premiere that Forsyth attended; he died only a month later. The ESO performances with the Richard Eaton Singers, conducted by ESO Music Director William Eddins, took place in November of that year.[19]

A Ballad of Canada can surely be ranked as one of Forsyth's most significant achievements as a composer. The commissioning orchestras represented not only a professional commitment but also an intensely personal one. First, his daughter, Amanda, served for many years as the National Arts Centre Orchestra's principal cellist and was married to Pinchas Zukerman; in Edmonton, Forsyth had a lengthy association with the ESO, as principal trombone and through a career-long record of commissions, premiere performances, and JUNO-winning recordings of his works by the ESO. *A Ballad of Canada* represents a pinnacle in Forsyth's compositional career in its highly evocative and idiomatic writing for the orchestra, Forsyth's true home base as a composer, and for the chorus.

NOTES

1. In addition to my own interactions with Forsyth, conductor Jon Washburn also commented on similar experiences with Forsyth in our personal communications (January 27, 2014).
2. Eitan Cornfield, "Forsyth Documentary," on *Canadian Composers Portraits: Malcolm Forsyth*, Centrediscs CMCCD 8802, 2002.
3. Larry Cook, personal communication, March 8, 2014.
4. Cornfield, "Forsyth Documentary."

5. See Roxane Prevost's study of this work in this volume.
6. These two settings, along with "In the Dying of Anything" (Brian Patten), remained in manuscript form until their collective publication as *Three Part-Songs* in 2004.
7. Dorothy Parker, *The Complete Poems of Dorothy Parker*. New York: Penguin Random House, 210. Used with permission.
8. Forsyth's source for his text is assumed to be Dante Gabriel Rossetti, Christina Rossetti, et al. *Poems: An Offering to Lancashire* (London: Victoria Press, 1863).
9. Malcolm Forsyth, *Annual Report*, University of Alberta, 1982–83, Forsyth archives, Taylor Family Digital Library, University of Calgary.
10. Brian Patten, *Love Poems*. Crows Nest, NSW, Australia: George Allen & Unwin, 1981. Used with permission.
11. Forsyth wrote a more extended setting of larger portions of this poem for solo soprano with piano in December 1983.
12. Both *Endymion's Dream* and *Three Love Poems of John Donne*, together with the earlier *The Sea* and *In the Dying of Anything*, are available on the CD *First Snow* produced by Pro Coro under the direction of Danish conductor Bo Holten in 1996 (Arktos 960014).
13. Inge Israel, *Unmarked Doors: Poems* (Vancouver: Cacanadadada Press, 1992).
14. "Robert Herrick (1591–1674)," Poetry Foundation, accessed January 7, 2016, http://www.poetryfoundation.org/bio/robert-herrick.
15. Pierre Grimal, *The Dictionary of Classical Mythology* (Hoboken, NJ: Wiley-Blackwell, 1986), 213.
16. Nora Bumanis, personal communication, January 29, 2014.
17. A CD recording of the cycle *Hesperides* is featured on a University of Alberta Madrigal Singers recording, *Hesperides: Works by Forsyth, Fauré, Holst, Pärt and Others*, featuring the Paragon Harp Duo with myself conducting, UAMS 200905, 2009.
18. See also Mary Ingraham's study of *A Ballad of Canada* in this volume.
19. Forsyth consulted frequently with me and with the chorus master of the Ottawa performance, Duain Wolfe, to ensure that his choral writing effectively combined his vision for these highly descriptive and intensely personal poems with effective and idiomatic vocal writing that matched the brilliance of his orchestral scoring.

Postlude

VALERIE FORSYTH

THE DAY I MET my late husband, Malcolm Forsyth, was the day that my life changed forever.

He stood there resplendent in his white tie and tails exuding the most extraordinary energy I had ever experienced. Malcolm was a large man but also had a "larger than life" presence.

What followed were 12 of the best years of my life.

Malcolm was a brilliant, artistic, well read, well travelled, accomplished, driven, funny, witty, articulate, and complex man. He could also be impossibly maddening and irritating. A paradoxical personality, he was a walking "contradiction in terms." Pompous at times, he could put people off, but Malcolm also had great insecurities and vulnerabilities. Hesitant to show his softer side, he carefully cultivated an aloof, sometimes harsh exterior. Argumentative to the extreme, he loved a good debate but, if taken too far, he would eventually get agitated and accuse one of exhibiting "hubris." As many of his students, colleagues, friends, and family could attest, he was not one to back down easily. Verbose and stubborn at times, he could also be easygoing and flexible.

His love (bordering on obsession) of language and grammar was, at once, fascinating and illuminating for those within earshot, but at the same time it could quickly become tedious and exhausting. Malcolm had a dry, razor-sharp wit, a razor-sharp mind, and sometimes a razor-sharp tongue. For those of us privileged enough to know him intimately, the good far and away outweighed the "bad" and we knew that each hour spent with him was a gift.

A teacher at his core, Malcolm was famous (infamous?) for correcting, chastising, and pointing out imperfections. What many people didn't realize was that he was the very hardest on himself—holding himself to very lofty standards—and he therefore held everyone else to the same. Malcolm was constantly striving and had an inquisitiveness and thirst for learning that I've yet to see in anyone else.

Then there was (is) Malcolm the Musician. Of course, music was his world and is his legacy. As varied and eclectic as his musical tastes and interests were, it was composing and performing that brought him as close to feeling "blissful" as was possible for Malcolm. It made him feel whole. The intention was always to make an indelible mark on his audience and change how they experienced the world. Feeling that this was possible gave him the utmost drive and incredible joy when he felt he had achieved his goal. Forever grateful for his gift, Malcolm never took it for granted. Always researching, questioning, and experimenting, he strove to make the most out of each day of each musical project.

Being with Malcolm wasn't always easy, but it was always worth the effort. My eyes and my world opened up and expanded exponentially the years following my fortuitous meeting of Malcolm Denis Forsyth. I am a much more questioning, broader-minded person because of my late husband, and I am honoured to carry his name.

I miss everything about him but most especially his laugh and how he made me laugh every day...the world is not quite as colourful a place without Malcolm. Thankfully, his music and his memory live on in our minds and in our hearts.

List of Works

This catalogue was compiled by Jean-Marie Barker, owner of Counterpoint Music Library Services Inc., publisher of Forsyth's works.

Orchestra

Overture "Erewhon" (1962) (withdrawn)

Jubilee Overture (1963, revised 1971)

Essay for Orchestra '67 (1967)

Symphony No. 1 (1968–72)

Sketches from Natal (1970)

Symphony No. 2 "*...a host of nomads...*" (1976)

African Ode (Symphony No. 3) (1981)

Images of Night (1981–82)

ukuZalwa (1983)

Atayoskewin: Suite for Orchestra (1984)

Springtide (1984)

Valley of a Thousand Hills (1989)

Natal Landscapes (1993)

Siyajabula! We Rejoice! (1996)

Morning's Minion (2000)

Requiem for the Victims in a Wartorn World at the Millenium (2002)

Orchestra with One or More Instrumental Soloists

Concerto for Pianoforte and Orchestra (1973–79)

Sagittarius (Concerto Grosso No. 1) (1975)

Quinquefid (Concerto Grosso No. 2) (1976–77)
The Salpinx (Concerto Grosso No. 3) (1981)
Concerto for Trumpet and Orchestra (1987)
These Cloud-Capp'd Towers: Concerto for Trombone and Orchestra (1990)
Tre Vie: Concerto for Saxophone and Orchestra (1992)
Electra Rising: Concerto for Violoncello and Orchestra (1995)
Andante from Sagittarius for Harp Duo and Strings (1999)
Concerto for Accordion and Orchestra (1999)
Double Concerto for Viola and Violoncello (2004, rev. 2008)
Ripsnorter Finale (from *Eclectic Suite*, aka *Pop's Cycle*) (2004)
Trickster Coyote-Lightning Elk for Violin and Orchestra (2006)

Vocal Solo with Orchestra

Three Métis Songs from Saskatchewan (1976) for solo low or high voice (melodies and texts collected by Barbara Cass-Beggs). I. Chanson du petit cordonnier (anon.); II. Adieu de la mariée (anon.); III. Chanson de la Grenouillère (Pierre Falcon)
Canzona for Voice and Orchestra (1985) for solo high or low voice
Sun Songs (1985) for solo high or low voice (text: Doris Lessing) I. Conchita, Conchita!; II. The Sun's Out!; III. Jupiter's Daughter
Evangeline (1993): A cantata for soprano voice, trumpet(=flugelhorn, natural trumpet) (text: Henry Longfellow)
Five Songs from Atlantic Canada (1989) for solo vocal duo, high and low voices. I. The False Knight on the Road (anon); II. Beau ciel (anon.); III. I Went to the Market (anon.); IV. Let Me Fish off Cape St. Mary's (Otto P. Kelland); V. Le grain de mil (anon.)

Chamber Music for Strings or String Orchestra

Eight Duets for Young Cellists (1974/2002) versions for 2 celli, or 2 violins/violas, or 2 doublebasses, or violin and viola. 1. Pitter, Patter, Mouse in Batter; 2. You & me; 3. The Mystery of a Cave; 4. The Funny-bone; 5. Two Giraffes; 6. The Sad Clown with a Happy Face; 7. Ambling Along; 8. Hop, step, skip
Pastiche (1981) for viola d'amore solo
Rhapsody for 14 Strings (1982)
Serenade for Strings (1985–86) for 12 solo strings
Little Suite for Strings (1988) for string orchestra, or quintet
Eclogue (1997) for solo cello

Chamber Music for Woodwinds

The Melancholy Clown (1962, rev. 1967). fl.cl.bsn. or 3 cl. (E♭, B♭, bass)
Le Scare du Printemps, or THE FRIGHT OF SPRING! (1983) for bassoon solo

Chamber Music for Mixed Instrumentation

Pastorale and Rondo for 4 Winds and Piano (1968–69). fl.cl.bsn.hn.pno.

Well-Meaning Recorder, or Tunes for Tootling (1976) for 4 recorders

Intimacies (1977). fl.vla.gtr. or fl.vla.hp.

Dark (1978) for tenor recorder solo, with electronics. Staged with solo dancer.

Mirrors (1978) for horn and marimba

Steps... (1978) for viola and piano

Fanfare & Three Masquerades (1979). Horn solo and 2 fl.2 ob.2 cl(II=bcl).2 bsn.hn., or horn and piano

Six Episodes after Keats (1979–80). vln.vlc.pno. I. A drowsy numbness pains my sense; II. I cannot see what flowers are at my feet; III. Lethewards had sunk; IV. No hungry generations tread thee down; V. Immortal bird; VI. Fled is that music

Suite for Haydn's Band (1980). 2 ob.2 hn.2 bsn.

Burlesque (1981). for cello and piano

Dreams, Drones and Drolleries (1981) for horn and piano

Quintette for Winds (or...) everythynge ye ever wanted to knowe about Essex (1986). fl(=picc).ob.cl(=E♭, B♭, A).hn.bsn.

Toccata (1986). 2 tpt.hn.tbn.btbn(or tba).org.

Caroline's Tune (1987) for clarinet and piano

The Swan Sees His Reflection (1987/2002) for cello and piano or vlc.hp.

Eclectic Suite (revised 1988), aka *Pop's Cycle* (1984) for cello and piano. I. Potpourri; II. Song of Light; III. Ripsnorter Finale

Rondo in Stride (1988) for cello and piano

Soliloquy, Epitaph and Allegro (1988) for trombone and organ

Andante from Sagittarius (formerly *Mexocello*) (1990) for cello and piano

The Kora Dances (1990) for 2 harps

The Tempest: Duets and Choruses (1990) for oboe and string quartet, or quintet. Duet I: Ariel; Chorus I: The Isle; Duet II: Caliban; Chorus II: Prospero; Chorus III: Miranda; Duet III: We are such stuff as dreams...

Breaking Through (1991) for alto saxophone and piano

Little Traveller before the Dawn (1991). fl.(or vln).vlc.pno.

Métis Songs from the Qu'Appelle Valley (1991). An arrangement of *Three Métis Songs from Saskatchewan* for soprano, cornet(=flhn), celtic harp, bodhran (celtic drum), org. I. Chanson du petit cordonnier (anon.); II. Adieu de la mariée (anon.); III. Chanson de la Grenouillère (Pierre Falcon)

Sonata for Trumpet & Piano (1995) for trumpet and piano or synthesizer

umGcomo (1999). 2 pno.2 perc.

Phantom Sketches (2000). cl.marimba.vln.

Concerto for Eight (2002–03). cl.hn.bsn.2 vln.vla.vlc.cb.

In Perfect Harmony (2004). vla.vlc.pno.

Lyric Essay (2007). ob.bsn.pno.

Andante from Sagittarius—arrangement (2009). 2 hns.pno.

Bis for Brahms (2011) for violin and cello

Concert Band and Brass Band

Colour Wheel (1978) for wind band

Songs from the Qu'Appelle Valley (1987) for brass band

Flourish of Welcome (1989) for 6 herald trumpets (or B♭ trumpets) with concert band

Kaleidoscope (1989) for wind band

The Oh Canada Thing, or, A Dominion's Dilemma (1992) for wind band

Tre Vie: Concerto for Alto Saxophone & Concert Band (1999)

Rondino & Tiddly Pom (2008) for solo soprano cornet and tenor horn, brass band

Brass Ensemble/Solo

Quartet '61 (1961). 4 tbns. (or 4 bsn. or 4 hn.)

Poem for Brass (1964–66). Version A: 1st choir: 3 tpt.4 tbn.; 2nd choir: 3 hn.euph.tba. Version B: 2 tpt.4 hn.3 tbn.tba. (1975)

Bachianas Capensis (1966). 3 tbn.

Aphorisms for Brass (1969–71). 2 tpt.hn.tbn.tba(or btbn.)

Five Fanfares (1970–78). 4 tpt.hn.atbn.tbn. I. Fanfare for Rodin (tpt.hn.tbn.); II. Flourish for the Humanities (4 tpt.); III. Gloria's Ta-raa (tpt.hn.tbn.); IV. Duet for François (atbn.tbn.); V. Ho-yo to Hoyt! (2tpt.atbn.)

The Golyardes' Grounde (1972). 2 tpt.hn.tbn.tba(or btbn.)

Triangles (1972). Now only available in Four Pieces for Brass Quintet. 2 tpt.hn.tbn.tba(or btbn.)

Quartet '74 (1974). 4 tbns.

Exploration Fanfare (1978). 4 tpt.4 hn.3 tbn.2 tba.

Four Dice = 40 (1979) for trumpet solo

Four Pieces for Brass Quintet (assembled 1979). 2 tpt.hn.tbn.tba(or btbn.) I. Intrada Olimpiada; II. Riverspirit; III. Renaissance Dance; IV. Triangles

Saltarello (assembled 1979). 2 tpt.hn.tbn.tba(or btbn.)

Two Gentil Knyghtes (1979). btbn.tba. I. Tucket; II. Sir Jeffrey, His Jest; III. L'après-midi d'un hippo; IV. Sir Roger, His Ricercar

Solemn Intrada (1980). 8 tbn.: 2 S.2 A.2 T.2 B. or 2 tpt.2 hn.2 tbn.2 tba.

Eclectic Altos with Pokerbass (1981). 3 atbn.G-btbn.

Miniatures for Brass Quartet (1982). 2 tpt.2 tbn.

Novum Spatium (1985). 4 tpt.4 hn.4 tbn.

Pfeifferfanfar für Pfeiffers (1985). 2 tpt.hn.tbn.tba(or btbn.)

Farinelli's Folly (1986, rev. 1988). 2tpt.hn.tbn.tba.

Zephyrus (1989). 2 flhn.hn.tbn.tba.

El Brazz! (Fanfare) (1993). tpt.hn.tbn.
Sonic Mobile for Trombone Choir (2003). 4 tbn.
Arcadian Panoply (2007). solo trombone and 3 tbn.btbn.
Gallimaufry (2010) for brass quintet

Choral

Music for Mouths, Marimba, Mbira and Roto-Toms (1973) for SATB (no text) and 1 percussion (marimba, mbira, roto-toms)
Three Part-Songs (1980–83) for SATB a cappella. I. The Sea (Dorothy Parker), SSAA; II. Sudden Light (Dante G. Rossetti), SATB; III. In the Dying of Anything (Brian Patten), SATB
Three Zulu Songs (text: Benedict W. Vilakazi) (1988) for SSA, fl.ob.handdrum. I. We moya! (Hail Wind!); II. Inyanga (The Moon); III. kwaDedangendhlale (Valley of a Thousand Hills)
Endymion's Dream (text: John Keats) (1993) for mixed choir (SATB) a cappella
Three Love Poems of John Donne (1994–95) for SATB a cappella. I. The Sunne Rising; II. Song; III. Holy Sonnet XVII
Northern Journey (text: Inge Israel) (1998) for women's choir (SSAA) I. Auyuittuq; II. Kluane Glaciers; III. Winter Sky
Blow!, Bugle, Blow! (text: Tennyson) (2000) for mixed choir (SATB) and brass (3 tpt.4 hn.3 tbn.tba.)
Glasnost (text: Inge Israel) (2000) for mixed choir (SSATB) and tape
Snug the Joiner as Lion Fell (text: Shakespeare, J. Lampe) (2000). A Musical Jest for Male Choir (TTBrB) a cappella
Hesperides (text: Robert Herrick) (2001) for mixed choir and 2 harps
Nursery Rhymes (text: Carl Hare) (2008–09) for unison children's chorus and piano
A Ballad of Canada (text: E.J. Pratt, Ralph Gustafson, Carl Hare, John McCrae) (2010) for mixed choir and orchestra. I. In the Yukon; II. In Flanders Fields; III. The Toll of the Bells; IV. On the Waverley Road Bridge; V. Newfoundland

Vocal

Wind and Rain (text: Anthony Delius) (1966) for low voice and piano
Three Métis Songs from Saskatchewan (1975) (melodies and texts collected by Barbara Cass-Beggs) for low voice, piano; mid-voice, piano. Also with orchestra accompaniment.
The Dong with a Luminous Nose (text: Edward Lear) (1979) for low voice, viola, piano
In the Dying of Anything (text: Brian Patten) (1983) for high voice and piano
Five Songs from Atlantic Canada (1989) for solo vocal duo (high and low voices) and piano. Also with orchestra accompaniment. I. The False Knight on the Road (anon.); II. Beau ciel (anon.); III. I Went to the Market (anon.); IV. Let Me Fish off Cape St. Mary's (Otto P. Kelland); V. Le grain de mil (anon.)
Incantation (anon., trad.) (1990) for solo voice (any type) and piano

Lines to Fanny Brawne (text: John Keats) (1991) for high voice and piano

Songs in Time of Crisis (2000) for baritone and cl.vlc.pno. I. The Orange Branch (Tennessee Williams); II. Lorelei (Sylvia Plath); III. Do Not Go Gentle into That Good Night (Dylan Thomas)

La Belle Dame sans merci (text: John Keats) (2006) for high voice and piano

Solo Piano

Strange Spaces (1978)

Tre Toccate per Pianoforte (1987)

Je répondrais... (1997) I. à Purcell: Fantazia upon One Note; II. à Schumann: Thumb-Piano; III. à Chopin: White-Key Study in African Mode

Preludio e Fuga/Glenn Gould (2007)

Arrangements: Orchestra

Orchestrations marked with an asterisk (*) were all commissioned by the South African Broadcasting Corporation, and are in the SABC Music Library, Johannesburg, South Africa.

March, Op. 12 (Prokofiev) (1967)

Dis Al * (S. le Roux Marais) (1967). hn.ob.hp.str.

Heimwee * (S. le Roux Marais) (1967)

Matrooslied * (S. le Roux Marais) (1967)

'n Simpel Liedjie * (Sidney Richfield) (1967)

Roseknoppies * (S. le Roux Marais) (1967)

O Canada (C. Lavallée) (1996)

Arrangements: Brass Ensemble

Dances from "Terpsichore" (Praetorius) (1963). 2 tpt.hn.euph.tbn.

Galliard, "Agatha" (Widmann) (1965). 3 tbn.

Magnificat Secundi Toni (Binchois) (1965). 3 tbn.

Chorus of Reapers "Eugene Onegin" (Tchaikovsky) (1969). 4 tbn.

Slavonic Dance No. 8 in G minor (Dvořák) (1969). 4 tbn.

Mazurka No. 47, excerpt (Chopin) (1970). 4 tbn.

"Norwegian Dance" from Lyric Pieces (Grieg) (1970). 4 tbn.

Song without Words in C, Op. 30, No. 3 (Mendelssohn) (1970). 3 tbn.

El Cumbanchero (Rafael Hemandez) (1976). 4 tbn.

Song without Words in B♭, Op. 62, No. 4 (Mendelssohn) (1977). 4 tbn.

Finlandia, Op. 26, No. 7 (Sibelius) (1979). Quintet (2 tpt.hn.tbn.tba.) and brass choir (6.4.4.2./tp.perc.)

Funérailles (Liszt) (1979). Quintet (2 tpt.hn.tbn.tba) and brass choir (4 tpt.6 hn.4 tbn.2 tba. (+optional tp. and perc.))

Slavonic Dance, Op. 46, No. 8 (Dvořák) (1979). Quintet (2 tpt.hn.tbn.tba.) and brass choir (4.4.4.1. (+optional tp. and 2 perc.))

Take Five (Desmond) (1982). 4 tbn.

Musical Priest (trad.) (2008) for brass band

Cantique de Noël (Adam) (2009) for brass band

I Want a Hippopotamus for Christmas (John Rox) (original 1953, arr. 2009) for brass band

Nocturne No. 16, Op. 55, No. 2 (Chopin) (2009) for brass band

All the things you are (Jerome Kern) (date unknown, ca. 1980s) for trombone quartet

Arrangements: Brass Quintet

2 tpt.hn.tbn.tba except where otherwise noted.

Prelude and Fugue in B♭ minor (Bach, WTC I/22) (1970)

Suite of Dances from "Terpsichore" (Praetorius) (1970) I. Entrée; II. Courante; III. Ballet; IV. La bourrée

Chôros No. 1, Typico (Villa-Lobos) (1971)

Suite de Symphonies I. Fanfares (Jean-Joseph Mouret) (1978). hn.2 tpt.tmb.btbn.

Arrangements: Brass and Woodwinds

Sarabande from *Suite pour le piano* (Debussy) (1965). 3 cl. in A.2 bsn.2 hn. in F.tba (and/or cbsn.)

Interludium from *Ludus Tonalis* (Hindemith) (1965). 2 cl.2 bsn.2 tbn.2 tpt.

Arrangements: Vocal

Two Songs, Op. 72, No. 3, Op. 43, No. 2 (Brahms) (2004) for mezzo-soprano and chamber orchestra

Stage and Film

Visage du Ballet (1965) (withdrawn)

The Last Chance (1974). Film score. 1 cl.3 tbn.1 perc./3 vlc.

Saltarello (1977). One-act ballet (scenario: Jeremy Leslie-Spinks). 3 brass quintets (one live, choreographed; two pre-recorded)

Music for Redford's "Wit and Science" (1982). Solo or unison voices, fl.vlc.gtr. or voice(s), recorder, gamba, lute. I. When travelles grete; II. Exceding mesure; III. O Lady deere; IV. March, Calypso & Galliard

Six Olympic Fanfares (1988) for orchestra, church bells, etc. I. Fanfare of Welcome; II. Fanfare of the Flags; III. Fanfare Greco; IV. Flag Fanfare; V. Fanfare of the Flame; VI. Fanfare for the Oaths

Breaking Joan (2000). Film score. Released by Riverside Film. First shown at Alberta Film Festival, 2002.

Early Works

Original manuscripts of these early works are held at the University of Cape Town, South Africa.

Impromptu (date unknown) for piano
Adagio (1961) for clarinet and piano
Tollites Portas (1961): motet for mixed choir
Oh Aching Heart (text: Hugo Wolf) (1962). Song for baritone voice.

Contributors

TOMMY BANKS (1936–2018), OC, AOE, a multi-talented and beloved colleague and artist, was a fixture of the Edmonton and Canadian cultural scenes for over 60 years. A renowned pianist, composer and improvisor, actor and politician, he served 12 years on the Canadian Senate as a member of the federal Liberals. Banks's legacy in Canadian cultural politics continue to resonate, but for many Canadians it is his musical practice as a band leader and pianist, TV personality, and participant at international and local musical celebrations that remains their most treasured memory of his life work.

ALLAN GORDON BELL is a composer who has created works for solo instruments, chamber ensembles, orchestra, band, and electroacoustic media as well as an opera. His music has been performed by soloists, ensembles, and orchestras throughout North America, Europe, and Asia. He is Professor of Music at the University of Calgary, an Associate Composer and Past-President of the Canadian Music Centre, a Fellow of the Royal Society of Canada, and a Member of the Order of Canada. He is the recipient of the 2014 JUNO Award for Best Classical Composition for *Field Notes.*

NORA BUMANIS & JULIA SHAW began their collaboration as Canada's first professional harp duo in 1988 when they were the principal harpists of the Edmonton Symphony and the Calgary Philharmonic Orchestras, respectively. Since that time, they have been heard frequently in recital and with symphony orchestras and choral groups across the country, as well as on CBC Radio and Television. They have recorded four CDS on the CBC Records label.

ROBIN ELLIOTT was appointed to the Jean A. Chalmers Chair in Canadian Music in the Faculty of Music at the University of Toronto in 2002. The main focus of his scholarly work is composed Canadian music; he has produced a dozen books and editions of music (as author or editor), and 100 articles of varying length. He co-edited (with John Beckwith) a selection of writings by the late Helmut Kallmann for Wilfrid Laurier University Press in 2013. He is a Senior Fellow at Massey College in the University of Toronto and the historian of the Women's Musical Club of Toronto.

AMANDA FORSYTH, a JUNO Award winner, is considered one of North America's most dynamic cellists. She achieved an international reputation as soloist, chamber musician, and principal cellist of Canada's National Arts Centre Orchestra from 1999 to 2015. Her intense richness of tone, remarkable technique, and exceptional musicality combine to enthrall audiences and critics alike. She has performed on international tours with the Royal Philharmonic and Israel Philharmonic Orchestras and appeared around the world with orchestras and in recital. She made her Carnegie Hall debut in 2014 with the Israel Philharmonic Orchestra. Born in South Africa and the daughter of Malcolm Forsyth, Amanda moved to Canada as a child and began playing cello at age three. She became a protégé of William Pleeth in London, and later studied with Harvey Shapiro at the Juilliard School.

VALERIE FORSYTH is the second of four daughters born to Harold and Audrey Simons, of Edmonton, Alberta. As a second-generation western Canadian of Prairie homesteaders, Valerie proceeded along the (mostly) typical pathways through high school, as cheerleader, baton twirler, and Beatles devotee. Valerie began her family at twenty-three and raised her two sons in her hometown of Edmonton. She is a proud grandmother to two grandsons, and two granddaughters. Though she did not pursue her musical training beyond the first attempts at "Blue Danube," Valerie always appreciated and recognized the muse in others. Malcolm was the spark that ignited and mirrored her passion for music and indeed, life itself.

ALLAN GILLILAND has a distinguished career as a composer, educator, and administrator. His music has been performed by some of the finest ensembles and soloists in the world and appears on over 20 CDs. He is currently the Dean of Fine Arts and Communications at MacEwan University where he has also been Head of Composition and Chair of Music.

CARL HARE has been a professor, actor, director, playwright, and poet. He founded the University of Victoria's Theatre Department, was the Artistic Director of Company One Theatre, taught at the National Theatre School in Montreal, and was Chair of the Drama Department at the University of Alberta. He has served on the Board of the Dominion Drama Festival, and was a BC member of the Canadian Conference of the

Arts and one of the founders of the National Screen Institute – Canada. In 2012 he won the Sterling Award for Outstanding Contribution to Theatre in Edmonton.

MARY I. INGRAHAM is Professor of Musicology and Dean of Fine Arts at the University of Lethbridge. She is an interdisciplinary teacher and researcher whose interests are historical and contemporary, critical, and pedagogical. Ingraham's work resonates within the fields of cultural studies, and includes critical approaches to coloniality, the politics of culture, identity studies, and discourse analysis that consider issues of ethnicity, race, gender, and spirituality. Recent activities include consideration of Indigenous resurgence in inter-arts collaborations.

EDWARD JURKOWSKI is currently Dean of the Desautels Faculty of Music at the University of Manitoba. His primary research interests include the study of compositional designs in twentieth-century music and the music of Scandinavia (in particular, Finland). He is the author of several books and articles on these topics and has presented his research at many venues throughout Canada, the United States, and Europe.

RYAN MCCLELLAND is Professor of Music Theory at the University of Toronto and also serves as Associate Dean, Academic and Student Affairs in the Faculty of Music. His research interests include rhythmic-metric theory, Schenkerian analysis, and performance studies. He has published on these subjects in several journals and in essay collections devoted to Brahms and to Schubert. McClelland's first book, *Brahms and the Scherzo*, was published in 2010, and with David Beach, he co-authored a textbook, *Analysis of 18th- and 19th-Century Musical Works in the Classical Tradition*, which appeared in 2012.

JOHN MCPHERSON has been Principal Trombone of the Edmonton Symphony Orchestra since Malcolm Forsyth retired from that position in 1980. The ESO has also engaged him as a soloist, arranger, and composer-in-residence. McPherson taught at the University of Alberta Department of Music and his compositions have been performed and broadcast all over Canada.

FORDYCE C. (DUKE) PIER came to the University of Alberta in 1973, where he taught trumpet and conducted wind ensembles, and eventually became Chair of the Department of Music. He continued to perform as a trumpeter, often sitting right next to his friend, Malcolm Forsyth.

ROXANE PREVOST is Associate Professor of Music Theory at the University of Ottawa. Her research interests include the analysis of post-tonal music, in particular the music of Canadian women composers. Her recent work focuses on the analysis of rhythmic structures in select post-tonal works, more precisely grouping structures rooted in tonal music. She is also interested in issues of music theory pedagogy.

KATHY PRIMOS is a retired Professor of Music at Wits University in South Africa. She lectured in history of music, while music education and musicology were her areas of research, including pioneering musicological research on Malcolm Forsyth and his compositions. Her contextual approaches to her history of music teaching met the changes in cultural demography and diversity of South African students' musical interests and needs. She was founding Director of the Travelling Institute for Music Research in South Africa (2000–2002) and served on many national committees, including the SA Musicological Society, SA Society for Music Education, and the SA Music Teachers Society.

TANYA PROCHAZKA (1952–2015) was a celebrated cellist, performing with major orchestras around the world. In 1986 she became Professor of Cello at the University of Alberta and Conductor of the University of Alberta Symphony and Academy Strings Orchestras. Highlights of her career include recitals for the ABC, BBC, and CBC, recitals in Carnegie Hall and in St. Petersburg, Russia, and world premieres of concertos by Alfred Fisher and Malcolm Forsyth with the Kingston and Edmonton Symphony Orchestras. In 2009 Prochazka was inducted into the Cultural Hall of Fame of the City of Edmonton, Alberta.

LEONARD RATZLAFF has been Professor of Choral Music at University of Alberta since 1981. His duties include supervising the Department of Music's graduate programs in choral conducting and directing the Madrigal Singers. He is also Artistic Director of the Richard Eaton Singers, Edmonton's symphonic chorus. Ratzlaff's research interests span the entire gamut of choral music, but his focus on Canadian music has resulted in premieres of works by Archer, Bevan, Estacio, Fisher, Forsyth, Hatzis, Krapf, Henderson, Martin, Raminsh, Rolfe, and Sirett. Honours include induction into the Alberta Order of Excellence, Order of Canada, and Royal Society of Canada, as well as the Distinguished Service Award from Choral Canada.

RAYFIELD RIDEOUT has spent most of his working life at CBC Radio as program host, news reporter, producer, and executive producer, and staff trainer. In his twenties, he was a high school teacher for four years. Rideout learned basic woodworking from his father and honed his skills by watching *This Old House* on television. It is fair to say that Malcolm learned most of his woodworking skills from Ray. The two of them often went tool shopping together and collaborated on dozens of projects.

ROBERT C. RIVAL was the Edmonton Symphony Orchestra's composer-in-residence from 2011 to 2014. Critics have described his work, written in a contemporary tonal style and inspired by the Canadian wilderness, literature, and classical and romantic musical forms, as "stirring and dramatic," "spectacular," "clever and evocative," "well crafted," "immediately appealing," "melodic and accessible," "memorable," and "sophisticated." His music for orchestra, chamber ensemble, and voice has been performed widely at home and abroad, including at Carnegie Hall, by leading orchestras, musicians, ensembles, and choirs. Also active as a writer on music, his scholarly publications include articles on Shostakovich and Nielsen. Rival has been teaching theory and composition at the University of Ottawa since 2016.

DALE SORENSEN is a passionate promoter of Canadian music who has premiered dozens of solo trombone works and chamber works, and recorded an all-Canadian CD of music for trombone. His doctoral dissertation (University of Toronto) was an annotated bibliography of Canadian solo trombone recital repertoire. As an orchestral musician, Sorensen performs regularly with Symphony Nova Scotia, the PEI Symphony Orchestra, and the Charlottetown Festival Orchestra, and has freelanced throughout Ontario and from St. John's to Winnipeg. Currently Assistant Professor of Brass at the University of Prince Edward Island, he has also taught at Dalhousie University, Mount Allison University, Memorial University of Newfoundland, and the University of Toronto.

CHRISTOPHER TAYLOR, a native of Edmonton, is a graduate of the University of Alberta where he studied bass trombone with former Edmonton Symphony Orchestra trombonist Malcolm Forsyth and later furthered his education in Los Angeles and Chicago. He has been a member of the ESO since 1975. Taylor was a founding member of the Malcolm Forsyth Trombone Ensemble and was involved with many premieres of brass and orchestral works by Forsyth. From 1981 to 2017, he held the position of Instructor of Bass Trombone in the Music Department of the University of Alberta.

Permissions

"In the Dying of Anything" from *Love Poems* by Brian Patten. Published by George Allen & Unwin, 1981. Copyright © Brian Patten. Reproduced by permission of the author c/o Rogers, Coleridge & White Ltd., 20 Powis Mews, London W11 1JN.

"In the Yukon" from *Selected Poems* by Ralph Gustafson is used by permission of Véhicule Press.

"The Sea" from THE COMPLETE POEMS OF DOROTHY PARKER by Dorothy Parker, copyright © 1999 by The National Association for the Advancement of Colored People. Used by permission of Penguin Books, an imprint of Penguin Publishing Group, a division of Penguin Random House LLC. All rights reserved.

Index

A drowsy numbness pains my sense. See *Six Episodes after Keats*

Adagio (1961), 240

Adam, Adolphe. See *Cantique de Noël*

Adieu de la mariée à ses parents. See *Métis Songs from the Qu'Appelle Valley*; *Seven Métis Songs of Saskatchewan*; *Three Métis Songs from Saskatchewan*

African musical influences, 2, 10, 11, 109–110, 123, 126, 187–189, 193, 202, 209, 216, 218

African Ode (Symphony No. 3) (1981), 16, 187–188, 193, 233

Alberta Chamber Players, 186

All the things you are (arrangement of Kern, ca. 1980s), 239

Also Sprach Zarathustra. See *Farinelli's Folly*

Andante from Sagittarius (formerly *Mexocello*) (1990), 235

Andante from Sagittarius—arrangement (2009), 236

Andante from Sagittarius for Harp Duo and Strings (1999), 234

apartheid, opposition to, xvii, 4, 11–12

Aphorisms for Brass (1969–71), 172, 200, 211, 236

Arcadian Panoply (2007), 209–210, 237

Archer, Violet, 10

Armenian, Raffi, 212

artistic credo, 9

Atayoskewin: Suite for Orchestra (1984), 6, 8–9, 12–14, 20, 81–82, 132, 166, 184, 187, 189–190, 192, 196, 221, 233

- harmonic resources, 82–83
- motivic unity, 82–83

Auyuittuq. See *Northern Journey*

Bach, Johann Sebastian. See Prelude and Fugue in B♭ minor

Bachianas Capensis (1966), 198, 236

- versions, 198

Ballad of Canada, A (2010), xv, xx, 5, 7, 21, 129–168, 155, 196, 216–217, 229, 230, 237
Canadian influences, 129
compositional style, 131–132, 135, 139
In Flanders Fields: analysis, 141–145
In Flanders Fields: musical structure, 141–144
In Flanders Fields: textual structure, 141
In the Yukon: analysis, 136–140, 166
In the Yukon: musical structure, 138–139
In the Yukon: textual structure, 136–138, 155
leitmotif, Northern Lights, 132, 134, 138–139, 159–161
Newfoundland: analysis, 154–161, 168
Newfoundland: musical structure, 159–160
Newfoundland: textual structure, 154–155, 158
On the Waverly Road Bridge: analysis, 150–154, 165, 167
On the Waverly Road Bridge: musical structure, 152, 154
overview, 130
poetic intent, 135
premiere, 129, 165, 229
summary of analysis, 161, 164
Toll of the Bells, The: analysis, 146–150, 167
Toll of the Bells, The: musical structure, 147, 149
Toll of the Bells, The: textual structure, 147, 154–155
vision, 130
Banff Centre, 201, 205
Banff Summer Festival of the Arts, 211
Banks, Tommy, 172, 241
Bartle, Jean Ashworth, 221
Bartók, Béla. See *Concerto for Orchestra*
Beau ciel. See *Five Songs from Atlantic Canada*
Bell, Allan Gordon, 10, 13, 241
Bernardi, Mario, 75, 85, 196, 201, 211, 221
Bernius, Frieder, 222
Binchois, Gilles de. See *Magnificat Secundi Toni*
Bis for Brahms (2011), 15, 236
Bläser Ensemble Mainz, 204
Blow! Bugle, Blow! (2000), 209–210, 216, 223, 237
premiere, 210, 223
Brahms, Johannes. See *Farinelli's Folly*; Two Songs, Op. 72, No. 3, Op. 43, No. 2
brass music overview, 197
Braun, Connie, 14
Breaking Joan (2000), 239
Breaking Through (1991), 235
Bring your Majicks, Spels and Charmes. See *Hesperides*
Bryant, Stephen, 23
Bryant, Sue Jane, 23
Budapest Brass Quintet, 211
Bumanis, Nora, 174, 225, 230, 241
Burlesque (1981), 235

Calgary Philharmonic Orchestra, 85, 196
Canadian Brass, 184, 191–192, 200–201, 211
Canadian Chamber Ensemble, 15, 212
Canadian Chamber Orchestra, 201
Canadian influences, 132, 164, 189
Canadian Music Centre, 7, 12–13, 15, 23, 48, 75, 211
Cantata Singers of Ottawa, 165
Cantilena Consort, 223

Cantique de Noël (arrangement of Adam, 2009), 239
Canzona for Voice and Orchestra (1985), 184, 221, 234
Cape Town Symphony, 4, 178, 184, 186
Caroline's Tune (1987), 235
Cass-Beggs, Barbara, xx, 49–53, 55–59, 62, 66–67, 70, 73, 75–77
See also *Seven Métis Songs of Saskatchewan*; *Three Métis Folk Songs from Saskatchewan*
CBC Vancouver Orchestra, 15, 49, 75, 85, 221
Chanson de la Grenouillère. See *Métis Songs from the Qu'Appelle Valley*; *Seven Métis Songs of Saskatchewan*; *Three Métis Songs from Saskatchewan*
Chanson du petit cordonnier. See *Métis Songs from the Qu'Appelle Valley*; *Seven Métis Songs of Saskatchewan*; *Three Métis Songs from Saskatchewan*
Chisholm, Erik, 3
Chopin, Frédéric, xx, 109
See also *Je répondrais...*; Mazurka No. 47; Nocturne No. 16, No. 2, Op. 55
Chor Leoni Men's Choir, 223, 224
choral music overview, 215–217
Chôros No. 1, Typico (arrangement of Villa-Lobos, 1971), 239
Chorus of Reapers "Eugene Onegin" (arrangement of Tchaikovsky, 1969), 238
Colour Wheel (1978), 236
colouration, 192–193
Composer of the Year (Canadian Music Council), 12, 183
Composer's Chair, The (podcast), 13–14, 211
See also Gray, John
compositional style, 1–2, 4, 7–9, 11, 18, 80–81, 83, 134, 161
Concerto for Accordion and Orchestra (1999), 196, 234
Concerto for Eight (2002–03), 235
Concerto for Orchestra (Bartók), 20
Concerto for Pianoforte and Orchestra (1973–79), 16, 187–188, 196, 233
Concerto for Trumpet and Orchestra (1987), 187, 192, 204–205, 234
percussion obbligato, 206
premiere, 205
Conchita, Conchita! See *Sun Songs* (1985)
Conquering Beauty: The Life and Music of Malcolm Forsyth, 13
Cook, Larry, 218, 229
Coop, Jane, 196

Da Camera Singers, 218
Daellenbach, Charles, 202, 211–212
Dances from "Terpsichore" (arrangement of Praetorius, 1963), 238
Dark (1978), 235
Debussy, Claude. See *Sarabande* from *Suite pour le piano*
Delius, Anthony. See *Wind and Rain*
Desmond, Paul, 190, 201
See also *Sagittarius*; *Take Five* (arrangement)
Dis Al (arrangement of le Roux Marais, 1967), 238
Do not go gentle into that good night. See *Songs in Time of Crisis*
Dong with a Luminous Nose, The (1979), 237
Donne, John. See *Three Love Poems of John Donne*
Double Concerto for Viola and Violoncello (2004, rev. 2008), 196, 234

Dreams, Drones and Drolleries (1981), 192, 204–205, 235
extended techniques, 205
premiere, 205
Dutoit, Charles, 205
Dvořák, Antonin. *See* Slavonic Dance No. 8 in G minor; Slavonic Dance Op. 46, No. 8

Eales, Lesley, 4, 14
early musical career, 4
early years, 2–3
Eclectic Altos with Pokerbass (1981), 202, 236
extended techniques, 203
theatrical elements, 202
Eclectic Suite (revised 1988), aka *Pop's Cycle* (1984), 235
Eclogue (1997), 234
Eddins, William, 229
Edinorodnyi Syne. See *Glasnost*
Edison, Noel, 224
Edmonton Children's Choir, 217
Edmonton musical activities, xvii, 5, 10, 172, 191, 199, 209
Edmonton Symphony Orchestra, 5, 10, 14–15, 85, 106, 165, 172, 178, 182, 184, 191, 199, 201, 216, 221, 229
Edmonton Wind Sinfonia, 210, 223
Edmundson, Morna, 222
Eight Duets for Young Cellists (1974/2002), 234
El Brazz! (1993), 236
El Cumbanchero (arrangement of Hemandez, 1976), 238
Electra Rising: Concerto for Violoncello and Orchestra (1995), xv, xx, 8–9, 12, 15–16, 79–107, 196, 234
aleatoric elements, 94
collection modulation, 97
cubic lattice plots, 86, 98, 101
first movement analysis, 86–96
fourth movement analysis, 98–104
Greek mythological allusions, 95–96, 105
harmonic resources and idioms, 85–86, 94–95
premiere, 85
reviews, 85
summary of analysis, 105
third movement analysis, 96–98
voice-leading relationships, 91, 98
Elektra Women's Choir, 222
Elliott, Robin, 242
Ellis, John, 204, 212
Elora Festival, 224
Elora Festival Singers, 224
emigration to Canada, xvii, 3–4
Endymion's Dream (1993), 221–222, 230, 237
premiere, 222
Essay for Orchestra '67 (1967), 186, 233
Evangeline (1993), 7, 15, 195, 204, 208, 234
premieres, 208
Ewashko Singers, 165
Exceding mesure. See *Music for Redford's "Wit and Science"*
Exploration Fanfare (1978), 236
extended techniques (including vocal), 203–205, 208, 218–219, 223

Falcon, Pierre. See *Métis Songs from the Qu'Appelle Valley; Seven Métis Songs of Saskatchewan; Three Métis Songs from Saskatchewan*
False Knight on the Road, The. See *Five Songs from Atlantic Canada*
Fanfare & Three Masquerades (1979), 6, 9, 15, 204, 212, 235
Farinelli's Folly (1986), 203, 236
Also Sprach Zarathustra quote, 203

premiere, 205
theme, Brahms Symphony No. 2, 205
theme, Myaskovsky Cello Concerto, 205
theme, Schumann Piano Concerto, 205
Fiedler, Arthur, 186
Finlandia, Op. 26, No. 7 (arrangement of Sibelius, 1979), 238
Five Fanfares (1970–78), 236
Five Songs from Atlantic Canada (1989), 234, 237
Fled is that music. See *Six Episodes after Keats*
Flourish of Welcome (1989), 236
form, 24–25, 27, 195
Forrester, Maureen, 49, 75, 184, 219
Forst, Judith, 6, 15, 75, 221
Forsyth, Amanda, xix, xx, 4, 8, 13, 15, 85, 95–96, 106, 229, 242
Forsyth, Donald, 3, 13
Forsyth, Valerie, xix, 6, 14, 21, 231, 242
Foster, Lawrence, 48
Four Dice = 40 (1979), 204, 236
Four Pieces for Brass Quintet (assembled 1979), 172, 200, 203, 211, 236
Funérailles (arrangement of Liszt, 1979), 238

Galliard, "Agatha" (arrangement of Widmann, 1965), 238
Gallimaufry (2010), 237
Gilliland, Allan, 10, 13, 176, 242
Glasnost (2000), 223, 237
electronic tape, 223
premiere, 223
Slavonic singing, 223
Glasser, Stanley, 3, 198
Goliard Brass Quintet, 172, 200
Golyardes' Grounde, The (1972), 191, 200, 211, 236
Gray, John, 12–15, 211–212
Great Lakes Brass Quintet, 203
Grieg, Edvard. *See* Norwegian Dance from *Lyric Pieces*
Grové, Stefans, 3
Gustafson, Ralph, xx, 166
See also In the Yukon under *A Ballad of Canada*

Hammerhead Consort, 181
Hannaford Street Silver Band, 206–207, 209, 212
Hare, Carl, xix, 5, 14, 170, 242
See also On the Waverly Road Bridge under *A Ballad of Canada*; *Nursery Rhymes*
harmonic resources and idioms, 23–24, 45, 47, 55–56, 58, 60, 62, 64, 66, 68, 70, 73, 82–83, 85–86, 94–95, 110, 114, 117, 121, 123–124, 126, 193–196
Harris, Don, 172
Heimwee (arrangement of le Roux Marais, 1967), 238
Hemandez, Rafael. See *El Cumbanchero*
Herrick, Robert. See *Hesperides*
Hesperides (2001), xxi, 175, 224–228, 230, 237
harp duo role, 225
premiere, 224
text choices, 225
Hindemith, Paul. See *Interludium* from *Ludus Tonalis*
Hoenich, Richard, 75
Holten, Bo, 230
Holy Sonnet XVII. See *Three Love Poems of John Donne*
Horn, Charles Edward, 227
How Roses came red. See *Hesperides*

How Violets came blew. See *Hesperides*
Hoyt, David, 204, 212
Humphreys, Wendy, 207–208

I cannot see what flowers are at my feet. See *Six Episodes after Keats*
I Want a Hippopotamus for Christmas (arrangement of Rox, 2009), 239
I Went to the Market. See *Five Songs from Atlantic Canada*
Iculabili. See *Music for Mouths, Marimba, Mbira and Roto-Toms*
Iculathathu. See *Music for Mouths, Marimba, Mbira and Roto-Toms*
Iculenya. See *Music for Mouths, Marimba, Mbira and Roto-Toms*
Images of Night (1981–82), 187, 191, 193, 233
Immortal bird. See *Six Episodes after Keats*
Impromptu (date unknown), 240
In Flanders Fields. See *A Ballad of Canada*
In Perfect Harmony (2004), 235
In the Dying of Anything (1983), 220, 230, 237
  premiere, 220
  See also *Three Part-Songs*
In the Yukon. See *A Ballad of Canada*
Incantation (anon., trad.) (1990), 237
Ingraham, Mary, 243
Interludium from *Ludus Tonalis* (arrangement of Hindemith, 1965), 239
intervallic cells, 193–194, 196
Intimacies (1977), 235
Inyanga (The Moon). See *Three Zulu Songs*
Israel, Inge. See *Northern Journey*; *Glasnost*

jazz influences, 28, 30, 33–34, 36–37, 188, 190
Je répondrais... (1997), xx, 16, 109–127, 238
  à Chopin: analysis, 123–126
  à Purcell: analysis, 110–117
  à Schumann: analysis, 117–123
  African musical influences, 109–110, 123, 126
  fortspinnung development, 124
  harmonic resources, 110, 114, 117, 121, 123–124, 126
  motivic events, 110
  ostinato, 114, 127
  ostinato-variation, 123–124, 127
  premiere, 109
  rhythmic idioms, 110–111, 114
  set theory, 110–111, 114, 117, 121, 123
  successive motives, variations on, 121
  summary of analysis, 126
Jones, Brian, 204
Joyce, James, 185
  See also *Portrait of the Artist as a Young Man*; Symphony No. 2
Jubilee Overture (1963, revised 1971), 6, 8–9, 15, 186, 233
JUNO Awards, xv, xvii, 10, 12, 85, 183, 196, 221, 229
Jupiter's Daughter. See *Sun Songs*
Jurkowski, Edward, 243

Kaleidoscope (1989), 236
kalimba. See thumb piano; *Je répondrais...*
Keats, John
  Ode on a Grecian Urn, 17–18
  See also *Endymion's Dream*; *La Belle Dame sans merci*; *Lines to Fanny Brawne*; *Six Episodes after Keats*
Kelland, Otto P. See *Five Songs from Atlantic Canada*

Kern, Jerome. See *All the things you are*
Kisses, The: A Dialogue. See *Hesperides*
Kitchener-Waterloo Symphony, 212
Kluane Glaciers. See *Northern Journey*
Kora Dances, The (1990), 16, 174, 235
kwaDedangendhlale (Valley of a Thousand Hills). See *Three Zulu Songs*
Kymlicka, Michael, 49, 75

La Belle Dame sans merci (2006), 238
Last Chance, The (1974), 239
Laughton, Stuart, 206, 208, 213
Lavallée, Calixa. See *O Canada*
Lavell, Carol, 212
Le grain de mil. See *Five Songs from Atlantic Canada*
Le petit cordonnier. See *Métis Songs from the Qu'Appelle Valley*; *Three Métis Songs from Saskatchewan*
le Roux Marais, Stephanus. See *Dis Al*; *Heimwee*; *Matrooslied*; *Roseknoppies*
Le Scare du Printemps, or THE FRIGHT OF SPRING! (1983), 234
Lear, Edward. See *The Dong with a Luminous Nose*
Lemelin, Stéphane, 109, 180
Leonard, Lawrence, 186
Lessing, Doris, 6
  See also *Sun Songs*
Let Me Fish off Cape St. Mary's. See *Five Songs from Atlantic Canada*
Lethewards had sunk. See *Six Episodes after Keats*
Lines to Fanny Brawne (1991), 237
Liszt, Franz. See *Funérailles*
Little Suite for Strings (1988), 234
Little Traveller before the Dawn (1991), 235
Longfellow, Henry Wadsworth, 7
  See also *Evangeline* (1993)
Loomer, Diane, 222–223
Lorelei. See *Songs in Time of Crisis*
Los Angeles Philharmonic Trombone Ensemble, 212
Lyric Essay (2007), 235

Magnificat Secundi Toni (arrangement of Binchois, 1965), 238
Mailing, Phyllis, 75
Malcolm Forsyth Trombone Ensemble, The, 182, 199, 211
Manitoba Chamber Orchestra, 208
March, Calypso & Galliard. See *Music for Redford's "Wit and Science"*
March, Op. 12 (arrangement of Prokofiev, 1967), 238
Maritzburg College, 3
Matrooslied (arrangement of le Roux Marais, 1967), 238
Mazurka No. 47 (excerpt, arrangement of Chopin, 1970), 238
McClelland, Ryan, 243
McCrae, John. *See* In Flanders Fields under *A Ballad of Canada*
McGill Symphony Orchestra, 75
McPherson, John, 177, 199, 210–211, 243
Melancholy Clown, The (1962, rev. 1967), 234
Mendelssohn, Felix. See *Song Without Words in C*, Op. 30, No. 3; *Song Without Words in B♭*, Op. 62, No. 4
Métis Songs from the Qu'Appelle Valley (1991), 207, 235
  See also *Songs from the Qu'Appelle Valley*; *Three Métis Songs from Saskatchewan*
Mill Creek Colliery Band, 209
Millne, Alan Alexander. See *Rondino &Tiddly Pom*
Miniatures for Brass Quartet (1982), 236

Mirrors (1978), 204, 235
choreography, 204
extended techniques, 204
premiere, 204
Montgomery, James, 207
Moravian Trombone Choir of Downey, 202
Morning's Minion (2000), 196, 233
Moses, Richard, 12
motivic events, 110
motivic unity, 82–83, 121
Mouret, Jean-Joseph. See *Suite de Symphonies I. Fanfares*
multiphonics, 202
Music for Mouths, Marimba, Mbira and Roto-Toms (1973), 16, 216, 218, 221, 237
ostinato, 218
premiere, 218
vocal effects, 218–219
Zulu phonics, 218
Music for Redford's "Wit and Science" (1982), 239
Musical Priest (trad. arrangement, 2008), 239
musical training, 3–4
Myaskovsky, Nicolai. See *Farinelli's Folly*

'n Simpel Liedjie (arrangement of Richfield, 1967), 238
Natal Landscapes (1993), 16, 233
National Arts Centre, 5, 21
National Arts Centre Orchestra, xv, 5, 8, 15, 48, 85, 165, 211, 216, 229
National Youth Choir of Canada, 210, 223
Newfoundland. See *A Ballad of Canada*
Newmark, John, 75
No hungry generations tread thee down. See *Six Episodes after Keats*
Noble, Willis, 207
Nocturne No. 16, Op. 55, No. 2 (arrangement of Chopin, 2009), 239
Northern Journey (1998), 222–223, 237
extended vocal techniques, 223
premiere, 222
Norwegian Dance from *Lyric Pieces* (arrangement of Grieg, 1970), 238
notation, 20
Novum Spatium (1985), 184, 236
Nowak, Grzegorz, 106
Nursery Rhymes (2008–09), 217, 237

O Canada (arrangement of Lavallée, 1996), 238
O Lady deere. See *Music for Redford's "Wit and Science"*
octatonicism, 25, 27–28, 36–37, 39, 41–43
Oh Aching Heart (1962), 240
Oh Canada Thing, The, or *A Dominion's Dilemma* (1992), 236
On himself. See *Hesperides*
On Julia's Breath/Cherrie-Ripe/To Anthea/On Julia's Lips. See *Hesperides*
On the Waverley Bridge Road, 165
See also Hare, Carl
On the Waverley Road Bridge. See *A Ballad of Canada*
Orange Branch, The. See *Songs in Time of Crisis*
orchestration, 18–20, 161, 172, 186–187, 191–193, 208, 225–226
Orchestre Symphonique de Montréal, 205
Order of Canada, Member, xvii, 12
ostinato, 28, 30, 36, 41, 47, 56, 83, 114, 127, 218
ostinato-variation, 123–124, 127
Ottawa Choral Society, 165

Ottawa Festival Chorus, 165
Otto, Dave, 172
Overture "Erewhon" (1962) (withdrawn), 186, 233
overview of works, 7

Paragon Harp Duo, 224
See also Bumanis, Nora; Shaw, Julia
Parker, Dorothy. *See* The Sea; *Three Part-Songs*
Pastiche (1981), 234
Pastorale and Rondo for 4 Winds and Piano (1968–69), 235
Patten, Brian. See *In the Dying of Anything*; *Three Part-Songs*
personality, 5–6, 172–174, 178, 180, 184, 195, 199, 231–232
Pfeifferfanfar für Pfeiffers (1985), 203, 236
Phantom Sketches (2000), 235
Pier, Fordyce (Duke), 178, 204, 209, 212, 243
Pinchin, Harry, 172
Plath, Sylvia. See *Songs in Time of Crisis*
Poem for Brass (1964–66), 198, 236
premiere, 198
versions, 198
poodle, 21, 174
Portrait of the Artist as a Young Man, 185
Praetorius, Michael. See *Dances from "Terpsichore"*; *Suite of Dances from "Terpsichore"*
Pratt, E.J. *See* Toll of the Bells and Newfoundland under *A Ballad of Canada*
Prelude and Fugue in B♭ minor (arrangement of Bach, 1970), 239
Preludio e Fuga/Glenn Gould (2007), 238
Prevost, Roxane, 243
Primos, Kathy, 244
Prince George Symphony Orchestra, 207–208
Pro Coro Canada, 222, 230
Prochazka, Tanya, 180, 244
programmatic connotations, 184–185
Prokofiev, Sergei. *See* March, Op. 12
Purcell, Henry, xx, 109
See also *Je répondrais...*

Quartet '61 (1961), 197–198, 236
versions, 198
Quartet '74 (1974), 199–201, 236
Quinquefid (Concerto Grosso No. 2) (1976–77), 187, 191–192, 201, 212, 234
premiere, 201
Quintette for Winds (or...) everythynge ye ever wanted to knowe about Essex (1986), 9, 235

Ratcliffe, Gloria, 172
Ratzlaff, Leonard, 5–6, 14, 165, 168, 210, 223, 244
"Remembering Malcolm Forsyth" (podcasts), 13
Requiem for the Victims in a Wartorn World at the Millenium (2002), 196, 233
Rhapsody for 14 Strings (1982), xix, 23–48, 187, 191, 234
Allegretto giusto: analysis, 28–34
Allegretto, leggero: analysis, 40–47
Bartókian influences, 32–33
colouration, 46
commission, 23
form, 24–25, 47
harmonic resources, 23–24, 45, 47
jazz influences, 28, 30, 33–34, 36–37
Lento, come prima: analysis, 34–40
Lento, pensato: analysis, 25–28
octatonicism, 25, 27–28, 36–37, 39, 41–43
ostinato, 28, 30, 36, 41, 47

overview, 23
premiere, 48
recordings, 48
rhythmic idioms, 41–42, 47
rhythmic idioms, 41–42, 47, 60, 62, 64, 66–67, 70, 110–111, 114, 189
Richard Eaton Singers, 165, 229
Richfield, Sidney. See *'n Simpel Liedjie*
Rideout, Rayfield, 181, 244
Rimsky-Korsakov, Nicolai. See *Scheherazade*
Ripsnorter Finale (from *Eclectic Suite*, aka *Pop's Cycle*) (2004), 234
Ritchie Trombone Choir, 210
Rival, Robert, 13, 245
Romm, Ronald, 201
Rondino & Tiddly Pom (2008), 197, 204, 209, 236
premiere, 209
representations, "Tiddly Pom" by Milne, 209
Rondo in Stride (1988), 235
Roseknoppies (arrangement of le Roux Marais, 1967), 238
Rosen, Robert, 10
Rossetti, Dante G. *See* Sudden Light; *Three Part-Songs*
Rox, John. See *I Want a Hippopotamus for Christmas*

Sagittarius (Concerto Grosso No. 1) (1975), 185, 187, 190–192, 201, 211–212, 233
jazz waltz style (Paul Desmond), 201
mariachi parody, 201
premiere, 201
versions, second movement (Andante), 211
Salpinx, The (Concerto Grosso No. 3) (1981), 184, 187, 192, 234
Saltarello (1977), 239
Saltarello (1982), 203
Saltarello (assembled 1979), 236
Sarabande from *Suite pour le piano* (arrangement of Debussy, 1965), 239
Scheherazade (Nikolai Rimsky-Korsakov), 3
Schöll, Klaus Rainer, 205
Schumann, Robert, xx, 109, 118
See also *Farinelli's Folly*; *Je répondrais...*
Scott Hoyt, Janet, 6, 14, 205
Sea, The, 219–221, 230
See also *Three Part-Songs*
Serenade for Strings (1985–86), 8, 187, 234
set theory, 110–111, 114, 117, 121, 123
Seven Métis Songs of Saskatchewan (1967), 49, 75
Jeannotte, Joseph Gaspard, 49, 51
overview, 49–53
Shakespeare, William. See *These Cloud-Capp'd Towers*; *Snug the Joiner as Lion Fell*
Shaw, Julia, 174, 241
shooe-tying, The. See *Hesperides*
Sibelius, Jean., 2, 13
See also *Finlandia*, No. 7 and Symphony No. 5, Op. 26, Op. 82
Simons, Valerie. *See* Forsyth, Valerie.
Six Episodes after Keats (1979–80), 235
Six Olympic Fanfares (1988), 239
Siyajabula! We Rejoice! (1996), 11, 16, 233
Sketches from Natal (1970), 10, 12, 16, 186–188, 192, 195–196, 233
Slavonic Dance No. 8 in G minor (arrangement of Dvořák, 1969), 238
Slavonic Dance, Op. 46, No. 8 (arrangement of Dvořák, 1979), 239

Snug the Joiner as Lion Fell (2000), 223–224, 237
choral theatre, 224
premiere, 223
Solemn Intrada (1980), 202, 236
Soliloquy, Epitaph and Allegro (1988), 204, 207, 235
Sonata for Trumpet & Piano (1995), 204, 208, 235
Song. See *Three Love Poems of John Donne*
Song without Words in B♭, Op. 62, No. 4 (arrangement of Mendelssohn, 1977), 238
Song without Words in C, Op. 30, No. 3 (arrangement of Mendelssohn, 1970), 238
Songs from the Qu'Appelle Valley (1987), 204, 206, 236
premiere, 206
versions, 206
Songs in Time of Crisis (2000), 238
Sonic Mobile for Trombone Choir (2003), 209–210, 237
Sorensen, Dale, 245
South African Broadcasting Corporation National Orchestra, 186
Springtide (1984), 233
ss *Greenland* disaster, 131, 146
See also Newfoundland under *A Ballad of Canada*
St. Cyr (Bunkal), Margaret, 205, 212
Steps... (1978), 9, 235
Strange Spaces (1978), 238
Strauss, Richard. See *Farinelli's Folly*
Streatfeild, Simon, 208
Sudden Light, 219–220
See also *Three Part-Songs*
Suite de Symphonies I. Fanfares (arrangement of Mouret, 1978), 239
Suite for Haydn's Band (1980), 235
Suite of Dances from "Terpsichore" (arrangement of Praetorius) (1970), 239
Sun Songs (1985), 6, 8–9, 15, 221, 234
Sunne Rising, The. See *Three Love Poems of John Donne*
Sun's Out, The. See *Sun Songs*
Swan Sees His Reflection, The (1987/2002), 235
Symphony No. 1 (1968–72), 187–188, 190, 192–193, 233
Symphony No. 2 *"...a host of nomads..."* (1976), 185, 187–188, 233
Symphony No. 3. See *African Ode* (Symphony No. 3) (1981)
Symphony No. 5, Op. 82 (Sibelius), 13, 190

Take Five (arrangement of Desmond, 1982), 239
Taylor, Christopher, 182, 199, 201, 210–211, 213, 245
Tchaikovsky, Pyotr. See *Chorus of Reapers "Eugene Onegin"*
teaching style, 17–20, 79–80, 176–177, 179, 182, 199, 232
Tempest: Duets and Choruses, The (1990), 180, 235
Tennyson, Alfred Lord. See *Blow! Bugle, Blow!*
These Cloud-Capp'd Towers: Concerto for Trombone and Orchestra (1990), 196, 204, 207, 234
extended techniques, 208
premiere, 207
reception, 207
Thomas, Dylan. See *Songs in Time of Crisis*
Thompson, James, 205–206, 212

Three Love Poems of John Donne (1994–95), 222, 230, 237
premiere, 222
Three Métis Songs from Saskatchewan (1975), xx, 49–77, 58, 206, 219, 237
Adieu de la mariée: setting, 60–67
Chanson de la Grenouillère: setting, 67–73
Chanson du petit cordonnier: setting, 55–59
harmonic resources, 55–56, 58, 60, 62, 64, 66, 68, 70, 73
ostinato, use of, 56
overview, 50
premieres, 49
programmatic connotations, 56–58
recordings, 75
rhythmic idioms, 60, 62, 64, 66–67, 70
summary of analysis, 73–74
versions, 75, 206
Three Métis Songs from Saskatchewan (1976), 6, 9, 234
Three Part-Songs (1980–83), 237
Three Zulu Songs (1988), 16, 221, 237
premiere, 221
Zulu language, 221
thumb piano, 117–118
Tiddly Pom. See *Rondino & Tiddly Pom*
To His Book: Another. See *Hesperides*
To His Mistresses. See *Hesperides*
To Silvia to wed. See *Hesperides*
To the Virgins, to Make Much of Time. See *Hesperides*
Toccata (1986), 203, 235
Toll of the Bells, The. See *A Ballad of Canada*
Tollites Portas (1961), 240
Toronto Children's Chorus, 221
Tre Toccate per Pianoforte (1987), 189, 238
Tre Vie: Concerto for Alto Saxophone & Concert Band (1999), 236
Tre Vie: Concerto for Saxophone and Orchestra (1992), 187, 234
Triangles (1972). See *Four Pieces for Brass Quintet*
Trickster Coyote-Lightning Elk for Violin and Orchestra (2006), 196, 234
Trudel, Alain, 207–208, 213
True North Brass, 203, 212
Tumanov, Alexander, 223
Two Gentil Knyghtes (1979), 202, 236
multiphonics, 202
Two New Hours (CBC Radio), 13
Two Songs, Op. 72, No. 3, Op. 43, No. 2 (arrangement of Brahms, 2004), 239

ukuZalwa (1983), 16, 184, 189, 233
umGcomo (1999), 13, 16, 181, 235
premiere, 181
University of Alberta, 1, 6, 10, 178, 182, 191, 204, 230
activities at, 5
University of Alberta Brass Ensemble, 198
University of Alberta Concert Choir, 218
University of Alberta Madrigal Singers, 230
University of Cape Town, 3, 4, 178, 198
Unmarked Doors. See Israel, Inge
Unsworth, John, 207
Upon Julia's breasts. See *Hesperides*

Valley of a Thousand Hills (1989), 16, 196, 233
Vancouver Chamber Choir, 221
Vilakazi, Benedict W. See *Three Zulu Songs*
Villa-Lobos, Hector. See *Chôros No. 1, Typico*

Visage du Ballet (1965, withdrawn), 239

Washburn, Jon, 221, 229
We moya! (Hail Wind!). See *Three Zulu Songs*
Well-Meaning Recorder, or Tunes for Tootling (1976), 235
When travelles grete. See *Music for Redford's "Wit and Science"*
Widmann, Erasmus. See *Galliard, "Agatha"*
Williams, Tennessee. See *Songs in Time of Crisis*
Wind and Rain (1966), 237
Winter Sky. See *Northern Journey*
Wits Chamber Choir, 220
Witwatersrand University, 220
Wolf, Hugo. See *Oh Aching Heart*
Wolfe, Duain, 21, 229–230
Wyner, Yehudi, 49, 75
Wynnyk, Theresa, 13

Young Mother, A, 165
  See also Hare, Carl

Zephyrus (1989), 203, 236
Zukerman, Pinchas, xvi, 15, 229
Zulu language, use of, 11

Other Titles from University of Alberta Press

Sonic Mosaics

Conversations with Composers

PAUL STEENHUISEN

With a colleague's candour, sympathy, and expertise, Steenhuisen discusses the creative process with thirty-two contemporaries.

Prairie Bohemian

Frank Gay's Life in Music

TREVOR W. HARRISON

Long-overdue biography of the enigmatic western Canadian luthier, musician, and guitar virtuoso Frank Gay.

Jane Austen Sings the Blues

NORA FOSTER STOVEL, *Editor*

GRAHAM GUEST AND GRANT STOVEL, *Producers*

Celebrate Professor Bruce Stovel's life with his two favourite subjects: Jane Austen and blues (book with CD).

More information at uap.ualberta.ca